Hussain S. Alsalmi

Oman's Basic Statute and Human Rights

Hussain S. Alsalmi

Oman's Basic Statute and Human Rights: Protections and Restrictions

with a Focus on Nationality, Shura, and Freedom of Association

KS
KLAUS SCHWARZ VERLAG • BERLIN

Bibliografische Information der Deutschen Bibliothek
Die Deutsche Bibliothek verzeichnet diese Publikation in der Deutschen Nationalbibliografie; detaillierte bibliografische Daten sind im Internet über *http://dnb.ddb.de* abrufbar.

British Library Cataloguing in Publication data
A catalogue record for this book is available from the British Library.
http://www.bl.uk

Library of Congress control number available
http://www.loc.gov

www.klaus-schwarz-verlag.com

First edition
Layout & Cover: J2P Berlin
Printed in Hungary on chlorine-free bleached paper
ISBN 978-3-87997-423-8

Abstract

Over the last three decades, Oman has emerged as a centre of political and economic stability in the Arab world, a stability which is an essential ingredient for any country to develop and flourish. Whereas democracy and public freedoms are at the core of stability in other parts of the world, the case in Oman is different. It is not a democratic state and it did not adopt the modern concepts of human rights and public freedoms into its legal-political system until 1996 when the Basic Statute of the State was promulgated.

The purpose of this study is to provide a general view of the current status of Human Rights under the Omani Basic Statute of the State with a specific focus on some civil and political rights. It illustrates the situation of human rights by assessing the implementation of the constitutional and legal safeguards into practice and finding out what hinders them.

It aims to evaluate the importance of the constitution in Oman, and the extent to which it has succeeded in incorporating international human rights' standards while walking the tightrope of reconciling this with core traditional social customs and Islamic values. It analyses the compatibility of constitutional and national laws and practice with international human rights standards and assesses current trends and policies.

Three case studies for different rights and freedoms are conducted to explore the guarantees and weaknesses of different rights in practice. These are the areas of nationality 'as individual right' which is very important under the Omani system as it is the direct link to enjoyment of other rights and freedoms. The *Shura* is the second case study as a political right or a collective right which represents public participation in Oman. Finally, the Freedom of Association, as an example for the freedom of expression and opinion, which represents individual and group rights together.

This research evaluation analyses in detail the developments since the promulgation of the Basic Statute in December 1996 but stretches to encompass progress till the developments to the end of July 2011. A summary of Human Rights Developments in Oman since then to early 2012 is covered under Appendix 3 of the book.

Acknowledgements

Throughout all stages of writing this thesis for my PhD in Law from the University of Manchester, I have received considerable support from various people who have been of immense assistance academically, emotionally and socially. I consider myself exceptionally fortunate and opportune to have these amazing people around me.

First and foremost I offer my sincerest gratitude to my supervisor Dr. Jackson Maogoto whose expertise, guidance, and patient supervision were invaluable to the completion of this study. Also, I would like to express my gratitude to my supervisor Dr. Paul Kearns for his comments and guidance. One simply could not wish for better or friendlier supervisors. My gratitude also goes to Jackie Boardman and Mary Platt, the Postgraduate Research Student Administration Office in the Manchester Law School for assisting me in many different ways.

I owe my deepest gratitude to Dr. Alexia Ellul Welsh, Lorna Nairn, and Dr. Salim Al Shukaili for their valuable inputs and comments.

Also, I wish to thank my best PhD colleagues, Timothy Umahi, Bader Al Sabah, Mahmoud Alamadani, Tariq Altawil, Maria Medina, Adrien De-hauteclocque, and all of those who supported me in any respect during the completion of the project.

I am indebted to my colleagues in the German University of Technology in Oman for their understanding and support, the most to mention is Prof. Burkhard Rauhut, the Rector, for his support and encouragement, and all other colleagues and staff for being supportive.

Lastly, I wish to thank my entire extended family for providing a loving environment for me. My wife Salwa, and my children Tasneem, Seereen and Anas must receive special thanks for the incredible amount of patience they had with me throughout all my PhD study. Uncle Abdulla whose encouragement, guidance and support from the initial days of my earlier studies to the final level of this PhD enabled me to develop in different areas. My brothers, sisters, and whole family for their understanding and for being supportive. I thank my parents for supporting me throughout all my studies. They bore me, raised me, supported me, taught me, and loved me. To my late father I dedicate this thesis.

Contents

Part II: Human Rights Case Studies: Nationality, Shura, and Freedom of Association

Table of Oman's Royal Decrees

Table of Oman's Court Decisions, Legal Opinions, and Ministerial Resolutions

Table of International Standards and Norms

List of Tables

Abbreviations

ACHR	American Convention on Human Rights
ACJR	Authority on Conflicts of Jurisdictions and Rules
CEDAW	Convention on the Elimination of All Forms of Discrimination against Women
CRC	Convention on the Rights of the Child
CRPD	Convention on the Rights of Persons with Disabilities
ECHR	European Convention on Human Rights
GCC	Gulf Cooperation Council
ICCPR	International Covenant on Civil and Political Rights
ICERD	International Convention on the Elimination of All Forms of Racial Discrimination
ICESCR	International Covenant on Economic, Social and Cultural Rights
ILO	International Labour Organisation
LoCA	Law of Civil Association in Oman (R.D. 14/2000)
M.R. 59/2010	Ministry of Manpower Resolution (59/2010) – Labour Unions' Regulation
NGO	Non-Governmental Organisation
OBSS	Oman Basic Statute of the State
OFTA	US-Oman Free Trade Agreement
OMR	Omani Rials (the Currency)
OPP	Office of the Public Prosecutor
R.D.	Royal Decree
ROP	Royal Oman Police
TIP	Trafficking in Persons
UDHR	Universal Declaration of Human Rights
UNDP	United Nations Development Programme
UNHRC	United Nations Human Rights Council
UPR	Universal Periodic Review
UAE	United Arab Emirates

1 General Introduction

"The political and civil laws of each nation ought to be only the parti-United Nations Chartercular cases in which human reason is applied. They should be adapted in such a manner to the people for whom they are framed that it should be a great chance if those of one nation suit another. They should be in relation to the nature and principle of each government; whether they form it, as may be said of politic laws, or whether they support it, as in the case of civil institutions. They should be in relation to the climate of each country, to the quality of its soil, to its situation and extent, to the principal occupation of the natives, whether husbandmen, huntsmen, or shepherds: they should have relation to the degree of liberty which the constitution will bear; to the religion of the inhabitants, to their inclinations, riches, numbers, commerce, manners, and customs".[1]
Montesquieu: The Spirit of Laws (1748)

1.1 Introduction

International human rights organisations' reports reveal that most of the Arab States are struggling because democracy still does not exist and the protection of human rights is still progressing very slowly in the region. This is especially so in the area of civil and political rights and freedoms. Arbitrary detention with the torture of detainees, strict control over freedom of opinion and expression and the right of assembly and association are examples of human rights violations in most Arab States. Most reports published in 2010 about freedoms and democracy, such as those from the Freedom House and the Economist Intelligence Unit, show that there have been minor or no changes

1 Montesquieu (1748). *The Spirit of Laws: Book I, chapter 3. Of Laws in General.* Retrieved 9 March 2011, from the Constitution Society website: <http://www.constitution.org/cm/sol_01.htm#003>

at all in the human rights status in the region during the last few decades. Most Arab States are still categorised by these entities as 'not-free' dominated as they are by 'authoritarian regimes', thus the low ranking on the analysis list.[2]

Different institutions within the United Nations have referred to widespread prevalence of human rights abuses in many countries of the world,[3] especially the Third World, due to a lack of commitment to the International human rights instruments.[4] In the case of Arab Middle East countries there are additional factors contributing to the lack of human rights' protection. These include:

- Lack of political and constitutional awareness, and insufficient attention to the fundamental rights and freedoms problems among the vast majority of the people in the absence of democratic institutions tasked with implementing protection of human rights, as well as a dearth of civic education.

---

2 Freedom House. (2011). *Map of Freedom 2011.* Retrieved 31 May 2011, from <http://www.freedomhouse.org/template.cfm?page=21&year=0&display= map> Economist Intelligence Unit. (2010). *The Democracy Index 2010.* Retrieved 9 May 2011, from <www.eiu.com/democracy> Also, World Audit. (2010). *Democracy Table November 2010.* Retrieved 9 April 2011, from <http://www.worldaudit.org/democracy.htm>

3 Such as the General Assembly of the United Nations and the United Nations Development Programme (UNDP); see United Nations High Commissioner for Human Rights (UNHCHR). (2010). *2009 Report: Activities and Results.* Retrieved 3 April 2011, from <http://unispal.un.org/UNISPAL.NSF/0/42FF510FF156E2FA85 25772900646CC7> UNDP. (2005). *Human Rights in UNDP: Practice Note.* Retrieved 13 April 2011, from <www.undp.org/governance/docs/HRPN_English.pdf>

4 The main International human rights instruments consists of the Universal Declaration of Human Rights (UDHR), the International Covenant on Civil and Political Rights (ICCPR) and its two optional protocols and the International Covenant on Economic, Social and Cultural Rights (ICESCR), the International Convention on the Elimination of All Forms of Racial Discrimination, the Convention on the Elimination of All Forms of Discrimination Against Women (CEDAW), the Convention Against Torture and other Cruel, Inhuman and Degrading Treatment or Punishment, and the Convention on the Rights of the Child. Check the UN publications website:<www.un.org/Pubs/CyberSchoolBus/briefing/rights/rights.pdf>

- Political instability due to often minority control over ethnic or sectarian majorities as well as other destabilising foreign influences.
- The allegation that human rights and democratic practices are a kind of intellectual luxury compared to more important issues such as the country's social and economic needs and developments.
- The use of stage-managed democracy methods, such as referenda and elections to deliver pre-set outcomes on a range of themes including the freedoms and rights discourse.
- Legally binding decrees that are antagonistic and often override explicit constitutional provisions that guarantee rights and freedoms, and that are geared to grant legitimacy to repressive regime policy by eviscerating fundamental guarantees.

The above-mentioned factors, enhanced by the allegation of western origin of the modern concepts of 'human rights' and 'civil liberties' traditionally influence the reaction of the political elite in Arab States towards adopting human rights and freedoms standards as recognised internationally.[5] All of them pay homage to the call for limited adoption of human rights based on cultural relativism though self-preservation is more of a factor. This is evident from their adoption of regional conventions: the Cairo Declaration on Human Rights in Islam[6]

5 Arab States can be broadly grouped under three main categories: one-party dictatorships, such as Libya and Syria; multi-party regimes, such as Iraq and Lebanon; and semi-Islamic regimes, such as Gulf States. The Saudi Arabia abstention to vote for the Universal Declaration of Human Rights in 1948 is an example that illustrates the criticism of some Muslim states to International Human Rights instruments of their failure to take Islamic cultural and religious context into the account.

6 The Cairo Declaration on Human Rights in Islam is a declaration of the member states of the Organisation of the Islamic Conference adopted during the Nineteenth Islamic Conference of Foreign Ministers in Cairo in 1990, which provides an overview on the Islamic perspective on human rights, and affirms Islamic Shariʿa as its sole source. This declaration is usually seen as an Islamic response to the United Nations' Universal Declaration of Human Rights of 1948. See the translated copy from Human Rights Library of the University of Minnesota website: <http://www1.umn.edu/humanrts/instree/cairodeclaration.html>

and the Arab Charter on Human Rights,[7] both of which disregard political rights to allow the states to follow their own interpretation of rights and freedoms without interference from western powers.[8]

Recent developments in several Arab states in 2011 in what is now dubbed the 'Arab Spring'[9] have refocused and placed human rights and freedoms norms at the forefront of many Arab states' agenda, on the one hand flagging major changes and developments in this arena, on the other a realisation that hard-nosed repression only solidifies the resolve of citizenry.

1.2 National Safeguards

Over several decades, the International Human Rights instruments have played a positive role in protecting rights and freedoms. However, the safeguards guaranteeing and protecting fundamental rights and freedoms at the national level can be more effective tools, because of their direct influence over individuals and groups, especially if the protection of rights and freedoms is linked and enforced through accountable and transparent national processes legitimised by a linkage to generally agreed international norms.

Safeguards at the national level cover different political, judicial

7 In January 2001, the Arab Commission on Human Rights recommended that the 1994 Charter, which no state had ratified it, should be revised, and on 22 May 2004 the Arab Charter on Human Rights was adopted by the Council of the League of Arab States and affirms the principles contained in the Universal Declaration of Human Rights and the Cairo Declaration on Human Rights in Islam. See the translated copy from Human Rights Library of the University of Minnesota website: <http://www1.umn.edu/humanrts/instree/ loas2005.html>

8 The Arab Charter on Human Rights has referred to the political participation under Article 19 but it has left the practice limited by the law.

9 Arab Spring is "a term that was used beginning in March 2005 by numerous media commentators to suggest that a spin-off benefit of the invasion of Iraq would be the flowering of Western-friendly Middle East democracies. The term took on a new meaning in early 2011, as democratic uprisings independently arose and spread across the Arab world" after the Tunisian and Egyptian revolutions. See: The Center for Media and Democracy (April 2011). *Arab Spring*. Retrieved 20 April 2011, from: <http://www.sourcewatch.org/index.php?title=Arab_Spring>

and social areas. For instance, having a democratic government, where sovereignty of people with free elections and control over the executive branch are the basis, tends to provide more protection than other political systems. On the other hand, the most effective judicial tool is the existence of a written constitution or legislation containing texts on the protection of rights and the freedoms protected.[10] The separation of powers, with the emphasis on the independence of the judiciary and the courts' control of the constitutional laws, in addition to the rule of law are the most important guarantees for the protection of human rights and essential "*if man is not to be compelled to have recourse, as a last resort, to rebellion against tyranny and oppression*".[11]

The propagation and perpetuation of a human rights culture is a safeguard and effective tool for protection. It helps people to be aware about their rights and freedoms, to activate control over public opinion, to supervise and to ensure the proper application of constitutional law. One need only recall that in the Declaration of the Rights of Man and of the Citizen in France in 1789, the forerunner of modern universal human rights asserted that:

> *"The representatives of the French people, organized as a National Assembly, believing that the ignorance, neglect, or contempt of the rights of man are the sole cause of public calamities and of the corruption of governments, have determined to set forth in a solemn declaration the natural, unalienable, and sacred rights of man, in order that this declaration, being constantly before all the members of the Social body, shall remind them continually of their rights and duties".*[12]

10 Of course merely having a text is not enough. It is its interpretation and implementation by which protection of human rights and freedoms are visible that can really add up to a written constitution where these rights are guaranteed.

11 The preamble of the Universal Declaration of Human Rights (United Nations 1948)

12 *The Declaration of the Rights of Man and of the Citizen.* (1789). Retrieved 2 April 2011, from <http://www.hrcr.org/docs/frenchdec.html>

1.3 Background of the Legal History and Rights in the Gulf Constitutions

From the 18th Century to the beginning of the 20th Century, most Arab states were subject to Ottoman rule. Consequently, despite the demise of the Ottoman Empire, it influenced Constitutions and it's laws permeate the Arab world more so as the Ottoman Empire was based on a inclusion of the principles of Islamic *Shariʿa* law.[13] This facilitated an easy identification by the Arab world who shared the same religion and principles. It is of note that subsequently the French and Italians were to exercise imperialism over this part of the world and they too left their footprint and importantly their legal doctrines and principles constituted the first nuanced foundations of contemporary Arab countries.[14]

Today, the legal systems in Arab states are not identical but do represent variegated quotients of Continental European legal systems, especially the French law, albeit the application of *Shariʿa* principles in the hereditary monarchies in the Gulf remains the bedrock. This is a natural extension of the reality that Arab Gulf States[15] not

---

13 The Ottoman Empire had expanded during its rule, which lasted for more than six centuries, to include many of Middle East lands, and the Ottoman's legal influence over Arab countries is evident today. One example is the adoption of the Ottoman legal and administrative terms in most of the Arab countries today. The Mecelle code, which formed the Ottoman Civil Code, is another example where it was the basis of Civil Law for several Arab States such as Iraq, Egypt, Jordan and Kuwait. See AlSulaiman, A. (2011). *Terminological differences between Morocco and other Arab countries.* Retrieved 23 June 2011, from Arabic Translators International website: <http://www.atinternational.org/index.php?option=com_content&view=article&id=49:2011-04-23-20-03-08&catid=36:2011-04-23-19-59-36>

14 Azzam, F. (1995). *Guarantees of Civil and Political Rights in Arab Constitutions (in Arabic).* Cairo: Cairo Institute for Human Rights Studies.

15 The Gulf States, Gulf Monarchies, Gulf Societies are terms used in this work to determine the group of 6 Arab countries with a coastline on the Persian Gulf (Oman, United Arab Emirates, Saudi Arabia, Qatar, Bahrain, and Kuwait). They have formed and are still members of the Cooperation Council for the Arab States of the Gulf (CCASG); also known as the Gulf Cooperation Council (GCC).

only consist of absolute or quasi-constitutional monarchies but share the same broad historical experiences. From the 19th Century most of them were British protectorates. Significantly the absolute monarchs, unlike all their neighbours, possess historical pedigree and thus legitimacy. The ruling families have been in power for centuries and survived many upheavals.

Over the last two decades or so there have been developments in the areas of human rights and freedoms. Substantial oil and gas revenues have served as a basis for social and economic development. Government largesse in providing basic needs has generally kept at bay demands for political freedoms in comparison to other parts of the world.[16]

Each Gulf State has its own constitution, but they are different to a certain extent in terms of detail and breadth of objectives and basic principles. However, all of them have determined the regulatory mechanisms of their governments in addition to listing the rights, freedoms and duties of citizens. Each Gulf State possesses a separate chapter for rights and freedoms with consensus over the general concepts of most rights.

The importance of Islam in these constitutions is ever dominant with most of them enshrining Islam as the State religion and *Shari'a* law as the source of legislation. Linkages of the importance of Islam and the political and legal systems of the state abound in constitution preambles and clauses. Basic principles such as *Shura* referring to *'traditional and Islamic term of public participation'*[17] abound. In others such as the Basic Law of Saudi Arabia the role of Islam is embed-

---

The term will exclude Iraq from this study, as it is not part of the Council and does not fall into a similar political system as other Gulf States.

16 Based on the 'no taxation and no representation'. See section 5.5 for more details.

17 Such as the case with Art. 9 (Oman), Art. 8 (Saudi Arabia), and constitutions' preamble (Kuwait and Bahrain).

ded with the Quran and *Sunnah*[18] the basis of the constitution.[19] The technicality of applying this in practice is another issue all together.[20] That said, it goes on to stipulate that the State protects human rights in accordance with Islamic law.[21] Other Gulf States' constitutions are more generalised in this area in an effort to be in line with the international human rights instruments. However, their reservations on the ratified conventions show a different attitude to limiting some rights and freedoms which may contradict with the Islamic law.

There are no direct references in any constitutions of the Gulf States regarding provisions of the seminal Universal Declaration of Human Rights or direct enshrinement of provisions of any international treaty or convention concerning human rights. Some constitutions have used terms like 'democracy' to show their tendency to open doors for more civil and political rights and freedoms which are very limited by the time those constitutions promulgated.[22] Nevertheless, other provisions within the constitution, such as the power of the ruler and the 'no tolerance' approach to political parties, show the reluctance in applying these terms in practice and convey a strong political message about the intention of maintaining absolute monarchy systems. Until today, only Kuwait and Bahrain have ratified International Covenant on Civil and Political Rights (hereinafter referred to as ICCPR) and International Covenant on Economic, Social and Cultural Rights (hereinafter referred to as ICESCR).[23]

18 Sunnah means statements, actions, approvals, characteristics and descriptions of the Prophet.

19 Art. 1 Saudi Basic Law.

20 It is difficult to consider Quran and Sunnah as a constitution in the precise meaning of its legal term, as they can be more as a platform for life.

21 Art. 26 Saudi Basic Law.

22 It has been used as a government system for Kuwait, Bahrain and Qatar. Art. 6 Kuwait, Art. 1 Bahrain, Art. 1 Qatar.

23 Kuwait adopted both conventions on 21 May 1996. Bahrain ratified ICCPR on 20 September 2006 and ICESCR on 27 September 2007. See United Nations Treaty Collection website: <http://www2.ohchr.org/english/bodies/ratification/index.htm>

One of the common concepts of the Gulf States' constitutions is the generality and simplicity aspect of the rights and freedoms set forth therein. For instance, all constitutions guarantee *'the right to freedom of expression'* in simple terms, without elaborating or determining the horizon of that freedom,[24] unlike the ICCPR for example, which makes the restrictions of this freedom specifically necessary for respecting the rights or reputation of others; or for the protection of national security, of public order, of public health or morals.[25] In contrast, the right or freedom in these constitutions is subject to regulation under the ordinary law and not to the constitution. In essence the political elite can interfere directly in the identification and interpretation of the law considering that most legislative powers are in the hands of an absolute monarch.

1.4 Oman and Constitutional Law

The constitution of a state is the most important legal document. The constitution is generally the supreme law as it outlines and regulates the limitation of powers for each branch of the government. It also serves as the basis of the guarantee of protecting fundamental human rights and freedoms. Alongside it constrains the tyranny of govern-

24 Once this provision is analysed in the light of the whole constitution as well as other ordinary legislations, the outcome of this right is simply limited and only provides a ray of hope or a legal mask.

25 Articles 19 and 20 ICCPR. Article 20 of the Covenant states that any propaganda for war and any advocacy of national, racial or religious hatred that constitutes incitement to discrimination, hostility or violence shall be prohibited by law. The UN Human Rights Committee (HRC), the body of experts tasked with interpreting the ICCPR, has specifically stated that these required prohibitions in Article 20 are fully compatible with the right of freedom of expression as contained in article 19. UN Human Rights Committee (HRC), *CCPR General Comment No. 11: Article 20 Prohibition of Propaganda for War and Inciting National, Racial or Religious Hatred*, 29 July 1983, available from: <http://www.unhcr.org/refworld/docid/453883f811.html> This is also echoed in the new General Comment on Article 19: *CCPR General Comment No. 34: Article 19 Freedom of Opinion and Expression*, 12 September 2011, available from: <http://www2.ohchr.org/english/bodies/hrc/comments.htm>

ment in part to facilitate realisation of fundamental rights and freedoms.[26]

Among the Gulf and Arab States, Oman was the last state to promulgate a constitution; other Gulf States have had their constitutions for more than 20 years.[27] The first written Omani Constitution, better known as the 'Basic Statute of the State', was promulgated by Royal Decree No. 101, issued on 6th of November 1996. The Constitution sought to formalise the extant political structure and officially give credence to governmental organs. Prior to this, governance being a prerogative of the Sultan was a malleable system that waxed and waned depending on the incumbent Sultan. The Constitution explicitly addressed key issues including previously taboo concerns such as the succession to the throne.

The Basic Statute of the State, as its name suggests offers a basic framework for the protection of human rights and regulates the organisational relationships between the various State's organs and mechanisms. The Constitution consists of eighty-one articles divided into seven sections. Since adopting the Basic Statute in 1996, the Omani legal system has changed dramatically.

Understanding the full potential of the Basic Statute is still a work in progress since a number of Royal decrees that pre-date the Basic Statute are still in force, and today, 14 years after its inception, some areas remain difficult to investigate and evaluate owing to absence of related law. For example, the establishment of the Administrative Court and the Higher Council for the Judiciary took place in 2000, four years after the promulgation of the Basic Statute. Moreover, other laws relating to human rights, such as the Labour Law and modifications to the Social Security Law, were declared in 2003 and 2005. November 2008 witnessed the establishment of the first Human Rights Commission in the country. Recently, in 2011, Oman has es-

26 Barendt, E. (1998). *An Introduction to Constitutional Law.* Oxford: Oxford University Press.

27 With the exception of Saudi Arabia which adopted its Basic Law in 1992.

tablished the independence of prosecution[28] and has for the first time granted parliament some important legislative powers.[29]

1.5 Research Question

This study seeks to answer the main question: To what extent is the application of human rights and freedoms set forth in the Omani Basic Statute of the State compatible with international conventions? It focuses a contemporary issue in the Arab and Gulf States – Human Rights. It does this through a detailed consideration of Oman's Basic Statute and its legal system. It describes and analyses the historical and cultural factors within a nuanced legal framework of the Omani legal structure.

Oman is distinct from other Gulf States historically and politically. It has been seen as, and is, progressive in seeking to track the rule of law, at least in terms of structure and organisation.[30] The Basic Statute's regulation of the relationship of individuals and the state power and the extent to which the principle of human rights are defined and codified constitutionally is one of the main themes.

This study proffers an overview of the Omani Basic Statute of the

28 By Royal Decree no. 25/2011. For more details see section 3.6.5.

29 Royal Decree No. 39/2011, which followed by Royal Decree No. 99/2011. See section 3.6.6 and Appendix 3.

30 The Rule of Law is an aspect that has been popularised by A V Dicey and it can be considered an important part of any State's constitution around the world that respects human rights and freedoms. "*Although there is a shared ideal or concept of the Rule of Law – marked in part by such traditional desiderata as that both ordinary citizens and public officials should be ruled by law – there is widespread confusion and uncertainty about the ideal's precise content*". Richard H. Fallon (Jan., 1997) "*The Rule of Law" as a Concept in Constitutional Discourse*, Columbia Law Review, Vol. 97, No. 1, pp. 1-56 from URL: <http://www.jstor.org/stable/1123446> Oman, however, is witnessing during this period the transition from its old system of unaccountable government to the new system where no one is above the law and everyone is equal before the law as the OBSS stated. However, such transition period will take time until the rule of law is fully recognised in practice. For more details about the Rule of Law in Oman see section 3.4.

State (hereinafter referred to as OBSS or the Basic Statute) relating to rights and freedoms with a specific focus on some civil and political rights. However, it is difficult to understand the situation of human rights without assessing the implementation of the constitutional and legal safeguards into practice and finding out what hinders this. Hence, an analysis on the factors that affect Omani citizens and residents from the actual enjoyment and exercise of such rights and freedoms forms another plank of this systematic analysis.

This work will examine the principles of the Omani constitution. It aims to evaluate the importance of the constitution in Oman, and the extent to which it has succeeded in incorporating international human rights' standards while walking the tightrope of reconciling this with core traditional social customs and Islamic values. It analyses the compatibility of constitutional and national laws and practice with international human rights standards and assesses current trends and policies.[31]

Three case studies for different rights and freedoms are conducted to explore the guarantees and weaknesses of different rights in practice. These are the areas of nationality 'as individual right' which is very important under the Omani system as it is the direct link to enjoyment of other rights and freedoms. The *Shura* is the second case study as a political right or a collective right which represents public participation in Oman. Finally, the Freedom of Association, as an example for the freedom of expression and opinion, which represents individual and group rights together.

In addition to the selection of these case studies based on their differentiation as a type of right or freedom (as individual or group rights or as civil or political rights) there are mainly three reasons for choosing those three rights as case studies for this work:

- Most constitutions of the Gulf States concentrate on the nationality right, as the first right guaranteed in the Public Rights and Du-

31 It should be noted that the use of the masculine in this research implies the feminine and vice-versa, unless mentioned otherwise.

ties Chapter of their constitutions (Kuwait, Oman, Bahrain), or by listing it at the first articles of the Constitution (UAE) or to give it a constitutional immunity (Qatar). Although most of them agree on the differentiation between the native national and the naturalised in terms of other rights and privileges, each state follow different practice with this rights. Hence, giving it special significance.

- Shura in Oman has a special status, different from the rest of other Gulf States. The OBSS focuses on the principle of Shura and the official statements asserts that Shura adopted in Oman is different from democracy, makes it important to analyse the reasons for such trend,
- Comparing the constitutions of the Gulf States on the freedom of association clearly highlights that the attention details paid by the OBSS on this right more than others, which gives it a special status to the study.

With the dearth of literature related to the Omani constitution and human rights, this study will be based mainly on analytical and comparative methodology of the articles of the Basic Statute and Oman's legislation. On the comparative spectrum, the prism of international and regional instruments, legal cases and opinions, secondary legislations, executive resolutions and constitutional provisions of other Gulf States will be referenced. Although there are few articles and textbooks about the Basic Statute, most of them lack fundamental analysis directed at the multifaceted externalities that inform the nature of the system and its main characteristics and shortcomings.[32]

The interrelationship between Gulf States in their legal and political trends can be helpful in understanding different aspects of Oman's Basic Statute and legislations. Other Gulf States' constitutions and legislations are juxtaposed to illustrate the similarities and

32 Such as the 'General Principles of the Basic Statute and Government System' (in Arabic) by Dr. Kamal Al-Rahim, and the articles from the Conference 'Features of the Basic Statute' (in Arabic) in 2004.

differences on the subject matter of protection of rights and freedoms. In this regard it is important to highlight that most issues relating to rights and freedoms in the Middle East are taken as a direct criticism of the regimes involved, thus it is one of the most sensitive areas of enquiry.

Official Interviews and the empirical analysis are beyond the scope of the study, due to the misconceptions about human rights in the region, which includes the pretexts of the special characteristics of the community with official secrets. The difficulties of this research also include finding relevant materials and court cases, while at the same time dealing with the problematic areas of lack of official translations of the Gulf States' constitutions and legislations.[33]

This research evaluation analyses in detail the developments since the promulgation of the Basic Statute in December 1996 but stretches to encompass developments to the end of July 2011 essentially because the 'Arab Spring' was so significant that the candidate felt compelled to revise some key themes and undertake a substantial rewrite to factor this in.[34] However, it does not cover pending Royal decrees pertaining to the Basic Statute in detail for reasons of practicality and research:

1. They are in a transitional stage with procedures outside the main framework of the current legal system making it difficult to obtain accurate information.
2. Article 75 of the Basic Statute emphasises that it does not affect the period prior to its issuance.

However, the earlier period might be exposed as necessary in different parts of the research, especially in chapters 1 and 2 to emphasise the basis of current legal and political frameworks and their developments.

33 Since there is no official translation of the Basic Statute yet, this research will be dependent on the translated copy from Oman's National Human Rights Commission website (not officially translated). See the Appendix 1.

34 See Appendix 3 for the developments occurred from August to November 2011.

1.6 Research Structure

This research aims to find a basis of human rights' studies in Oman, enlighten researchers, and educate students about the importance of human rights and the relationship of the Basic Statute or the Constitution in protecting rights and freedoms. Accordingly, the research plan has been developed based on dividing the two components into two parts in addition to the general introduction as Chapter 1, and the general conclusion as Chapter 7:

Part I: Introduction to the Basic Statute of the State in Oman covering the constitutional, legal and political safeguards to protect human rights. This part is divided into two Chapters.

Chapter 2 'Introduction to Oman's Basic Statute': It explains the historical, social and political backgrounds that influenced the promulgation of the Basic Statute and the political system in Oman. It covers the process of promulgating it and analyses its most important characteristics. It will also highlight the most important observations about the system.

Chapter 3 'Human Rights Protections and Safeguards under the Omani System': This constitutes one of the central themes of the study about the current status of human rights in Oman in general. It enumerates all rights and freedoms set forth under the Basic Statute. It lists other interlinked laws, legislations and regulations for each right, if any. Most important principles of protecting human rights and freedoms, such as the separation of powers and rule of law will be covered, with summaries of each branch of the government and its power. The Omani judicial system will be explained in more detail, especially with regard to the role and the importance of the Constitutional and Administrative Courts.

It will also examine the international human rights reports about Oman and their role in promoting human rights. Finally, it will highlight the most important regulations and legislation with the latest developments that have a significant impact in supporting the rights and freedoms in Oman.

Part II is an analytical showcase of the three case studies or models of civil and political freedoms and rights, which are contained and protected in the Basic Statute. This part is limited to a study of three specific categories of rights: Nationality, *Shura*, and Freedom of Association. It will examine each of this subjects in detail both descriptive but more importantly incisive in order to reflect the way that the Basic Statute protects each right, and to explain how each right relates to other rights and freedoms.[35] Therefore, each case study (right or freedom) will be studied independently over three substantive Chapters; 4, 5 and 6 culminating in a general overview and conclusion in Chapter 7.

Chapter 4 'Omani Nationality and Human Rights': deals with the Right to Nationality. It has been introduced as the first case study of this research to demonstrate the importance of this right, because it is the first-mentioned right in the Basic Statute under Part Three (Rights and Duties), and the fact that most of the fundamental rights and freedoms mentioned in the Basic Statute are associated with this right.

This chapter will explain how the Omani system paid great attention to the nationality right, and the way that nationality is obtained and lost according to the legislation that governs this right, and how other rights and freedoms are affected by it, such as the rights of women and children. Dual nationality, adoption, mixed marriage, and the situation of statelessness will be part of the study too.

Chapter 5 'Democracy, *Shura* and Public Participation': *Shura* as one of the most important political rights granted to Omani citizens by

35 The rest of the rights and freedoms, as abovementioned, will be discussed generally within part of the study whenever is necessary. For example, women's rights have been mentioned in different parts, such as under the nationality and Shura Chapters. Overall, the Second Chapter of the research will give an overview of all rights and freedoms set forth in the Basic Statute of the State.

representing the right of public participation, representation, and election will be covered with related articles in the Basic Statute and other legislations. It will show the differences between *Shura* and democracy and the reason for resorting to the term '*Shura*'. It will indicate the current status of *Shura* in Oman and the evolution of public participation, and the role of Parliament in human rights. Hence, the power of elected council, the prevention of political parties in the Gulf States and the role of civil society and women in Oman's elections will be discussed in general.

Chapter 6 'Freedom of Association': will focus on the right of association as one of the fundamental rights which stem from the freedom of opinion and expression, as an individual right as well as a collective one. This chapter shows the most significant hurdles facing this right in practice under the Omani legislation with an explanation and analysis of the different protections guaranteed for Non-Governmental Organisations compared to labour unions based on their respective regulation.

Chapter 7 'General Conclusion': will present an indication of the most important recent developments in Oman with an analysis of the main obstacles facing human rights in Oman and the recommendations.

In summary; currently there is very little known about Oman's constitution. On the one hand, this project will yield valuable information about Oman's system and its constitutional and legal system. On the other hand, fundamental rights and freedoms is another field which is worthy of research because of the lack of academic and national studies on the subject. This study, hopefully, can be the basis for future human rights studies in Oman.

Part I:
Basic Statute and Human Rights

2 Introduction to Oman's Basic Statute

2.1 Oman before the Constitution: 'A Historical and Political Overview'

2.1.1 Introduction[1]

In general, the Arab Gulf States share the same broad historical experiences which include religion, language, area, and tribal affiliation. Oman, however, is different from neighbouring Gulf States in many ways: geographically, economically and traditionally.

Geographically, Oman has a unique position in the Arabian Peninsula with a diverse natural environment. By virtue of its coastal position, Oman controlled the movement of gulf trade for centuries developing one of the strongest navies in the Gulf. As well the mountains surrounding the country's land borders kept neighbours away and the Omani people insulated from outsiders. It enjoyed prosperity as a commercial empire. Today it has more limited oil reserves than most of its neighbours but foreign workers add up to a lower percentage of the population in Oman than in other Gulf States giving a more homogenous society and lessening tensions.

Traditionally, Oman is the only country in which the *Ibadi* School of Islam is predominant. The *Ibadi* movement has its own unique governing system distinct from other Islamic sects (*Sunnism* and *Shiʿism*). *Ibadism* has influenced the country in subtle but distinctive ways for centuries.[2] The *Ibadi* School, while in the minority

---

1 The constitution of Oman called the Omani Basic Statute of the State or the Basic Statute.

2 *Ibadi & Ibadism:* The jurisprudence school of Islam, a distinct sect of Islam that is neither Sunni nor Shiʿai, existing mainly in Oman, East Africa and in some parts of Algeria, Libya and Tunisia. See: Hoffman, V. (2001). *Ibadi Islam: An Introduction* [online]. [Accessed 25 March 2007]. Available from: <http://www.uga.edu/islam/ibadis.html>

in other parts of the world, is the predominant sect in Oman.[3] The *Ibadi* movement is one of Islam's earliest fundamentalist movements, founded less than fifty years after the death of Prophet Muhammad.[4]

The aforementioned factors within the historical development of the country have influenced Omani society for hundreds of years as will be discussed in this Chapter. Thus, components such as the constitution, the political and legal system are underpinned by historical antecedents. This is coupled with the present Sultan, who has ruled the country for more than 40 years and overseen seismic changes in guiding Oman from an underdeveloped state to a modern country.[5]

2.1.2 Historical Development before the Constitution (until 1996)

The contemporary Sultanate of Oman was formerly known as Muscat and Oman. It is situated on the South East Arabian peninsula, bordered by Yemen, Saudi Arabia and the United Arab Emirates (UAE). Oman forms one political, economic and social unit, and this is one of the important facts noted by researchers into the history of the Arabian Peninsula.

Oman was among the first parts of the Arabian Peninsula whose people embraced Islam during the life of Prophet Muhammad in the first generation of the Islamic era in the 7th Century. They elected

3 There are no official statistics. However, the current estimation between 50% and 75% of citizens. See Katz, M. (2004). Assessing the Political Stability of Oman. *Middle East Review of International Affairs* [online] 8, Accessed 29 April 2007, pp. 5, 6. from: <http://meria.idc.ac.il/journal/2004/issue3/katz.pdf>.

4 Prophet Muhammad (570–632) was the political leader and the chief of the first Muslim State in Arabia. However, the arguments with the debate after his death and during the first four Caliphs, known as *the Rightly-Guided Caliphs*, and the different understanding of the Qur'an and the Sunnah has resulted in the emergence of different schools of thought and sects; such as Ibadism, Sunnah, Shi'ite and Mu'tazila.

5 Hence, the necessity of exploring the legal and political developments under his rule from 1970 until the promulgation of the constitution in 1996 will be discussed in the second part of this Chapter.

their first Imam as ruler in 748 AD.[6] Oman managed to remain relatively free of Abbasid[7] and foreign control until 1506, when the Portuguese occupied it for more than a century before being expelled in 1650.

In 1744 Imam Ahmed bin Said, founder of the present dynasty, succeeded in uniting the country, ending internal disputes and civil wars. In the early 19th Century, the ruler took the title of Sultan to encompass his authority as both a spiritual and political leader. Oman's power extended to control of portions of the East African Coast, the Indian subcontinent, and much of the coasts of Iran and Gwadar (in Pakistan).

Although never formally a British protectorate, from the mid-19th Century British influence over Oman's affairs was prevalent due to the British interests in securing the shipping lanes between Europe and India.[8] The British signed several treaties with Omani Sultans over four generations,[9] as well as truces with the tribal leaders on the

---

6 *Imam*: in Islam, a recognised leader or a religious teacher; it is used in several senses. In general use, it means the one who lead prayers and has been used as an honorary title; but the word is also used under the *Ibadi* sect to mean the elected leader of the Islamic country.

7 Abbasid Dynasty: "Second of the two great dynasties of the Muslim Empire of the Caliphate. It overthrew the Umayyad caliphate in ad 750 and reigned as the ʿAbbāsid caliphate until destroyed by the Mongol invasion in 1258". ʿAbbāsid Dynasty. (2011). In Encyclopedia Britannica. Retrieved from <http://www.britannica.com/EBchecked/topic/465/Abbasid-dynasty> The Abbasid State influences in Oman started from 750 with the first Ibadi Imamate in Oman, and the Abbasid domination over Oman's coast oscillated with the weakness of the Imamate until the year 986 with the end of the Abbasid state influence in Oman. See Ministry of Education. (1997). *Oman and the Abbasid State (in Arabic).* In Social Studies, "History", Middle School, 9th Edition. Muscat.

8 The weakness of Oman began with the separation of the Omani empire into two; Oman and Zanzibar with the Oman Sultan's financial weakness stemming from being separated from his source of wealth in the African part of his empire.

9 The British involvement after the separation between Oman and Zanzibar in 1856 continued with both Sultans; one leading Oman and one leading Zanzibar.

other coasts of the Gulf, which were under the nominal control of the Sultan of Oman.

A new *Ibadi* Imamate emerged in the interior of Oman, after which the Sultans and Imams of the interior tribes clashed continuously throughout the 20th century. With the discovery of oil in the 1930s, Gulf States became a theatre of competition between the United States and Britain. In 1938 Sultan Said bin Taimur, came to power and, with British assistance, put down the Imamate supporters by 1959.[10]

Sultan Said, in his bid to limit external influence, curtailed developments in education, health care and other services while more open neighbouring countries progressed. Even in representing the country in international organisations and diplomatic circles, Sultan Said delegated his authority to Great Britain.[11] This period ended in 1970 when he was overthrown by his only son, Qaboos bin Said Al Said, in a bloodless palace coup. The new ruler focused on economic development along with changing the name of the country from Muscat and Oman to Oman to symbolise its unity.

Sultan Qaboos ousted his father Sultan Said bin Taimur on 23 July 1970 and has ruled ever since. His extensive modernisation programme rapidly opened up the country to the outside world. Elham Manea avers that Sultan Qaboos succeeded in using the state's agencies to get his subjects to do what he wanted and his regime emerged

---

10 Oman under the Imams was governed by Islamic Law with *Ibadi* doctrine as its socio-legal basis with traditional and tribal customs supplementing this. It is also noteworthy that some treaties have had a significant legal influence. Such as the treaties signed between the Sultan and the British in 1822 and 1845 which forbade the Sultan from engaging in the slave trade are two examples. Also known as Moresby Treaty (1822) and the Hamerton Treaty (1845). See: Ghubash, H. (1997). *Oman – the Islamic Democratic Tradition: An Islamic Democracy* (in Arabic) pp. 197-201

11 Manea, E. (2005). *Regional Politics in the Gulf: Saudi Arabia, Oman and Yemen*, p. 87.

to become a model in the Arab world for its control of society.[12] In part the Sultan's power is based on his personality and charisma bolstered by the perception of being a saviour from his father's wobbly regime. He solidified his national hero status when Oman triumphed in the *Dhofari* war in 1974.[13] Moreover, he is credited for unifying all the diverse elements of the country, and for using the country's natural resources to spur development and growth. In the view of the common people he is fair and just.

As a new Sultan, Qaboos concentrated his efforts on developing and uniting the country, building infrastructure and providing essential services such as education, health care, water, electricity, transport and communications. With rapid development and expansion, there was a need to legislate and establish laws to associate and to organise the relationship between the people and the activities of the State, as there were no laws or regulatory systems to define how institutions functioned, their principles and goals, or the rights and duties of people.

In 1970, the Ministry of Justice was instituted as one of the first four ministries in the country. It was responsible for regulating and supervising the courts which applied traditional Islamic Law. Between 1970 and 1974 the Sultan issued several Royal decrees geared to maintain the stability of the national development. This includes the Nationality Law,[14] the Omani Passport Law,[15] the Traffic Law,[16] the Commercial Company Law,[17] the Press Law,[18] the Labour

12 Manea, *ibid*, p. 88.

13 The first pressing problem that Qaboos faced as Sultan was an armed Communist insurgency from South Yemen, the Dhofar War. The Sultan quickly defeated the incursion with help from the Iranian and some other Arabs armies, and the British Royal Air Force.

14 Law (1/72).

15 Law (2/72).

16 R.D. 37/73.

17 Law (4/74).

18 R.D. 3/75.

Law,[19] the Banking Law,[20] and the Penal Law.[21] However, there were still no laws or regulatory systems to define how public institutions functioned, their principles and goals, or the rights and duties of their employees.

The formalisation and delineation of authority amongst government organs began in the mid-1970s, when a committee of consultants and under-secretaries headed by a minister was established to examine laws promulgated between 1970 and 1974. In July 1975, Royal Decree 26/75 introduced laws to regulate administration pursuant to one of the committee's recommendations. It was the first law to set out the powers and responsibilities of the Council of Ministers and other governmental bodies, in tandem with the Civil Service Law of Royal Decree 27/75, which outlined civil servants' rights and duties.[22] The year also saw the establishment of the Diwan (Bureau) of Legislation, which was responsible for reviewing all draft laws and decrees before they were issued by the Sultan. Other responsibilities of the Bureau were reviewing all international treaties and contracts to which the government was party before they were signed.

The State Administrative Apparatus Law[23] was the supreme referential text in the State for all regulations, laws and legal principles for many years, until November 1996, when the new constitution, called the Basic Statute of the State, came into force.

2.1.3 Factors Influencing the Omani Society

The Gulf societies have been influenced over the years by different factors which have had different effects on the recent political systems. These factors, which exert a general influence over all states,

19 R.D. 34/73.

20 R.D. 7/74.

21 R.D. 7/74.

22 Al Shukaili, S. (2006). *The Mediator in Explaining the Omani Basic Statute* (in Arabic) pp. 85-87.

23 R.D. 26/75.

vary from one country to another. They include the Royal Family, merchants, tribes and religion. This section aims to give a nuanced overview of the most influential elements in the Omani society, which as aforementioned are different from those in other Gulf States.

The Ibadi Doctrine and Imamate System

Since Islam was embraced by Omanis centuries ago, it has had great influence on Omani society. It will be seen later how Islam influences the Omani legal system and the Constitution and in particular *Ibadi* doctrines and tenets.

The *Ibadi* sect is distinguished by its conservative doctrine and a distinctive system of governance. It is impossible to make a serious study of Oman's political and legal experience without addressing the influences of Islam, especially the *Ibadi* Imamate system that prevailed for over a millennium. Some scholars have described it as an Islamic Democracy.[24]

Oman was governed for over 1200 years by a theocratic stratum of the *Ibadi* sect. This school of thought believes in the institution of Imamate, where the ruler of the country (Imam) is elected by a Council called *'Majlis Ash-Shura'*[25] or *'Ahl al-Hall wa al-Aqd'*. Most members of the Council are community notables, such as religious people, scholars, and respected members of the public. The Council was seen as a representative of people's opinion, and had a consultative role as well as the power to appoint and remove the ruler. All its decisions were taken by majority.[26] This was complemented by the 'Common Council', which had a consultative role, drawing its members from the tribal leaders, regional governors, and respected members of the public. The Imam could call meetings of this Council. However, no

---

24 Ghubash, H. (1997). *ibid.*

25 Or the Shura Council.

26 Al-Hashmi, S. (2000). *Shura in Oman (in Arabic).* ed. Muscat: Unpublished Article, pp. 50-51.

important issues could be decided unless the tribal leaders consulted their people.[27]

There are many strict requirements for the Imam to be selected, such as personal qualities (behaviour and conduct) and knowledge of religion. The Council must select the most worthy leader whom it supposes to be just and fair, capable of protecting the people's rights and interests, and best able to defend the community and rule it according to religious principles. After the Imam is elected he is entitled to receive homage from the public. The Imam has executive, judicial and legislative powers, however, his power is always limited by the *Shura* Council and by the *Shari'a* law, and he will be treated as a normal person in so far as he is subject to the law.[28] There is no limited period for his governance, as long as the Imam still fulfils the necessary criteria for his position or until he proves himself unworthy of it.

It is also important to distinguish between two types of Imam under the *Ibadi* jurisprudence: The *Weak* and the *Strong* Imams. The Strong Imam is one who used to be a religious scholar before being elected, while the Weak Imam is one who does not fulfil this criterion. While the Imam must be elected by the *Shura* Council in both cases, his legislative and executive powers are very much limited by the Council if he is known as a Weak Imam.

The *Ibadi* doctrine does not accept the hereditary system of monarchy as a way of ruling and this often led to civil wars and conflicts between the Imams and the monarchs throughout history. However, if the monarch is fair and just, even if he is not elected, mutiny and rebellion are prohibited.[29]

One aspect of the *Ibadi* influence in the current Basic Statute can

27 Ghubash, H. (1997). *ibid*, pp. 78-81.

28 The rule of law was implemented under the Imamate system, and there were some historical cases where individual citizens have lodged a complaint against the Imam, brought him as a defendant under the court and won the case. See Ghubash, H. (1997). *ibid*, pp. 85-112.

29 Ghubash, H. (1997). *ibid*, pp. 67-75.

be seen in the implementation of a bicameral parliamentary system whose two chambers are the *Majlis Ash-Shura*, which represents the people and is elected, and the *Majlis Ad-Daula*, which consists of scholars or experts appointed by the Sultan. Additionally, the taking by the Sultan of an oath and the way in which he is elected by the Royal Family under the Basic Statute follows to some extent the pattern of the election of the Imam. Statutorily, the influence of the *Ibadi* School can be seen in legal areas which are related to society and the people, such as Personal Status Law.

Another aspect of the *Ibadi* sect's interpretation of Islam is 'tolerance' of others, even with non-Muslims, which has its clear influence in the Omani society. This has been adopted as part of the State's political system and foreign policy by maintaining peaceful and friendly relationship with all countries of the world, especially with neighbouring countries. Even when the international relations of other Gulf States wither, Oman usually tries to peacefully maintain its international relations, such as the case with Egypt after its peace agreement with Israel in 1979, and with Iraq and Iran before and after the Gulf Wars in 1980, 1991, and 2003. Such events have drawn clear principles for Oman's foreign policy as well its political system as they are stated under the Omani Basic Statute.[30]

Tribal Society and Hierarchy[31]

Most of the population of Oman is Arab, and these people belong to various tribal groups. Society in Oman, like other Gulf States, is viewed as tribal; rules and regulations of daily affairs and marriage are significantly governed by tribal rules and etiquette. Usually, there are small clans which belong to a mother tribe and their administrative structure will consist of individual local sheikhs and a Chief Ar-

30 Art. 10 OBSS.

31 Al Mukhaini, A. (2002). Stepping into Democracy: The Shura in Oman. *Qatar Conference on Democracy and Free Trade, 26-27, March 2002, Doha, Qatar*, pp. 1-4.

bitrator from the mother tribe. Each tribe will have its consultative council called Sablah or Majlis, which will advise the Sheikh on the tribe's own affairs.

Historically, it was difficult to survive in the desert alone, so related families joined together to form a tribe. The tribal nature of society has caused civil clashes in Oman as well as in other Gulf Countries. Arab tribes have attacked each other since before Islam whose advent prohibited such attacks and prevented them from turning into random violence. However, tribal interests such as the domination of water or lands, and tribal revenge are prickly issues.[32]

Its Arabian attribute came historically when two of the Arabian tribes moved from the southwest and centre of the Arabian Peninsula to Oman in the 2nd century BC. The first of these tribes, known as the *Yamani*, succeeded in expelling the Persians from Oman; the other tribe was the *Nezaari*. The effects of these two tribes continued with Oman's history, as in the 18th century, the two influential ethnic groups who polarised into the political divisions of the *Hinawis* of *Yamani*, and the *Ghafiris* of the *Nezaari*. Today, most Arab tribes in Oman are affiliated with one of these groups. According to Peterson and Siegfried: "An Omani ruler has to be accepted by both confederations in order to rule effectively ... the 'Albusaid', the ruling family since 1744, does not belong to either of these confederations. Hence, both alliances can accept a ruler from this family more easily than from opposite groupings, but at the same time the Sultan's power is inherently endangered since he can only "buy" legitimacy and cannot rely on historical family linkage".[33]

The conflict between these groupings continued into the twentieth century, "tribes often changing their positions, collapsing into tribal

32 Imam Ahmed, founder of the present dynasty, succeeded in using the tribal society of Oman by unifying the warring factions and tribes and leading them to victory against the Persians who then occupied parts of the country.

33 Siegfried, N. (2000, October). *Legislation and Legitimation in Oman: The Basic Law*. Islamic Law and Society, 7 (3), p. 363.

offshoots or forming alliances under the leadership of an Ibadi Imam against outside aggressors, whether Portuguese, Persians, Sunni caliphs, Qarmatians, Wahhabi or British. An atmosphere of tension lasted over centuries during which the structure of society was constantly changing. Geographical isolation led to the continuance of feuds which lasted for generations".[34]

The old tribal structure was alive and very strong in Oman when Sultan *Qaboos* assumed power. He faced a very difficult task to establish his new State while the tensions between tribes existed from ancient disputes. He had to peacefully unite the tribes, and put an end to old disputes and to convince the tribal Sheikhs to cooperate with the State in building the country again.

This in many ways dictates Oman's politics and government which are largely dictated by tribal structure, as in the Imamate system, which usually depends on the tribes to stabilise the state. The Royal Family, indeed, has usually ruled on the basis of the protection and support of elite tribes.[35]

Oman's Remoteness

The west of Oman is flanked by the desert *al Rub al Khali*, or the Empty Quarter, which is difficult to cross even with modern desert transport, and the sea surrounds most of the country with the rest ringed by mountains forming a barrier between Oman and its neighbours. Because of geographical and political remoteness from other neighbours, Oman has developed a unique culture and traditions which have survived hundreds of years. Even when it was occupied

34 Popp, Georg (2008). *Tribal Society in Oman.* Retrieved from <http://www.omantours.com/about-oman/people-overview/tribalsociety>

35 Today, the Sultan makes a yearly progress through the interior and southern parts of the country, meeting tribal leaders and local notables. Tribal influence over general elections is still strong, but in the modern democratic era it is also transparent.

by others, such as Abbasids, Portuguese and Persians, they usually occupied the coast, while the vast interior of Oman remained insular.

This has led the people on the coast towards sea-trade and maritime power, so that Oman became a powerful commercial empire. It has also made the country the object of foreign covetousness when it has been weak, because of its important location, controlling the sea and regional trade.

During times of weakness, Oman has lost many lands which were semi-geographically connected to it, such as the Sheikdoms along the western coast, or non-geographically connected, such as Zanzibar and Gawadr. The consequences of this weakness and isolation are still felt today.

The remoteness promoted the tribal society life and enabled the *Ibadis* to survive as a group long after they had vanished from other parts of the Muslim world. This gave Oman the opportunity to establish its governments under the Imamate system for many years undisturbed.

Some ethnic groups and minorities are established as Indians, Iranians, Iraqis, freed slaves from Africa, mercenaries and others. This diversity changed the population structure along the coast in light of the fact that these arrivals come in by sea. Merchants who hold the economic power are mostly *non-Ibadi* and some are non-Muslim which has played its own role in national politics for decades.

Some regions of the country are independent by their nature, for example, the Southern Region, also known as Dhofar, has held the status of special territory for two historical reasons: It was the link between Northern Oman and Africa for many years, and it was also the source of a rebellion fighting for communist rule in the 1960s and 1970s.

Administratively, the natural features combined with the diversity of population structures have divided the country into 11 governorates, which are further subdivided into 61 *Wilayats* (provinces).[36] Although the nomination of the governor is by a Royal Decree and the *Wally* (province ruler) by the Minister of Interior's Decision, both nominations usually takes the tribal and land structure into account.[37]

Oman's Economy

The nature of the economic influence in yesteryears has influenced the legal and political aspects of modern Oman. As a commercial empire it has extended its domination on other parts of Asia and Africa contributing to the stability of the Monarchy. After the Zanzibar separation, which was the economic capital in mid-19th Century, Oman faced a large economic and internal crisis which led to more reliance on British support to maintain its stability and spawned a strong British presence in the Sultanate's policies.

In the 20th Century with the discovery of oil, the ruling families in the Gulf States enjoyed more financial independence from elite tribes as well as support from foreigners, which was the case in Oman too.[38] Economic, and specifically oil revenue, could be considered as the major reason for political stability under absolute monarchy rulers in Gulf States these days. Though Oman is not a major oil producer in the Gulf States, oil still forms a central pillar of the government revenue.[39]

National figures show that 35.2% of the Omani population is under

36 According to R.D. 114/2011.

37 By nominating a governor who does not belong to the same governorates.

38 Until the commercial production and export of oil in 1967, Oman's budget was totally dependent on custom duties, religious alms giving (zakat), and British loans and subsidies. When Sultan Qaboos assumed power in 1970, he expended the oil revenue on country developments as well as ensuring tribes' support which led the country to more stability.

39 According to 2010 figures, the net oil revenue composes 69.10% of the total revenue, with 5470.1 million Omani Rials. See Ministry of National Economy (2011) *Facts & Figures 2010*, downloadable from: <http://www.mone.gov.com/PublicationAttachment/F&F%20BOOK2011.pdf>

the age of 15.[40] With the young generation seeking employment, and the country's dependency on foreign workforce, this does present a major challenge for the Omani government.

One year before promulgating the Basic Statute, the government addressed some of these challenges in the 'Vision Conference: Oman 2020',[41] with the aims of achieving economic and financial stability, reshaping the role of the government in the economy, broadening the private sector participation, diversification of the economy, globalisation and human resources' development.[42]

2.2 Basic Statute and Constitutionalism

2.2.1 Introduction

Gulf States have a tradition of absolute monarchs who hold most of the legislative, executive, and judicial powers without limitations. Despite the fact that customs and traditions of society could present some form of restriction, the ruler can nonetheless override them. The second boundary is Islamic tenets which influence the community's behaviour. However this could be ignored by the ruler's interpretation of Islamic doctrines. This poses questions as to the extent of applicability of a constitution in a society which has been ruled by such tradition and mind-set for centuries.

Most constitutions around the world are drawn up for a country

40 Based on the Final results of General Census of Population and Housing, and Establishment in 2010, announced by Minister of National Economy in January 2011, the total number of Omani population under the age of 15 is 690,701 from a total population of Omani citizens of' 1,957,336. See the Oman Census Summary from Ministry of National Economy: <http://85.154.248.117/MONE2010/>

41 In June 1995.

42 This is addressed under the Omani Basic Statute, Article 11, entitled 'The Economic Principles'. However, international economic treaties have their legal and political effects too. Such as the case with U.S.-Oman free trade agreement which was signed in January 2006. Legally, the agreement was the leading motive for changing the Labour Law and allowing the existence of labour unions. As will be discussed in Chapter Six.

making a fresh start, whether to emancipate it from colonialism or to establish fundamental principles for a new system of government, or to bring different nations into a single union. When Oman implemented a constitutional document for the first time in its modern history, it was done for the reason of establishing a new system of government. Among the Gulf and Arab States, Oman was the last to promulgate a constitution.[43]

It is believed that the need to establish an Omani constitution at that time was a step to start a new developmental era through legal and institutional reforms,[44] as the preamble of the Royal Decree stated.[45] Rule of Law was introduced as the main objective of the next governmental era, with emphasis on a bill of rights echoing international human rights and civil liberties norms. This was on the back of unrest that had happened two years prior to the promulgation of OBSS.[46] In May 1994, hundreds were arrested and then released, including a number of high-ranking officials and prominent families. The individuals were charged with being members of a secret, violent group attempting to destabilise the country. This incident raised the alarm regarding political opposition to the Sultan's regime; hence, the severe restriction on the freedom of association under the Basic Statute.[47] Another motive for adopting the Basic Statute followed a Sep-

43 Other Gulf States have had their constitutions for more than 20 years, with the exception of Saudi Arabia which adopted its Basic Law in March 1992. Kuwait was the first State to have a constitution in the Gulf which was adopted in 1962, followed by Qatar, United Arab Emirates, and Bahrain in 1970, 1971, and 1973 respectively. Moreover, some of them have adopted new amended constitutions such as was the case in Bahrain in 2002 and in Qatar in 2004.

44 The Sultan had intended to issue the constitution in his silver jubilee, which was supposed to be in 1995 after his 25 years of ruling the country. However, it was announced a year after. See Miller, J. (1997). *Creating Modern Oman: an interview with Sultan Qabus.* Foreign Affairs, p.16.

45 Royal Decree (101/96) which promulgated the Basic Statute.

46 The Omani Basic Statute of the State.

47 Art. 32 OBSS. Please refer to Chapter Six.

tember 1995 car accident involving the Sultan.[48] The Sultan who has no successors and has not nominated any of his relatives as a crown prince, faced the crucial need of establishing a system where the monarchy could move peacefully and flexibly within a specific root of the ruling family.[49]

On 6 November 1996, Sultan Qaboos promulgated the most important piece of legislation, the 'Basic Statute of the State',[50] which is also known as 'the White Book' symbolising a new era in socio-economic and political.[51]

2.2.2 Adopting the Constitution

Oman did not follow basic democratic avenues in adopting the constitution, neither by Constituent Assembly or Constitutional Referendum as the U.S. 1787 and France 1791 constitutions, nor by a semi-democratic way as a contract between the Constituent Assembly and the monarch as in the case with the Kuwaiti and Bahraini Constitutions of 1962 and 1973. It was promulgated by Royal Decree without an iota of public participation.

In an interview, the Sultan himself described the process he followed to adapt the constitution: "*I got together four of my most trusted people – all Omanis, I sat with them and told them exactly what I had in mind. I gave them a year to formulate it in a legal document. Then*

48 The Sultan who was driving at that time was injured and his Finance Minister who was the dominant economic figure in the country was killed.

49 In his ruling era, the Sultan has managed to gain a majority support from his people by unifying the country's diversities. That successfully rehabilitates legitimacy to the Royal Family which was almost lost under his late ascendants. Therefore, a constitutional document recording all the Sultan's objectives, success, and intentions would be necessary.

50 vide Royal Decree No. 101.

51 The 'white book' term could be derived from the Islamic terminology 'white page' which stand for pure, and clearness. It is usually used to describe a new starting life without sins under religious meaning.

we had a second review, and then a final session".[52] The Omani people, the Consultative Council and the Cabinet did not know what was decided about the constitution until the Sultan announced it on his annual 'Meet the People' tour a few months before its adoption. Thus they were never involved in drafting or giving their opinion on its articles, indeed, they did not know about its contents or structure. Moreover, the four trusted people as the Sultan referred to them are as yet unknown to the public, nor are their roles and backgrounds which reflected on the drafting; hence illustrating, the Basic Statute's provisions.

Compared with other Arab and Gulf States' constitutions the OBSS is informed by various aspects of the Kuwaiti constitution, which is also provides the basic model for other Gulf region's constitutions as its principles were also adopted in the later Gulf constitutions. Being the oldest constitution among Gulf States, the Kuwaiti Constitution, which is itself based on the Egyptian constitution with modifications, suits to some extent the tribal communities as well as helps to maintain the power of the monarchy system as is the case in the Gulf States.[53]

The influence of the Kuwaiti Constitution on the Omani Basic Statute is not merely in the general formation and meaning. A number of provisions are almost identical.[54] In addition to the influences of the Kuwaiti and Egyptian models, the French, the United States and the Universal Declaration of Human Rights of 1948 have their influences too; especially with regard to the articles dealing with fundamental

---

52 Miller, J. (1997), *ibid.*

53 Ballantyne, W.M (1986); "The Constitutions of the Gulf States: a comparative Study". *Arab Law Quarterly,* p. 160.

54 As the cases of Articles (62, 64, and 68) of the Omani Basic Statute with Articles (164, 167, and 172) of Kuwaiti Constitution. The comparison used the original Arabic manuscripts for both constitutions; example for the similarities of the Omani (Art. 68) with Kuwaiti (Art. 172); "*The Law shall regulate the procedure for settlement of conflict of jurisdiction between judicial bodies and in cases of conflict of judgments".*

rights and freedoms known in the OBSS as 'Public Rights and Duties'.[55]

A key question that arises is why the choice of the term 'the Basic Statute of the State' instead of the most common term 'Constitution'?[56] This is of some significance when one considers that besides Saudi Arabia all other Gulf States used the term 'constitution' including Kuwait,[57] Bahrain,[58] Qatar,[59] and United Arab Emirates.[60] An insight is offered with a quick overview of the terminologies in Arabic terms *dustur* (Constitution) and *netham asasi* (Basic Law). According to Siegfried, N. (2000) "*... the connotation of the term dustur bears a European influence. Therefore, governments wanting to emphasise the importance of Islamic principles in the basic law also avoid the term dustur*".[61] Arguably the use of this term in Oman may be in part due to the current Sultan's efforts to keep the Arab language and culture alive by avoiding the use of any foreign words.[62]

55 An example of similarities Art. 11 of the Universal Declaration of Human Rights, (Art. 22) OBSS, and (Art. 34) Kuwaiti constitution which are about Presumption of Innocence and Right to Trial.

56 The 'Basic Statute of the State' term is used in most of the translated versions of the Original Arabic one, such as the one provided by the Ministry of Legal Affairs or by the State Council. It is worth mentioning that 'the Basic Law' term is usually used as an alternative expression of the constitution, while 'Basic Statute' term is rarely used as it is the case of Oman and the 'Provisional Amended Basic Statute of the State' of Qatar of 1972.

57 1962.

58 2002.

59 2003.

60 1971.

61 Siegfried, N. (2000, October). Legislation and Legitimation in Oman: The Basic Law. *Islamic Law and Society*, 7(3), p. 362. However, the Arabic term *dustur* is actually not Arabic, it is originally Persian that came to Arabic via Turkish, and means Basic or Fundamental; thus it is not mentioned in all old Arabic lexicons before 1869. See al-Shukaili, S. (2006), *ibid*, pp. 12-14.

62 One of the well-known practices of the current Sultan is his orders to change the foreign or non-correct Arabic words to their Arabic origins, such as changing the terms 'unemployment' and 'cyclone' from their vernacular usage.

2.2.3 The Basic Statute Structure

The Royal Decree (101/96) promulgating the OBSS consists of two parts; the first part includes two articles that the Sultan has decreed as the Basic Statute of the State formally published in the Official Gazette, while the second part is the main document which is the Basic Statute consisting of seven chapters and 81 articles. The first chapter 'The State and the system of Government' consists of 9 Articles, and it follows the same formats as other Gulf States constitutions and somewhat the Egyptian model by setting the State's religion, language, and the basis of legislation. It emphasises the hereditary Sultanate (Monarchy) as the system of government, and provides the system for choosing the next successor to the throne.

'Principles Guiding State Policy' is the second chapter, and lists 5 Articles of Political, Economic, Social, Cultural, and Security headings. They are no more than guiding principles, and enforcing them legally poses a question, especially since their common principles are difficult for the courts to rely on as definite law articles; nevertheless, they give some direction to the government to follow in all of its policies, decisions, and regulations. There are two main differences between this chapter with its parallels in other Gulf States and Egyptian constitutions, namely that Oman is the only one who names it the 'Principles Guiding State Policy', which suggests that emphasis on the government's higher responsibilities over maintaining the 'Basic Constituents of Society', named by other constitutions. Table 1 below sets out comparisons and contrasts with other Gulf State constitutions and includes the Egyptian version which forms a basis for Gulf States.[63]

---

63 United Arab Emirates named it 'The Fundamental Social and Economic Basis of the Union' because of its union attribute, the 'Saudi Arabia' constitution divided it into two chapters the 'Constituents of Saudi Society', and 'The Economic Principles', while the rest named it the 'Basic Constituents of Society'. Also, the Omani model has fewer numbers of articles than its parallels; actually it combines most of the separated listed articles on other constitutions into a few articles with more details.

Table 1: The Constitution Structure of Gulf States and Egypt

	Kuwait 1963 (183 Articles)	**Egypt** 1971 (211 Articles)	**UAE** 1971 (152 Articles)	**Saudi Arabia** 1992 (83 Articles)	**Oman** 1996 (81 Articles)	**Bahrain** 2002 (125 Articles)	**Qatar** 2003 (150 Articles)
Chapter 1	The State and System of Government (6 Articles)	The State (6 Articles)	the Union (12 Articles)	General Principles (4 Articles)	The State and the System of Government (9 Articles)	The State (3 Articles)	The State and the Bases of the Rule (17 Articles)
Chapter 2	Fundamental Constituents of Kuwaiti Society (20 Articles)	Basic Constituents of Society (33 Articles)	The Fundamental Social and Economic Basis of the Union (12 Articles)	The System of Government (4 Articles)	Principles Guiding State Policy (5 Articles)	Basic Constituents of Society (13 Articles)	Basic Constituents of Society (16 Articles)
Chapter 3	Public Rights and Duties (23 Articles)	Public Freedoms, Rights and Duties (24 Articles)	Freedom, Rights and Public Duties (20 Articles)	Fundamental Constituents of Saudi Society (5 Articles)	Public Rights and Duties (26 Articles)	Public Rights and Duties (15 Articles)	Public Rights and Duties (25 Articles)
Chapter 4	Powers (124 Articles)	Sovereignty of the Law (9 Articles)	The Union Authorities (65 Articles)	Economic Principles (9 Articles)	The Head of State (17 Articles)	Public Authorities General Provisions (75 Articles)	Organization of Powers (82 Articles)
Chapter 5	General and Transitional Provisions (10 Articles)	The System of Government (112 Articles)	Union Legislations and Decrees and the Authorities having Jurisdiction Therein (6 Articles)	Rights and Duties (21 Articles)	The Oman Council (1 Article)	Financial Affairs (13 Articles)	Final Provisions (10 Articles)
Chapter 6		General and Transitional Provisions (9 Articles)	The Emirates (4 Articles)	The Authorities of the State (28 Articles)	The Judiciary (13 Articles)	General and Final Provisions (6 Articles)	
Chapter 7		New Provisions (18 Articles)	Union and Emirates Jurisdictions (6 Articles)	Financial Affairs (7 Articles)	General Provisions (10 Articles)		
Chapter 8			Financial Affairs of the Union (11 Articles)	Control Bodies (2 Articles)			
Chapter 9			Armed Forces and Security Forces (7 Articles)	General Provisions (3 Articles)			
Chapter 10			Final and Transitional Provisions (9 Articles)				

As can be seen from the table, almost one third of the Omani constitution, which is composed of 26 articles, is listed under the third chapter 'Public Rights and Duties'.[64] There are 22 articles relating to

64 This part of the document is mostly influenced by the western constitutions and the Universal Declaration of Human Rights.

Public Rights and Civil Liberties with only four articles about the Public Duties, which could result in the question arising about the rights being conditional on meeting obligations.[65] As noted above it follows broadly the same structure and format of the Egyptian and Kuwaiti models with the distinction of Omani model having less articles listed than others.

The powers and the government branches are usually discussed under one chapter in most of Gulf constitutions. It is remarkable that Oman is the only one which gives a chapter for each branch. However three articles list the Sultan's powers and functions, under the fourth chapter 'The Head of the State' which consists of 17 articles divided into 5 sections namely 'The Sultan', 'The Council of Ministers', The Prime Minister, His Deputies and Ministers', 'Specialised Councils', and 'Financial Affairs'. Listing those institutions under the 'The Head of the State' could be regarded as a sign that they are manacled by the Sultan more than Oman Council and the Judiciary.[66]

Chapter five is the shortest chapter, with only one article about the 'Oman Council', saying that it is a bicameral chamber and consists of *Majlis Ash-Shura* (Consultative Council) and *Majlis Ad-Daula* (State Council). Unconventionally, it was left for external statute to determine each Council's powers, sessions, procedure.[67] It was the

65 Siegfried, N. (2000), *ibid*, p. 370. The view that rights and duties are correlative used to be the dominant one among philosophers. "Many rights theorists, including Feinberg, Lyons, Martin and Nickel, and McCloskey, take different standpoints against this position". Although, most of the arguments are based on the four Hohfeldian categories; "which are claims (or rights proper), privileges (or liberties), powers, and immunities". See Alison Renteln (1988) The Concept of Human Rights, Anthropos, Bd. 83, H. 4./6, pp. 343-364. Downloadable from <http://www.jstor.org/stable/40463371>; and Nikolai Lazarev (2005) Hohfeld's Analysis of Rights: An Essential Approach to a Conceptual and Practical Understanding of the Nature of Rights, Murdoch University Electronic Journal of Law, from: <http://www.austlii.edu. au/au/journals/MurUEJL/2005/9.html>

66 *ibid*

67 See the changes on this Chapter about Oman Council on the Appendix 3.

first constitution in the Gulf which established the bicameral chamber followed by Bahrain in 2002.

Judiciary is dealt with under the 13 articles of chapter six; and among other constitutions it was the first one to establish the Public Prosecution and Attorney General as parts of the legal system constitutionally. It is also worth mentioning that the words 'Law' and 'Laws' have been repeated on the OBSS 94 times within its 7 Chapters which highlights the rule of law as one of the constitution targets to be implemented during the next era.

The Basic Statute follows other constitutions by making the last chapter of the constitution for 'General Provisions' with 10 articles that give the importance of international treaties in the local law, as well as regulating the relationship between the OBSS and extant laws, and any amendments to the constitution.

What is notable under the structure of the Basic Statute, as mentioned above under Chapters Four, Five, and Six, is that the institutions seem separated. Instead of a separation of powers divided between the executive, legislative, and judicial branches of the government, the Basic Statute has different separations which are namely Head of State, consultative, and judicial. Even with such structured separations, it is actually the powers of one, 'The Sultan', with the assistance of the others.

Instead of the legislative as a branch, the OBSS mentioned the Oman Council without any clarifications of any of its legislative powers and left it for external statutes, which suggests that this could give a flexible development for the Council to be powered from time to time in accordance with the community development and without the need to amend the Basic Statute, which needs to be stable for years until it is recognised by the government and the people.[68] However, such flexibility could agitate the issue inversely, such as em-

68 Marashaha, M. (2005). Views over the Basic Statute. *The Basic Statute Characteristics (in Arabic).* Muscat: School of Law, p. 14.

powering the Council by normal statute depending on the ruler's enunciations that are not constrained by the constitution.

2.3 The Characteristics of the Basic Statute

Each constitution has its own unique characteristics that set it apart from other constitutions. In general, the Basic Statute can be classified as written, codified, and flexible geared to an undemocratic, absolute monarchical, and unitary system.

To some extent the Basic Statute is a flexible constitution that makes it possible to amend it without any restrictions such as time limit, mandatory principles or protective articles.[69] It is also modern, and respects international law by recognising the international treaties and agreements and incorporating them as part of the Omani law.[70] By examining it, we find several characteristics that have been influenced by the Omani Society factors.

Arabic and Islam as major constructions for the territory and its people will be discussed first, followed by some other remarkable characteristics that makes the Basic Statute different. The branches of the government and the separation of their powers will be introduced with a detailed analysis in the following Chapter.

2.3.1 Arabic Character

The First Article of the Basic Statute states that "*the Sultanate of Oman is an Arab, Islamic, independent State*". This stresses the historical and cultural background of Omani society. Although Arabic is the main spoken language, and it is taught in schools, there are some

69 Such as the case with the 1971 UAE constitution which was declared as interim for five years (Art. 144) and the Kuwait, Bahrain and Qatar constitutions which prevent any discussion for amendment provisions concerning rights and public freedom unless in cases where the purpose is to grant more rights and guarantees in the interests of the citizens. (Art. 175 Kuwait Constitution, Art. 146 Qatar Constitution and Art. 31 Bahrain Constitution).

70 Art 76.

other languages in use in Oman.[71] English is widely spoken in the capital area especially in the economic and commercial fields. In addition, minorities speak their own languages. For example, Asian languages such as Hindi, Urdu, Persian, and Baluchi are used. Swahili is spoken by some Omanis who came from Zanzibar and elsewhere in East Africa. In addition to other Semitic languages, Bathari and Mehri are spoken in the South of the country.[72]

Most states specify their own official language through legislation. Article 3 of the OBSS lays down that: the '*state's official language is Arabic*'. Therefore, Article 26 of the Civil and Commercial Legal Procedures Law and Article 3 of the Criminal Procedures Law came later to determine that Arabic is the language used for legal and judicial proceedings. Thus, all documents, scripts, and legal instruments have to be written in or translated into Arabic, and in case of listening to non-Arabic speakers, the court can use interpreters under oath.[73]

Some constitutions in other parts of the world do not indicate the state's official language such as is the case with the United States, and Germany's constitutions. On the other hand the French constitution, which indicates French as its official language, as mentioned is an influence on the model for most Arab constitutions.

The Basic Statute is not different from most Arabian constitutions in making the first few articles focus on the country's Arabian nature and thus its official language. Distinguishably, the Basic Statute does

71 The Arabic language is still the main source of the definition of Arab; according to Britannica Encyclopaedia "An Arab is someone whose native language is Arabic. The term was first used to describe people who lived in a part of southwestern Asia called the Arabian Peninsula. Today the word Arab also refers to Arabic-speaking people who live in the Middle East, North Africa, and other places" Arab. (2011). In Encyclopaedia Britannica. Retrieved from <http://www.britannica.com/EBchecked/topic/31348/Arab>

72 Lewis, M. (2005). *Languages of Oman.* Retrieved 04 May 2007, from Ethnologue: Languages of the World: <http://www.ethnologue.com>

73 Criminal Procedures Law (R.D. 97/99), Civil and Commercial Legal Procedures Law (R.D. 29/2002). See Al Shukaili, S. (2006), p. 88.

not give emphasis to the Arabic Union or Arab Nation unlike other Gulf and Egyptian models where the State is 'part of the Arab *Umma* (nation)' and the final goal of the government is the establishment of a pan-Arab Nation.[74] It seems that the OBSS's goal was more realistic and not that of propounding the Pan-Arab nation as a dream to implement but rather that of stating the reality of the Omani society's affiliation to the Arab world.[75]

2.3.2 Islamic Character

Islamic and tribal traditions have dominated the Arabian Peninsula's people for a long time and Islam is a central basis of the community. In addition to specific mentions by most of the Islamic countries constitutions, the ruler is also designated as the protector of Islam which also serves a central role in providing legitimacy to rulers.

The word 'Islam' and 'Islamic' have been mentioned five times in the Basic Statute, mainly in the first articles which also state that "*the Sultanate of Oman is an Arab, Islamic and independent State*";[76] and "*The State's religion is Islam and the Islamic Shariʿa is the basis of legislation*".[77] Other references are in regard to the Principles Guiding State Policy, politically and economically.

However, the most outstanding feature in the Basic Statute is that "*the Islamic Shariʿa is the basis of legislation*" while in all other Gulf States and Egypt, with the exception of Saudi Arabia, make the Islam-

74 UAE (Art. 7); Saudi (Art. 25); Bahrain (Art. 1); Qatar (Art. 1); Egypt (Art. 1); Kuwait (preamble & Art. 157); it is notable that the Pan-Arabism as a movement is less than 100 years old and was first pressed to seek independence from the Ottoman Empire.

75 It is worth mentioning that the main driving factor for the Pan-Arab nation or the Arabic Union is of Arabic language whereas the European Union is of the continent and the Islamic Union is of the religion. Such belongingness influences the states, to a certain extent, even without indicating this in legal documents.

76 Art. 1 OBSS.

77 Art. 2 OBSS.

ic *Shariʿa* as the *main* source of legislation.[78] Such distinction should give the *Shariʿa* Law a higher ranking over other statutes in Oman.[79]

From the early 1970s following the ascent to power by Sultan Qaboos, the judiciary system changed dramatically from a fully traditional Islamic law to be influenced by western systems. Before implementing the Basic Statute there were *Shariʿa* and *non-Shariʿa* courts, the later functions were in relation to the commercial disputes and penal cases. Today, the role of *Shariʿa* Law is reduced but it still forms the basis of family and personal laws.[80] As well, professing Islam is

---

78 UAE (Art. 7); Bahrain (Art. 2); Qatar (Art. 1); Egypt (Art. 2); Kuwait (Art. 2). However, the case of Saudi Arabia is different where the Holy Quran and the Sunnah of the Prophet Muhammad are mentioned as its own constitution (Art. 1).

79 Legislation is a main source, particularly in civil law systems. Case law, precedent, is equally important in common law. In the Islamic states, the *Shariʿa* is also designated a source of law and afforded a primary or secondary status in their constitutions or civil codes. In some Gulf States, the Shariʿa remains predominant not only in local and family relations but in other areas as well. Conflict with overlapping statutory enactments is not uncommon. Such as the case of the UAE Supreme Court of the UAE in 1984, ruled that the penal statute providing for the imposition of a fine and imprisonment for drunkenness in a public place did not preclude the sharia punishment of flogging as well. (UAE Official Gazette, No. 135, Vol. XIV (February 1984)). "The court chose to uphold the divine injunction over the statutory, which, skirting the issue of personal freedom and privacy, concerned itself with what seemed more appropriately the state's concern, that is public order and safety. The problems posed by the existence of a duality in the law, with the Sharia in this instance representing the 'higher law', and the impact this has had on the legislative process and the development of fundamental rights". See Sfeir, G (Summer, 1988) Source of Law and the Issue of Legitimacy and Rights, Middle East Journal, Vol. 42, No.3, pp.436-446, from <http://www.jstor.org/stable/4327779> For further expansion on this matter please refer to: Brown, N. (Aug., 1997) Sharia and State in the Modern Muslim Middle East, International Journal of Middle East Studies, Vol. 29, No. 3, pp. 359-376, from www.jstor.org/stable/164585 and Layish, A (2004) The Transformation of the Shari'a from Jurists' Law to Statutory Law in the Contemporary Muslim World, Brill, Die Welt des Islams, New Series, Vol. 44, Issue 1, pp. 85-113 from <http://www.jstor.org/stable/1571336>

80 Siegfried, N. (2000), p. 367.

still one of the main requirements a person must have to be chosen as a successor to the Sultan[81] and to hold the post of a judge in courts.[82]

Islam plays an important role in some personal rights, such as the right of inheritance. It has been mentioned separately from other rights and freedoms in the Third chapter of the Basic Statute, which are more connected to the international human rights. The Basic Statute has clearly stated that the *Shari'a* of Islam is the law governing the right of inheritance.[83] The Islamic *Shari'a* law has different methods of dividing inheritance among heirs,[84] and under its division of the inheritance portions, there could be a clash with Article 17 of the Basic Statute that relates to Citizen Equality and non-Discrimination rights.

Under Article 10, another major influence of Islam in the Basic Statute is the *Shura* principle. The establishment of the *Shura* Council was the choice of several systems in Gulf States as a parliament. There are a lot of arguments regarding the distinction between *Shura* in Islam and Democracy under western theory. It is inappropriate to examine such clues in the Basic Statute without enlightening briefly the *Shura* in Islam which will be discussed in Chapters 3 and 4. In Oman, *Shura* has been part of the political principles "*by establishing*

81 Art. 5 OBSS.

82 Art. 21 of the Judicial Authority Law (R.D. 90/99).

83 Art. 11 OBSS.

84 The dividing method under *Shari'a* have different considerations for each heir and his or her relation to the inherited, the discrimination between male and female does not mean the male always gets more than female. There are some cases where the female gets more or all the inheritance. The UN Human Rights Special Procedures reports claim that male heirs are favoured in adjudicating inheritance claims, and that many women are reluctant to take an inheritance dispute to court for fear of alienating the family. See document (E/CN.4/2003/75/Add. 1) the Report of the Special Rapporteur on violence against women, its causes and consequences 'Integration of the Human Rights of Women and the Gender Perspective Violence against Women, submitted in accordance with Commission on Human Rights resolution 2002/52 Addendum 1 International, regional and national developments in the area of violence against women'.

the pillars of genuine Shura Consultation, based on the national heritage and its Islamic Shari'a".[85] The Shura term is used not just to give a parallel to democracy; it serves more as a substitute. Therefore, it is connected to Article 9 where "*the rule in the Sultanate shall be based on justice, Shura, and equality*" and it limited the citizens' right to participate in public affairs "*in accordance with this Basic Statute and the conditions and provisions stipulated by the law*".

2.3.3 The Succession System[86]

Succession to the throne was one of the most important motives for adopting the Basic Statute in Oman. The method of choosing the successor in Oman is unique, which makes it one of the main characteristics of the Omani Basic Statute. It does not have much in common with the other Gulf States, as it mixes the monarchy and tribal methods with the influences of Islam, especially tenets of the *Ibadi* sect.[87]

What is unique about contemporary succession in Oman as opposed to other Gulf State monarchies is that there are no apparent heirs; in essence the next Sultan is still unknown. Article 6 of the Basic Statute describes how the next Sultan is chosen "*within three days of the position of Sultan becoming vacant, the Ruling Family Council shall determine upon who will succeed to the throne. If the Ruling Family Council does not agree upon a successor, the Defence Council shall confirm the appointment of the person designated by the Sultan in his letter to the Family Council*".[88]

85 Art. 10 OBSS.

86 Articles 5-7 OBSS.

87 On October 2006, Saudi Arabia announced the Homage System which is similar in a way to the Omani Ruling Family Council idea, with clear vote system; however it has never been examined yet.

88 The Sultan explained that: "*When I die, my family will meet. If they cannot agree on a candidate, the Defence Council will decide, based on a name or names submitted by the previous sultan. I have already written down two names, in descending order, and put them in sealed envelopes in two different regions*". See Miller, J. (1997), p. 17.

Its monarchical side can be viewed from its hereditary Sultanate's attribute as a system of government, and the Royal Family as a monarchy which excludes any other families, as well as any other systems such as the traditional Imamate, from ruling the country in the future. While its tribes' perspective came from making the Royal Family Council the main authority for choosing the next ruler, the council itself follows the traditional Omani tribal system where the main key members of the tribe gather to decide.[89]

The influences of Islam are clear from the successor's requirements. Article 5 requires that the successor is a "*Male, adult, Muslim, of sound mind, and a legitimate son of Omani Muslim parents*", which follow in a way the requirements for an Imam. Similarly, as the ruler under the Imamate system is chosen by *'Ahl al-Hall wa al-Aqd'* Council, the Sultan as the ruler is chosen by the Royal Family Council.[90] Also, the new Sultan shall take an oath before exercising his powers, in front of a joint session of the Oman and Defence Councils which is similar to the oath done by the Imam in front of the council.[91]

However, the Royal Family Council and the succession process are still ambiguous which could lead to anxiety about the system's stability for choosing the next Sultan. Throughout history, there are examples of some disagreements inside the Royal Family, whereby certain members demanded to rule. One of the conflicts could come from the Royal Family Council, whose voting and decision making systems, as well as its members, are unknown to the public.[92]

---

89 The succession system under Art. 5 of OBSS excludes other root descendants of the main Royal Family by limiting the successor under the descendants of *Turki bin Said bin Sultan*; the third grandfather of the current Sultan.

90 Art. 6.

91 Art. 7.

92 The Sultan describes such process as always known, as a Monarchy convention, and for the first time it is publicised in a formal document 'the Basic Statute'. There is no heirs apparent system in *Al Said* ruling, and the key members of Royal Family and other leading tribes approve the ruler. See Miller, J. (1997) *ibid.*

Thus several concerns and uncertainties about the successor system abound. These concerns cover areas such as the nominations and their ruling ability, the Royal Family Council's conflict with the Defence Council when they do not agree on a candidate and do not accept the Sultan's nominations, the possibility of different nominations in different envelopes, and also the question of the successor system under the Sultan's rule while he is alive but can no longer fulfil governing functions.

2.3.4 The Oman Council[93]

Another distinguishing feature of the Basic Statute is related to the parliamentary system represented by the Oman Council, which was the first bicameral set-up among the Gulf States. It follows to some extent the English model where the Upper House, the State Council members, are nominated by the Sultan similar in some ways to the House of Lords, while the Lower House, *Ash-Shura* Council members are elected by the people as for the House of Commons.

The Basic Statute has left the system of the Oman Council flexible, enabling it to be developed from time to time without the need to amend the Basic Statute. Essentially it is left for ordinary statutes to determine and elaborate the whole system. In the past years, the system has been examined and it seems that the development of the Council is in progress.[94] However, such flexibility means the Oman Council does not enjoy constitutional guarantee.

93 The discussion about Oman Council will be covered in several parts of this work, as the case needed here to highlight the most important features about the OBSS and on section 3.3.2 about its power compared to other branches. However, a comprehensive analysis on different aspects of the Oman Council will be covered on Chapter Five and Appendix 3.

94 Although such developments do not reach the expectations of parliament as a legislative body yet.

2.4 'Basic Statute' in Practice

For more than 20 years,[95] the State Administrative Apparatus Law[96] was the supreme reference text in the state for all regulations, laws and legal principles. This law had given the state the basis needed for organising the administrative and government bodies. But its structure, characters and articles did not follow the Basic Statute. Furthermore, the main issues relating to the State' and the system of government, the Judiciary, or civil liberties were not addressed.

The promulgation of the Basic Statute has been a magnificent legal move in Oman for the government and society as well. The Basic Statute's legal success is attributable to how it combines many customs, traditions, social and religious rules while at the same time adding the fundamental human rights and liberties into the legal document. Moreover, it succeeds in highlighting the construction of national unity as identity instead of the "*heterogeneity of Omani culture*".[97]

A year after the Basic Statute had been promulgated, it was developed further by other decrees including Royal Decree (84/97) which brought about significant changes to the Cabinet departments as well some ministerial positions. One result of the decree was that the Ministry of Justice, Awqaf (Endowments) and Islamic Affairs was divided into two separate ministries. Firstly, it established the Ministry of Justice to implement the rule of law as a governmental target for the next era, with the intention of establishing the new judicial system as described in the Basic Statute. Secondly it established the Ministry of Awqaf (Endowments) and Religious Affairs, as its name had been changed from Islamic to Religious Affairs. Such changes to the name were unacceptable for a conservative community where Islam as a religion is the most important issue. Even within a community known for its tolerance, a change in the name was seen as a

95 From 1975 to 1996.
96 Issued by the Royal Decree 26/75.
97 Siegfried, N. (2000), p. 371.

change in respect for the religion. Nevertheless, the changes were necessary to prove the government's commitment to freedom of religion and to organise it as stated in the Basic Statute. However, it has taken the people time to understand the purpose of such changes.

Such changes were followed by enormous developments in the legal system. Most notably is the independence of the courts,[98] by instituting the Judiciary Higher Council in 1999,[99] the Public Prosecution and the Attorney General in 1999,[100] the legal profession in 1996[101] and regulating the types and grades of the Law Courts in 1999.[102] Such developments succeeded in moving the country from a traditional legal system to a modern one and since 1997 the country has had its first law school. Establishing the administrative court system under Article 67 has had its impacts too. For the first time citizens were granted the right to complain legally against government procedures, decisions and administrative disputes which usually were not recognised earlier.

Another important aspect of the Basic Statute is human rights which was an unfamiliar term in the past, and of which people never really had an awareness of. Formally enshrining these rights and duties should have an influence on educating the people and developing the courts. Over the years since the promulgation of the OBSS progressive developments are visible,[103] and the importance of the rule of law has been recognised. Several laws have been amended, changed or repealed. At the same time new laws have been published, and are often modern and specialised taking into consideration the recognition of international standards.

---

98 Art. 60.

99 Art. 66.

100 Art. 64.

101 Art. 65.

102 Art. 62.

103 Such as the unification of judicial authorities and the independence of the judiciary and the public prosecutor.

On the other hand, there are other issues where the Basic Statute is supposed to safeguard the rights and liberties. It is however constrained by the assertion "*in accordance with the exigencies of the public interest*" (Preamble). Some of these issues are related to the Basic Statute in general, while others are related to specific articles. When it was promulgated, it fell short of expectations, and did not fulfil what most educated people desire. However as opposed to the 1971 UAE Constitution, for example, the OBSS is not a temporary constitution. Indeed, it was a turning point in Oman's history, bringing about a number of developments and leading people to think more in terms of public participation, freedoms, and governmental accountability.

Instead of a constitutional monarchy, the state remains an absolute monarchy. Freedoms exist more in theory than in practice, and parliament does not have power over the executive branch. Moreover, many people have not read the OBSS, some being unaware of its importance or even of its existence. This raises the question of education and the media's role in spreading awareness. Is it a special document intended merely for the use of courts or is it a personal responsibility to find out about it? Some specific articles will be set out for the purposes of aspects of the thesis with a snapshot. This will be progressively examined in detail.

Article 78 of the OBSS states that "*the competent bodies shall take steps for issuance of non-existing laws necessitated by this Basic Statute within two years from the date of its coming into force*". In fact the required laws have taken more than two years to be promulgated such as the case of instituting the Judiciary Higher Council,[104] the Public Prosecution and the Attorney General,[105] and regulating the types and grades of the Law Courts in 1999.[106] According to the Sultan's interview in 1997 he admitted the difficulties in implementing those laws

104 Art. 66.
105 Art. 64.
106 Art. 62.

within that period, but which he hoped would be implemented by 2000.[107] However, there are other main statutes which came after 2000 such as the Labour Law in 2003,[108] the State's Flag, Emblem, National Anthem Law in 2004,[109] and the independence of Public Prosecutor in 2011. In addition, there are other important legislations which have not been declared yet, such as the relevant terms of reference for the constitutional body 'the Authority on Conflicts of Jurisdictions and Rules'.[110]

Although the flexibility is regarded as one of the characteristics of the Basic Statute, Article 58 about Oman Council could be reaping negative results. This is mainly because it allows the ordinary statute to determine the council's power, membership, and rules of procedure. The ordinary statute does not give the council constitutional protection. Thus, its powers could be reduced instead of strengthened by an ordinary law.[111]

The Independent Constitutional Court is meant to be established by Article 70, with the aim of "*settling disputes arising from the incompatibility of laws and regulations with the Basic Statute of the State and ensuring that the latter's provisions are not contravened*". Also, it was one of the Sultan's priorities as he described it as "*the guardians of the law, without that you cannot have a proper government, they are the ones to say what is right and wrong*".[112]

Similar to the flexibility in Oman Council, the OBSS has given the determination of such institution and its membership to an ordinary statute without having it as a part of the Basic Statute itself. Moreover, under article 10 of the Judicial Authority Law,[113] the authority

107 Miller, J. (1997), p. 16.
108 Art. 12.
109 Art. 4.
110 See section (3.4.4) for more details.
111 Refer to Appendix 3 for the recent changes.
112 Miller, J. (1997), p. 16.
113 R.D. 90/99 which came into force in June 2000.

of that judicial body has been granted to a panel which consists of eleven of the highest ranking judges from the Supreme and Administrative courts. Article 11 of the Judicial Authority Law has given that body the authority to hold the specialisation of the Constitutional Court as mentioned in Article 70 of the Basic Statute but it is still not tantamount to a Constitutional Court.[114]

Today, fourteen years after promulgating the Basic Statute and ten years after establishing the Judicial Panel responsible for Constitutional Court issues, all the important constitutional issues between the Basic Statute and the Constitutional Court have still not been discussed. This is mainly attributable to the lack of a related statute that should clarify the competence of the Judicial Panel responsible for Constitutional Court issues and the procedures it follows.[115] It is difficult to leave such a crucial judicial gap for a longer period without establishing such an important statute, especially if one takes into account cases of crisis and emergency.

The main crucial issue regarding the Basic Statute is related to its amendments which are found in the last article of the Basic Statute (Article 81). It "*can only be amended in the same manner in which it was promulgated*". This provision is different from normal statutes where the government, cabinet, and Oman Council are all involved. The amendment of the Basic Statute is left solely as the right of the ruler, without any other powers to restrict him, which means he could change or amend any or all articles of the Basic Statute. The Basic Statute involves neither the people's referendum, nor the participation of parliament or councils. This means that the Sultan will still have ultimate power unless an amendment is introduced to restrict it. This is considered unlikely under the current Sultan who has issued it according to his own desires. However, if this right is not limited, it would be easy for the next Sultan to make any change

114 For more details see Chapter Three (3.4.4) 'The Constitutional Court'.
115 Article 11 of the Judicial Authority Law.

whatsoever, thus creating problems if the changes made are against people's rights or undermine the developments achieved.

2.5 Conclusion

The Basic Statute has brought a new era for Omani people to gain more rights and freedoms giving them constitutional protections and guarantees that did not exist earlier. The Basic Statute, however, is still lacking in important areas and it seems it was drafted as a transitional constitution designed to last no longer than the next Sultan's rule. The demand for changing the Basic Statute comes from educated people and the young generation with the increasing use of the internet as a source of information.

In December 2009, a group of writers and bloggers expressed their interest in presenting the Sultan with a petition to adopt a new constitution, which they called a 'contractual constitution'. The invitation for the new constitution began via email and internet blogs, and later it was sent as a formal letter to the Sultan signed by 50 people[116] asking him to change or amend the current Basic Statute to a new one based on fundamental changes in the separation of powers and increasing the power of the parliament. It suggested that the constitution should be put forward for public referendum to get its 'contractual status between the ruler and people'. This step was remarkable for several reasons:

1. It used the internet to spread the willingness for change, which is not possible under any normal publication in Oman.[117]
2. It spread the awareness about the Basic Statute, as many people are still not aware about the importance of the supreme law of the land.
3. It was the first public demand to amend the constitution.

116 On 3rd July 2010 and most of the group were educated youth.

117 The freedom of expression in the media and publications is very weak in Oman due to the strictness of the Press and Publications Law (R.D. 49/84).

One of the prominent petitioners had listed six reasons for asking for the new constitution:[118]

- First: The rights contained in the OBSS are formulated in a way that does not represent sufficient safeguards to protect them, but they are left in the hands of the government and its sole discretion.
- Second: The OBSS does not recognise the people as a source of authority, and the absence of this recognition takes away from the people the ability to grant legitimacy under their free will.
- Third: The OBSS does not restrict the powers of the ruler and governmental institutions and subject them to be held accountable to the people, which is part of the absolute power problem.
- Fourth: The OBSS does not contain a chapter for the legislative branches as it is practised by the executive and both powers are concentrated in the hands of the Sultan.
- Fifth: The OBSS can be modified or repealed by Royal Decree, and it was promulgated without discussing its contents with the people and without putting it in a referendum.
- Sixth: There is no constitutional court which monitors the laws issued by the State and to ensure compatibility with the principles and provisions of the OBSS, and therefore there is no clear mechanism or specific institutions working to activate the system.

The importance of such a petition lays in its legal and political principles, such as guaranteeing human rights and freedoms, and asserting the progression of the absolute monarchy to a constitutional one as necessary for the long term stability of the State. The petition however, was not successful, and did not receive any support either from government or people. The petition did not gain widespread acceptance for several reasons: public awareness; society structure; and tribal and traditional support. In any case the petition could not gener-

118 Al Kiumi, B. (12 December 2009). *The Petition for Contractual Constitution: Why do we sign?* Retrieved 3 January 2010, from Alharah AlOmania: <http://alharah.net/alharah/t13995.html>

ate government or the Sultan's support as it demanded a reduction in their power. However it gained some attention because it was so unexpected, though it would have gained more if it had been built on solid ground and if the above-mentioned reasons had been taken into account.

The petition ignored the general public awareness, as they had focused their demand through the internet, while many people around the country were unaware of the meaning of the Basic Statute and its importance. Hence, they did not know what the request was for. It also ignored the society structure, where the link between the ruler and his people cannot be achieved through internet invitations, though it gained more publicity. It should be linked in more formal ways which the Sultan feels are appropriate. It must be taken into account that most developments and freedoms granted to citizens in Oman were based on the Sultan's willingness and not by a request from his people. This is in addition to the fact that the petitioners' list of names did not attract many of the public, the elite and the tribes as many of them were youths and liberals who ignored the importance of the traditional social structure without taking the influence of Omani factors into account.

Despite the failure of the first attempt of this petition, it must be noted that it was an unprecedented step to open the way to understand the Basic Statute more broadly for the general public. Even though the government ignored this petition at the beginning, it attracted its attention.

However two years later, amidst the event of the 'Arab Spring' demonstrations that took place in February and March 2011 demanding better standards of living and more jobs, the earlier petitioners realised it was a golden chance to reclaim the 'contractual constitution' as part of other demands listed by the demonstrators. This time it succeeded in getting greater attention from the government and the public. In part the events and the now reinvigorated petition had a role in the Sultan proclaiming Royal Decree no. 39/2011. This granted the Council of Oman some legislative and auditing powers by establishing a constitutional committee from specialists to develop draft amendments to the Basic Statute State in order to give the Council the legislative powers; this is to be announced before the new period of *Ash-Shura* Council starting in October 2011. This step does not satisfy the people who demanded a contractual constitution as drafted. But, no doubt, they had a role in the changes that took place.

The Royal Decree provides power to the Council of Oman as a Parliament and not to the elected lower house *Ash-Shura* Council as representatives of the people, this indicates that the process of making laws would be distributed by the two houses, *Ash-Shura* Council and the State Council. The Royal Decree also has not specified the range of the legislative power granted and may include other roles for the Council of Ministers as well. Overall, it is expected that the system will follow the Kuwait's parliamentary system in its way of legislation, so that the consent of the Sultan remains decisive in the issuance of laws.[119]

119 Refer to Appendix 3 on the latest updates regarding *ash-Shura* Council.

3 Human Rights Protections and Safeguards under the Omani System

3.1 Introduction

Public rights and freedoms are one of the most important issues addressed by constitutional law and political systems. Public rights and freedoms are defined by Article 4 of the 1789 *Declaration of the Rights of Man and of the Citizen* as: the ability "*to do anything that does not harm others*", and, according to the same proclamation, the "*limits on that freedom is not permissible except by law*".[1] Evaluating human rights in any country cannot be done without examining the rights protected and the legal framework within which they operate. It is indispensable that in every system, there is a group of guarantees through which society's fundamental rights and freedoms are protected.

This chapter examines human rights protections and safeguards under the Omani system. The main issues discussed in this Chapter relate to whether the OBSS adequately references basic human rights and freedoms in its text; whether it adopts the principle of separation of powers and the 'rule of law' in the respective branch of the government; and whether the laws under the OBSS are subject to the examination of its constitutional review of the legality of administrative decisions. It will also analyse how human rights conventions and reports influence the protection of human rights and freedoms. Finally, it will consider the latest human rights developments in Oman in order to give some indication of Oman's prospective path along with a general overview of the limitations and obstacles that weaken the protection of human rights in Oman today.

1 The Declaration of the Rights of Man and of the Citizen (in English) Available from: <http://www.hrcr.org/docs/frenchdec.html>

3.2 Constitutional References to Basic Human Rights

In countries like Oman where the constitution is the supreme law, the OBSS serves as the fundamental framework in maintaining the country's peace and order. On one hand, the Constitution is the foundation of the authoritative function of any governmental entity; it determines how the government should be organised and defines the duties and powers that can be exercised by governmental branches as well as the rights of citizens. On the other hand, it provides the legal basis for citizens' rights and outlines all the freedoms that citizens can enjoy. Thus the OBSS is the fundamental legal framework in Omani society.

Most modern constitutions list several rights and freedoms that limit the government's power against its people, thus protecting their rights and freedoms. In some totalitarian states, the listing of such rights equates to no more than having a document with no tangible results. However, this is a generalisation which is not absolute as the promulgation of the OBSS in 1996 does seek to promote the protection of human rights and enhanced awareness in Oman.

3.2.1 Human Rights Restrictions and Guarantees under the Basic Statute

Oman followed the constitutional structure of other Gulf States, where rights and duties were incorporated in the OBSS thereby rendering them legally binding as part of the supreme law of the land. However, in their reference to 'democracy', it did not follow Kuwait, Bahrain and Qatar which described the governmental system of the state.[2] Instead, the OBSS placed more emphasis on the term '*Shura*', a principle derived from the country's religious and traditional background, which calls for the right to public participation in Oman. Contrary to western constitutions that attempt to reach a "*voluntary*

2 Also, the preamble of the UAE constitution states that a parliamentary democratic regime is a step cherished by the rulers of the Emirates.

accommodation between incommensurable values and interests",[3] the OBSS aims to impose a particular system of values, mainly the Islamic and traditional values, while attempting to reconcile that system with international human rights norms.

The OBSS introduced several civil, political, social, economic, cultural and even the so-called 'third-generation solidarity rights'. This was the first step in promoting and protecting human rights in Oman via a modern legal document. Such a document had never been part of the system before and the majority of Omani citizens were unfamiliar with its intended outcomes. It is worth noting that Oman has neither signed nor ratified the International Covenant on Civil and Political Rights (ICCPR), nor the International Covenant on Economic, Social and Cultural Rights (ICESCR).[4] Nevertheless, the OBSS is influenced by the concept of human rights as well as most civil, economic, social and cultural rights that are enshrined in these international human rights instruments. Chapters 2 and 3 of the OBSS most clearly demonstrate these influences as set out in Table 2 in the following section.

Of particular note is that the OBSS makes no explicit references to certain basic rights and freedoms that are found in international human rights instruments. In particular, the OBSS does not mention a person's right to life or political rights such as the right to choose and change the government.[5] Though a number of other rights are missing, they are protected under several Omani statutes and regulations such as the rights relating to motherhood, childhood, marriage and the prohibition of slavery.[6]

3 Alder, J. (2007). *Constitutional and Administrative Law* (6th ed.). Basingstoke: Palgrave Macmillan. p. 19.

4 United Nations. (2011). Retrieved from *Treaty Collection*: <http://www2.ohchr.org/english/bodies/ratification/index.htm>

5 It was one of the observations of the Report of the Special Rapporteur on extrajudicial, summary or arbitrary executions (A/HRC/17/28). From <http://www2.ohchr.org/english/bodies/hrcouncil/docs/17session/A-HRC-17-28.pdf>

6 In the OBSS it is clear that the drafters had a tendency to avoid mentioning

Similar to other Gulf States' constitutions, the right to life is not guaranteed under the OBSS or any other law. The purpose for excluding this right is to avoid conflict with the state's use of capital punishment. However, it is important to at least limit the use of capital punishment in the constitutional text by forbidding its application on children and pregnant women.[7] In comparison, Article 6 of the ICCPR does not prohibit the death penalty, but restricts its application to the '*most serious crimes*', whilst strongly recommending that the death penalty be abolished. However, most Gulf States' constitutions allow the head of government the right to pardon or commute the punishment of a citizen.[8] Oman still uses the death penalty for several cases, especially under Penal and Anti-Terrorism laws.[9]

Rights are not absolute but are subject to derogation and some limitations,[10] provided that they "*do not amount to the undermining of such rights, or eliminate their object and purpose, or contradict the essence of constitutional provisions*".[11] Several rights and freedoms listed in the OBSS include limitations that restrict their application for reasons related to public order, public morals and national security. Omani rights and freedoms are also limited by a clause that requires

---

political rights at that time, although the future possibility for such rights is left open under Chapter 5 of the OBSS.

7 Art. 6.5 ICCPR.

8 Art. 42 OBSS.

9 Such as Articles 123, 124, 127, 131, 140-144, 149, 237 of the Penal Law (R.D. 7/74), and Articles 2-7, 9-11 of the Anti-Terrorism Law (R.D. 8/07).

10 Mostly based in the interests of national security, public safety and order, protection of health and morals, protection of the rights and freedoms of others, preventing disorder or crime, and necessary for democratic society. Such as the derogations under Article 4 of ICCPR, and limitations under Articles 18 and 19 of ICCPR, and Articles 4 and 8 of ICSECR.

11 Al Roken, M. (1997). Human Rights under the Constitution of the United Arab Emirates: Guarantees and Restrictions. *Arab Law Quarterly*, 12 (1), p. 101.

them to be 'within the limits of the Law',[12] or 'specified by the Law'.[13] Many of these laws lack explicit definitions in relation to human rights or contradict the spirit of the right itself.[14]

Moreover, Oman has not followed the constitutions of Qatar, Bahrain and Kuwait in preventing the amendment of provisions related to human rights and public freedoms, unless the amendment aims to enhance and widen the guarantees thereof.[15] Rather, it leaves the amendment to be determined "*in the manner in which it was promulgated*"; namely a Royal Decree (Article 81).

3.2.2 Human Rights and Freedoms under the Basic Statute

The significance of enshrining rights and freedoms in the Omani Basic Statute is that no enacted statutes or secondary legislations and procedures should violate the rights and freedoms provided therein. What is notable under the OBSS is its categorisation of rights and freedoms under 'direct protected rights' and 'guiding principles'. Thus, most of the economic, social and cultural rights are listed under the *'State's Policy'* heading. Understanding these rights in a judicial context is still under question. As the title of this section suggests, policies for moving forward are mere guidelines rather than rights and freedoms with legal protection.[16]

---

12 Art. 11 'Freedom of Economic' and 'Private Ownership', Art. 15 'Nationality Right', Art. 29 'The Freedom of Opinion and Expression' and Art. 32 'Right to Assemble'.

13 Art. 31 'Freedom of the Press', Art. 30 'Freedom of Correspondence'.

14 Thus, by inserting such phrases, the OBSS reflects the following statement by W.M Ballantyne: "*Thus preserving to the government from time to time discretion to legislate on acceptable levels of freedom. This contrasts sharply with the absolute terms of the U.S.' First Amendment*". Al Roken, M. (1997). p. 102.

15 Art. 146 Qatar, Art. 175 Kuwait, Articles 31 & 120 Bahrain.

16 The distinction between direct protected rights and guiding principles has parallels in other legal systems, such as the case of the constitutions of Ireland, India, and Nigeria which have called them as Fundamental Rights and Directive Principles. Similar to Oman's Guiding Principles (or the Basic Constituents of Society in other Gulf States constitutions), the Directive Principles of State Policy are

Table 2: Rights and Freedoms under the Basic Statute and international instruments[17]

Rights/Freedoms	UDHR	ICCPR	ICECSR	Oman 'OBSS'
The right to life	Art.3	Art.6	–	–
Right to liberty and security of person	Art.3	Art.9	–	Art.18
Freedom from slavery, servitude and forced or compulsory labour	Art.4	Art.8	--	Art.12
Freedom from torture, inhuman or degrading treatment or punishment	Art.5	Art.7	–	Art.20
Right of deprive persons to be treated with humanity		Art.10	–	Art.20
Right to recognition as a person before the law	Art.6	Art.16	–	–
Freedom from imprisonment for inability to fulfil a contractual obligation	–	Art.11	–	–
Non-retroactive application of criminal law	–	Art.15	–	Arts.21, 75
Equality before the law without any discrimination	Art.7	Art.26	–	Art.17
Right to an effective remedy by national tribunals	Art.8	–	–	Art.24
Freedom from arbitrary arrest, detention or exile	Art.9	–	–	Arts.16, 18
Right to a fair trial	Art.10	Art.14	–	Art.24
Right to be presumed innocent until proved guilty according to law	Art.11	–	–	Art.22
Right to privacy, family, home or correspondence	Art.12	Art.17	–	Arts.30, 12
Right relating to motherhood, childhood, marriage and the family	–	–	Art.10	–
Freedom of movement and to choose residence	Art.13	Art.12	–	Art.16
Right to seek asylum from persecution	Art.14		–	Art.36
Freedom of aliens from arbitrary expulsion	.	Art.13	–	–
Right to a nationality	Art.15		–	Art.15
Right to marry and found a family	Art.16	Art.23	–	Art.12

guidelines for the framing of laws by the government. However, Article 37 of the Indian Constitution explicitly declares that these Directives Principles "are not enforceable by any court" and "it shall be the duty of the State to apply these principles in making laws".

17 The table shows the articles of human rights in international instruments such as the UDHR, ICCPR and ICESCR. It also shows explicit reference to these rights in the OBSS, although some of the rights and freedoms are implicitly mentioned.

Right to own property	Art.17	–	–	Art.11
Freedom of thought, conscience and religion	Art.18	Art.18	–	Art.28
Freedom of opinion and expression	Art.19	Art.19	–	Arts.29, 31
Right of peaceful assembly	Art.20	Art.21	–	Art.32
Freedom of association and to form and join trade unions	Art.20	Art.22	Art.8	Art.33
Right to take part in the conduct of public affairs, to vote and to be elected	Art.21	Art.25	–	–
Right to social security	Art.22	–	Art.9	Art.12
Right to work	Art.23	–	Art.6	Art.12
Right to just and favourable conditions of work	–	–	Art.7	Art.12
Right to rest and leisure and periodic holidays with pay	Art.24	–	–	–
Right to adequate food, clothing, housing and standard of living and freedom from hunger	Art.25	–	Art.11	–
Rights of the child	Art.25	Art.24	–	–
Right to physical and mental health	–	–	Art.12	–
Right to education; including a plan for implementing compulsory primary education	Art.26	–	Art.13	Art.13
Undertaking to implement the principle of compulsory education free of charge	Art.26	–	Art.14	–
Right relating to science and culture	Art.27	–	Art.15	Art.13
Prohibition of propaganda of war	–	Art.20	–	–
Rights of minorities	–	Art.27	–	–

Most directly protected rights and freedoms come under Chapter Three of the OBSS under the sub-title *'Public Rights and Duties'*, which comprises nearly one-third of the articles in the OBSS. Twenty-two of these articles are related to public rights and civil liberties, while only four articles relate to public duties. This imbalance results in questions surrounding the conditional nature of rights.

The rights and freedoms contained in the OBSS can be classified as follows:

- The Right to Nationality and the Prohibition of Exiling Nationals
- Equality before the Law and the Prohibition of Discrimination
- The Right to Liberty and Security of the Person, including the Prohibition of Torture

- The Right to a Fair Trial
- The Right to Respect for Private Life
- The Freedom of Thought, Conscience and Religion
- Freedom of Expression and the Media
- The Freedom of Peaceful Assembly and Association
- Political Rights
- Economic, Social and Cultural Rights

However, it should be noted that some of the existing statutes and regulations in Oman today undermines the original principles of the rights and freedoms as stipulated in the OBSS and international instruments and norms. Some of these difficulties derived from the old-dated statutes which came before the promulgation of the Basic Statute,[18] or to avoid the contradiction with other traditional and Islamic values,[19] or because of the current government's interpretation of the rights and freedoms are contradict or not in-line with the international understanding of the rights and freedoms.[20] Hence, the need of more human rights activities in different levels (NGOs, governmental, national, and international) to highlight the short comes.

The Right to Nationality

The right to nationality is one of the primary personal rights mentioned in all Gulf constitutions.[21] The OBSS gives this right priority and is the first right guaranteed under the *'Public Rights and Duties'* chapter.[22] Article 16 of the OBSS prohibits the deportation or expulsion of citizens, including preventing them from returning to Oman.

Significantly, the OBSS explicitly guarantees some basic rights and

18 Such as the Nationality right.

19 Such as the right to life and the limitations or the penalties and criminal offences for those that "commit an affront to religious groups by spoken or written word" and "abuse a person's dignity or rights".

20 Such as the freedom of expression, conscience and information.

21 Art. 27 Kuwait, Art. 17 Bahrain, Art. 8 UAE, Art. 4 and 41 Qatar, and Art. 35 Saudi Arabia.

22 Art. 15 of the OBSS.

freedoms for Omani citizens, but leaves non-nationals without constitutional rights or protections such as the principle of equality before the law, non-discrimination, and the right to assembly.[23] In other words, the Sultan's obligation to safeguard rights and freedoms is explicitly limited to citizens.[24] This is regulated by the Law on the Organisation of the Omani Nationality (R.D. 3/83) which governs nationality right. However, based on the 'supremacy' of nationality affairs this law is outside the jurisdiction of the courts. This will be discussed further in the Chapter Four on 'Omani Nationality and Human Rights'.

Equality before the Law and the Prohibition of Discrimination

Rather than being a general bill of rights that belongs to all individuals in Oman, regardless of their nationality and citizenship, the OBSS is oriented toward the needs of the Omani people. The principle of equality before the law is guaranteed, under Articles 10 and 17, which explicitly cater for all citizens who share the same public rights and duties. Although Article 35 grants personal and property protection to foreigners with legal residency in Oman, other related rights and freedoms, such as the alien's freedom from arbitrary expulsion, are absent from the OBSS.

Article 17 does not discriminate between citizens '*on the ground of gender, origin, colour, language, religion, sect, domicile or social status*'.[25] The OBSS seeks to accommodate all mixed diversities that exist in Oman, which is unique among other Gulf States' constitutions. The basic principle of equality behind Article 17 is a motivation

23 Articles 10, 17 and 32.

24 Articles 7, and 42.

25 The Committee on the Elimination of Racial Discrimination recommends including "race", "descent" and "national or ethnic origin" among the prohibited grounds of discrimination in the OBSS. See point 12 of the report 'Concluding observations of the Committee on the Elimination of Racial Discrimination: Oman' (19 October 2006). Geneva: United Nations. Available from: <www2.ohchr.org/english/bodies/cerd/docs/CERD.C.OMN.CO.1-new.pdf>

to change old statutes and practices that are incompatible with it. An example of such a change is the Establishment Law in Civil and Commercial Transactions (R.D. 68/2008), which states that the testimony of men and women is equal in court proceedings. A second example is R.D. 125/2008, which has amended the System of Entitlement to Government Land, ensuring that Omani women have an equal right to own residential plots without any discrimination. Nevertheless, other statutes contain vestiges of gender discrimination including the core nationality law.

The Right to Liberty and Security of the Person, Including the Prohibition of Torture

The right to liberty, the security of the person, and the prohibition of torture are explicitly outlined in the OBSS under several articles. Article 18 stresses that '*Personal freedom is guaranteed according to the Law*'.[26] It is, therefore, unlawful to arrest, search, detain or imprison any person or restrict his freedom of movement or residence except in accordance with the provisions of the law.

Article 20 stipulates that: "*No person shall be subjected to physical or psychological torture, inducement or demeaning treatment*". It provides punishment for any person who commits such an offence and voids any statement or confession proven to have been obtained under torture, inducement, demeaning treatment or threats of any such acts. Such prohibition also includes harming "*an accused either bodily or mentally*".[27] Article 24 complements Article 20 of the OBSS by stressing that an arrested or detained person must be promptly informed of the reason for their arrest or detention and of any charge against them. This protection is applicable even in critical situations such as under Martial Law, as stipulated in Article 7 of the State of Emergency Law (R.D. 75/2008).

26 Art. 18.
27 Art. 22.

Article 26 is also unique among Gulf States' constitutions by making the conduct of any "*medical or scientific experiment on any person without his freely given consent*" an explicit violation of human dignity. According to the Law of Prisons (R.D. 48/98), the protection of the prisoner extends to specifying the places designated for detention or imprisonment where health and social care are provided.[28]

Referencing Articles 2 and 7 of the ICCPR,[29] the OBSS acknowledges the primacy of effective procedural safeguards where absolute rights, such as the prohibition of torture or inhumane treatment, are concerned.[30] Including such details as explicit features of the OBSS is a positive reaffirmation on the protection of the person.[31] In the light of these constitutional references, a group of significant legal principles have been applied in the other statutes such as the Criminal Procedures Law (R.D. 97/99), which has led to a practical application and confirmation of the protection of the person.[32]

The Right to a Fair Trial

The OBSS has established mechanisms relating to fair trial principles. As previously mentioned, it stresses the rights of the person during pre-trial detention, including the principle that "*the accused is innocent until proven guilty in a legal trial*".[33] Furthermore, Article 24 guarantees the person's right to contact "*whoever he wants to inform of what has taken place or get assistance in the manner regulated by the Law*" and to petition the court against the action restricting their personal freedom.

28 Art. 19 of the OBSS, and the Law of Prisons (R.D. 48/98).

29 States should provide effective procedural remedies in their domestic legislation to protect individuals from torture.

30 Oman has not yet signed or ratified the United Nations Convention against Torture and Other Cruel, Inhuman or Degrading Treatment or Punishment.

31 Among Gulf States, only Bahrain has an identical approach in its constitution (Art. 19).

32 Articles 41 and 192 of the Criminal Procedures Law (R.D. 97/99).

33 Art. 22.

Article 25 of the OBSS confirms that "*Litigation is a protected right and is guaranteed to all people*".[34] During trial, this guarantee includes the right to defend oneself in person or to appoint a person capable of undertaking their defence. This also includes the person's right to obtain free legal assistance if they do not have the financial resources to pay for such services.[35] The Criminal Procedures Law stresses that the accused person should be allowed to talk freely and his right to silence should not be considered a confession.[36]

The OBSS also contains the '*no punishment without law*' principle. This means that punishment is personal, no crime or penalty is cognisable as such except by virtue of a law and a person cannot be punished under a law that criminalises conduct that was not criminal at the time it was committed.[37] Finally, all trials should be public but the court may take into account public order and morality; however, the pronouncement of judgment in all cases must occur during an open session.[38]

The Criminal Procedures Law and the Civil and Commercial Legal Procedures Law[39] regulate these rights in practice.[40] Nonetheless, some of the articles contained in these laws have the potential to impact a person's freedom and, therefore, need to be reviewed. An example is allowing for the arrest and detention of an accused person for 48 hours before being charged.[41]

34 Same article also add the provision of "*The State as far as possible will guarantee approximation of judicial bodies to litigants and speedy settlement of cases*".

35 Articles 22, 23 of the OBSS, Articles 13, 14 and 314 of the Criminal Procedures Law (R.D. 97/99), and Articles 3 and 52 of the Legal Profession Law (R.D. 108/96).

36 Articles 188 and 189 of the law.

37 Article 21.

38 Article 63 of the OBSS, and Article 177 of the Criminal Procedures Law (R.D. 97/99).

39 R.D. 29/2002.

40 In addition to other related laws as the case.

41 Although Articles 50-59 of the Criminal Procedures Law give the detained the right to petition the court against the action restricting their personal freedom,

The Right to Respect for Private Life

Article 18 in the OBSS stipulates the right to free movement and residence deeming it unlawful to restrict such rights, except in accordance with the provisions of the law. However, the provisions of the law may not lead to the expulsion or deportation of a citizen, as this would be equivalent to eliminating another basic right guaranteed in Article 16. The Penal Law indicates that a foreigner may be deported in the case of terrorism or if the crime was egregious or disrupted the country's security or public morality, or if it was proven to be a mass crime.[42]

Article 27 of the OBSS confirms that a person's dwelling place is inviolable and should not be entered or trespassed without their permission, except in the circumstances and in the manner prescribed by law. The law punishes any person, including officials, who trespass a person's residence without permission or in accordance with the law with up to 2 years imprisonment.[43]

Similarly, Article 30 protects and guarantees a person's correspondence by any means of communication as this is considered private; *"Hence it is unlawful to monitor, search, disclose the confidentiality, delay or confiscate the same except in cases specified by the Law".*

However, this freedom is not absolute as the government has the right to control communication if duly designated by the law. Article 5 of the Law of Organising Communications (R.D. 30/2002) allows the authority to do so if such communication involves a breach of public order or morality or if it amounts to an assault on the rights of others. In order to violate this right, it is necessary to obtain permission from the prosecution before monitoring takes place. This permission should be based on the interest of revealing a felony or a misdemean-

---

It is limited by the provisional seizure and the judicial body who has to decide within three days, which does not provide necessary protection yet (Art. 59).

42 Art. 48 of the Penal Law (R.D. 7/74).

43 Articles166 and 262 of the Penal Law.

our punishable by imprisonment for more than three months and the permission must be reasoned and must not exceed the duration of thirty days.[44]

The Freedom of Thought, Conscience and Religion

Article 28 of the OBSS declares that the "*freedom to practice religious rites according to the recognized customs is guaranteed, provided it does not disrupt the public order or contradict with morals*". Islam is the official religion of the Omani State and Islamic *Shari'a* is the basis for legislation contained in the OBSS, which also prohibits discrimination based on religion or sect.[45]

With the exception of land that must be specifically approved by the Ministry of Endowments and Religious Affairs, non-Muslims are allowed to practice their religion without interference. However, Article 209 under Penal Law establishes penalties (imprisonment or fine) for those who publicly blaspheme God or His prophets, commit an affront to religious groups by spoken or written word, or breach the peace during a lawful religious gathering.

The right to change one's religion or belief is not explicitly mentioned in the OBSS, although, it is guaranteed indirectly. According to articles 172, 228 (7) and 239 under the Personal Status Law (R.D. 32/97), citizens may face various difficulties when committing apostasy (converting from Islam to another religion) such as the loss of parental or guardian rights over children and the loss of eligibility from wills or inheritances. However, this law exempts non-Muslims provisions by allowing them to follow their own religious rules pertaining to family and personal status.[46]

44 Articles 90-99 under Criminal Procedures Law, Articles 6 and 13 under Post Offices Services Law (R.D. 27/80) and Article 5 under the Law of Organising Communications (R.D. 30/2002).

45 Articles 2 and 17.

46 Article 282 under Personal Status Law (R.D. 32/97).

Freedom of Expression and the Media

The OBSS protects the freedom of opinion and expression and freedom of the press, printing and publishing under articles 29 and 31. However, interferences with these rights may be permitted if they are prescribed by law. The statutes that regulate these areas are older than the OBSS itself and are not in line with its principles; moreover, they are less restrictive than their latest amendments and regulations.[47] Hence, Oman faces the greatest difficulty in protecting basic rights in this area as previous statutes and provisions are extremely strict and limit the practical application of newly attained rights and freedoms.[48]

The Press and Publications Law (R.D. 49/84) contains restricted procedures and penalties in almost every respect. This law allows the government to prevent publications if they are politically, culturally or sexually offensive, in all domestic and imported publications. Furthermore, it does not allow for the printing of any content in public or private print outlets without the permission of the Ministry of Information.[49] Libel is treated as a criminal offense and journalists can

47 Such as the Amendments on the Press and Publications Law in 2004 or the Law of Organising Communications in 2008 which came with more restrictive provisions than the original laws in different areas.

48 Such as the case about the journalist who was summoned by the Prosecution Office and charged with "slander against the police apparatus" and "false testimony", for his refusal to reveal his source of information. For more information see the documents (E/CN.4/2006/7), (A/HRC/14/23/Add.1) and (A/HRC/16/44/Add.1) the Reports of the Special Rapporteur on the promotion and protection of the right to freedom of opinion and expression, available from: <http://www2.ohchr.org/english/bodies/hrcouncil/docs/14session/A.HRC.14.23.Add.1_AV.pdf>, <http://www2.ohchr.org/english/issues/defenders/ docs/A.HRC.16.44.Add.1_EFSonly.pdf> Also, the cases of a poet and journalist and another former Member of Parliament who have been arrested in 2005, for their expression and publicly questioned the Government's willingness to undertake democratic reforms. See (E/CN.4/2006/55/Add.1) UN Economic and Social Council: Civil and Political Rights, Including the Question of Freedom of Expression, 27 March 2006, from: <http://daccess-dds-ny.un.org/doc/UNDOC/GEN/G06/121/12/PDF/G0612112.pdf>

49 Art. 12 of the Press and Publications Law (R.D. 49/84).

be fined or imprisoned for up to three years for criticising the Sultan[50] or for printing material that leads to "*public discord, violates the security of the state, or abuses a person's dignity or rights*".[51]

The Law of Organising Communications (R.D. 30/2002) allows the authorities to prosecute individuals for any message sent through any means of communication that violates public order and morals or is harmful to a person's safety. The government restricts freedom of expression via the Internet and media[52] and restricts access to many websites considered pornographic, culturally or politically sensitive, or competitive with local telecommunications services.[53] Thus the law also requires internet cafes to record their visitors' identifications and activities.[54]

Article 61 of the same law has been amended several times to cope with the telecommunications developments and to tighten restrictions on the use of new technology. It extends criminal liability to those operating communications facilities and services, such as websites and blogs. This law has been heavily criticised by various lawyers, human rights activists and bloggers as it has been used as a means to criminalise several website owners as well as moderators

50 Articles 25 and 35 of the Press and Publications Law.

51 Article 31 of the OBSS.

52 Confidential government instructions relating to a popular phone-in radio programme, which were leaked and widely publicised, included directives to move from live to pre-recorded broadcasting and exclude calls about military, security or judicial matters or concerning the head of state. See: Amnesty International. (1 June 2009). *Amnesty International Report 2009 on Oman.* Retrieved January 2011, from <http://www.buzzle.com/articles/amnesty-international-report-2009-on-oman.html>

53 Bureau of Democracy, Human Rights, and Labor. (2010, March 11). *2009 Human Rights Report: Oman.* Retrieved January 2011, from U.S Department of State: <http://www.state.gov/g/drl/rls/hrrpt/2009/nea/136077.htm>

54 Articles 6 and 7 of the Decision 166 of the Telecommunications Regulatory Authority. See: *Digital Repression in the Sultanate of Oman (in Arabic).* (2010) Retrieved January 2011, from Human Rights in Oman Blog: <http://humanrightsinoman.blogspot.com>

and administrators of forums based on their responsibility for the content published by their users. According to the *Freedom of the Press Report 2008*, this serves to create a highly censored and cautious media environment making it one the most restrictive in the Arab world.[55]

The Freedom of Peaceful Assembly and Association

The right of association and freedom of assembly are guaranteed by the OBSS. Article 32 is the shortest article concerning a right or a freedom in the OBSS and upholds the right to association within the limits of the law. However, currently, there is no single statute in Oman legislations that can regulate this right in a theoretical or practical sense.[56] The government usually uses provisions of different legislations, which are very broad, to restrict this right, and usually do not accommodate most forms of assembly.[57]

On the other hand, the right to freedom of association is one of the most descriptive articles contained in the OBSS since the term 'association' can refer to all varieties of associations, including civil associations such as non-governmental organisations (hereinafter re-

55 Freedom House (April 2008). *Freedom of the Press 2008 – Oman.* Retrieved January, 2011, available at: <http://www.unhcr.org/refworld/docid/4871f6242.html>

56 Such as the Public Order Act in the UK, or the Law of Public Meetings and Assembly in Kuwait.

57 Such as Article 137 of the Omani Penal Law (R.D. 7/74), Article 51 of the Police Law (R.D. 35/90), and Article 40 of the Traffic Law (R.D. 28/93). The lack of recognition of peaceful assembly was reported through the Communications Report of Special Procedures Report (A/HRC/18/51) about alleged killings and detention of protestors in the context of peaceful demonstrations. According to the report 2 was killed when police fired rubber bullets on protesters. On 27 March 2011, one person working in a local newspaper and another lecturer were reportedly arrested and questioned about their links with foreign organizations as they participated in the protests. Few days later, a number of protesters were allegedly arrested by security forces. Other individuals who took part in the protests were allegedly arrested at their homes. See <http://www2.ohchr.org/english/bodies/hrcouncil/docs/18session/A.HRC.18.51_en.pdf>

ferred to as NGOs), trade unions, and political parties. The Omani system only recognises the first two types of association since political parties are prohibited by the Law of Civil Association issued by Royal Decree No. 14/2000, which also regulates most types of associations. Trade unions are regulated through Oman's Labour Law R.D. 35/2003 as well as its amendments and Ministerial Resolutions. Both statutes have regulated this type of association via different approaches and restrictions.[58]

Political Rights

In the OBSS, political rights fall into two categories: The right to participate in public affairs, and the right to submit petitions and complaints, also known as the right to address authorities. The first category is confirmed by Article 9, which states, "*The citizens have the right in accordance with this Basic Statute and the conditions and provisions stipulated by the Law – to participate in public affairs*". However, this right does not give citizens the right to change the government which remains an exclusive prerogative of the Sultan.[59] It does include the citizen's right to vote and stand for election, but these rights are not part of the OBSS's text; instead they can be found in an ordinary statute that regulates the elections of the *Ash-Shura* Council, which represents public participation as the main political right granted to Omani citizens today.[60]

The second category concerns the means by which individuals may express their viewpoints regarding personal matters or matters relevant to public affairs; these are guaranteed by Article 34 under the OBSS. This includes the citizen's right to address these matters

58 For more details about the freedom of association in Oman please refer to the respective Chapter Six.

59 Art. 42 OBSS.

60 Art. 58 OBSS, and 'the Council of Oman Affairs' (R.D. 86/97). Please refer to Chapter Five to know more about the public participation in Oman.

directly with the executive department or the judicial court, as well as the *Ash-Shura* Council.

Economic, Social and Cultural Rights

Economic, social and cultural rights are guaranteed under Chapter 2 of the OBSS, which does not fall under the same category as the directly protected rights in Chapter 3. They are framed more akin to policies or strategies that the state should follow, although they have some direct influences on the rights of the citizenry.

The economic principles, which the OBSS refers to in Article 11, are in accordance with most individual and collective rights and freedoms stipulated in international human rights instruments. These principles can be generally categorised into three pillars:

- The freedom of economic activity and the principle of the free economy of the State; This includes raising the standard of living, encouraging savings, supervising the regulation of credit, the inviolability of public property, and to confirm that natural resources are the property of the State.
- The right to private ownership and inheritance, and the prohibition of confiscating property except by judicial order and in accordance with the law. This is currently controlled by several statutes, such as the Confiscation of Property Law (R.D. 64/78) and the Personal Status Law (R.D. 32/97).
- Taxes should be just and imposing new taxes should be in accordance with the law, and retroactive taxes are not permitted. This is currently regulated by the Income Tax Law (R.D. 28/2009).

In terms of social principles, Article 12 specifies the following rights:

- The right to family: This is currently governed by the Law of Personal Status (R.D. 32/97), which is controlled by the Islamic *Shariʿa*. However, non-Muslims are governed by their own systems unless they request to apply this law.[61]

61 Art. 282 of the Personal Status Law.

- Social Security of the citizen and family, in cases of emergency, sickness, disability and old age, which is currently governed by the Social Security Law (R.D. 84/87) and its amendments.
- Health: The Ministry of Health provides health services free of charge to all citizens.
- The right to work and the prohibition of forced labour except by virtue of a law and in return for a fair remuneration for any person working in the private sector is enshrined by the Omani Labour Law (R.D. 35/2003).[62]
- The right to hold public office: The Civil Service Law (R.D. 120/ 2004) is the main law governing those who are working for the government, in addition to other military and police laws.

The cultural principles in the OBSS guarantee some of the most important cultural rights, and most importantly, emphasise the right to education for all, albeit it lacks the compulsory status and free education for all.[63] Article 13 references the fight against illiteracy and encourages the establishment of private and public schools. It stipulates that it is the State's duty to preserve the national heritage and to encourage the propagation of science, art, literature and scientific research, a role currently distributed across several governmental agencies.

---

62 Most GCC States follow the sponsorship system known as Kafala, and the High Commissioner for Human Rights, Navi Pillay, highlighted during her visit to these States, that this system rigidly binds migrants to their employers, enabling the latter to commit abuses, while preventing workers from changing jobs or leaving the country" and requested the Gulf States with updated labour laws to do so at the earliest. See 'Encouraging' changes under way in Persian Gulf countries, says UN rights chief' from: <http://www.un.org/apps/news/story.asp?NewsID=34404>

63 It was one of the comments from the CRC and CEDAW committees in this regard. See documents (CRC/C/OMN/CO/2) 'Consideration of Reports Submitted by States Parties under Article 44 of the Convention: Concluding observations: OMAN'. Forty-third session, 29 September 2006; and (CEDAW/C/OMN/CO/1) 'Concluding observations of the Committee on the Elimination of Discrimination against Women: Oman'. Fiftieth session, Geneva, 3–21 October 2011.

There are other rights and freedoms under the aforementioned principles that represent what are called third-generation solidarity rights. Some of these rights require the State to conserve and protect the environment and prevent pollution (Article 12), to promote peace and security among States and peoples (Article 10) and to promote economic and social development in order to increase production and raise the standard of living (Article 11).

3.3 Separation of Powers

> *"There would be an end of everything, were the same man or the same body, whether of the nobles or of the people, to exercise those three powers, that of enacting laws, that of executing the public resolutions, and of trying the causes of individuals"*
> Baron de Montesquieu – The Spirit of the Laws (1748)[64]

The principle of the separation of power is considered to be one of the most important principles in maintaining basic human rights. The aim of the separation of power is to prevent any single power, person or group from dominating the government by holding two or more functions (legislative, executive or judicial), as the outcome is likely to be tyranny. As the French Declaration of the Rights of Man (1789) asserted: "*A society where rights are not secured or the separation of powers established has no constitution*".[65]

This concept has taken on various meanings for different purposes, including the separation of *function* between different government branches, the separation of *personnel* between different governmental branches and *checks and balances* between different government branches.

Most Gulf countries, except the UAE, have adopted a unitary gov-

64 Montesquieu, B. (1748). *The Spirit of the Laws*. Retrieved January 2011, from Historical Documents: <http://www.graves.k12.ky.us/schools/gchs/bleonard/html/hd/doc7.htm>

65 Article 16 of the Declaration.

ernmental system where power is concentrated at the centre; more accurately, it appears that the power in each country is concentrated in one person. The current constitutional structure of the OBSS provides that the three pillars of the government include the Head of State (Chapter 4), the Oman Council (Chapter 5), and the Judiciary (Chapter 6). Below the thesis sets out a Table that encapsulates the structure of the OBSS.

Table 3: Structure of the Omani Basic Statute[66]

Chapter	Title	Articles
I	The State and the System of Government	9
II	Principles Guiding State Policy	5
III	Public Rights and Duties	26
IV	The Head of State	3
	The Council of Ministers	4
	The Prime Minister, His Deputies and Ministers	8
	Specialized Councils	1
	Financial Affairs	1
V	The Oman Council	1
VI	The Judiciary	13
VII	General Provisions	10
Total		**81**

There is a separation between the personnel and functions in each group; however, this alone does not achieve separation of power as a concept, nor provide checks and balances for each branch. While the OBSS structure indicates the Omani Council as the legislative branch; nonetheless the Council lacks this power. The government's legislative and executive powers are defined under the Head of State (Chapter 4), which means both functions are chaired by the Sultan. Moreover, the judicial branch, which is explicitly referred as "independent" under Article 60 of the OBSS, is headed by the Sultan as the head of

66 Table from Siegfried, N. (2000) p. 369.

the Supreme Judicial Council.[67] Thus, no separation of powers can be said to exist in Oman today, which reconfirms its status as an absolute monarchy.

The OBSS mentions two other councils, the Ruling Family Council and the Defence Council in the successor system (Article 6) with defined but limited roles. In addition the OBSS allows for the existence of specialised councils under the Head of State chapter, through Royal Decrees.[68] Such specialised councils allow the Sultan to distribute some of his executive power to different bodies by giving them a framework to work within while maintaining his status as the final decision-maker for important policies.

The way in which Oman separates power appears to be complex but most power, if not all, still rests with the Sultan who is the ultimate authority by enacting laws and heading the Council of Ministers, the Supreme Judicial Council, the Defence Council and other specialised councils. The complexity of the system is the result of distributing executive powers among different branches of government, rather than a system of clear distinction between governmental branches. Equally the Sultan remains the final arbiter of any disputes between the branches of the government. The theory behind it is that the Sultan will maintain a harmonised government, but this harmony is the result of domination and the weakness of each branch, rather than a profitable interrelationship between governmental bodies. After more than 14 years from the promulgation of the OBSS legislation initiatives repose in the hands of the Sultan and away from the mandate of both houses of the Oman Council. For instance, the upper house is nominated by the Sultan and is usually selected from retired high-ranking civil servants who may serve as trustworthy legislators. The Sultan's supreme role can also be seen in the executive branch

67 Art. 1 of the Supreme Judicial Council (93/99).

68 Art. 56.

where, for nominations to the Council of Ministers, some of the most important ministerial posts fall under his control.

3.3.1 The Sultan's Rule

Article 5 of the OBSS states that "*The system of government is a hereditary Sultanate*", meaning that Oman continues to be an absolute monarchy where all important powers are vested in the Sultan. The Sultan is the Head of State, the Supreme Commander of the Armed Forces, and the Prime Minister. Additionally, he is the Chairman of several important Councils, such as the Supreme Judicial, the Defence, the National Security, the Monetary Governors, the Financial Affairs and Energy Resources, and other councils and committees. The Sultan also holds the key ministerial positions of Defence, Finance, and Foreign Affairs.[69]

The Sultan's prerogatives are wide-ranging and numerous. He is tasked with many functions such as guiding general policy, representing Oman in all international relations, presiding over the Council of Ministers and other Specialised Councils, appointing chairmen for them, appointing and dismissing the Prime Minister, Ministers and high-ranking government positions and appointing and dismissing senior judges.[70] He is immune from prosecution and judicial review, and all court decisions are announced in his name.

Neither the Parliament, nor the Courts, nor the Council of Ministers nor any Executive Council in the country has the right to question the Sultan's authority or power, or to veto or question his decisions. Their authority does not exceed the submission of suggestions and recommendations, and executing his orders. In practice, he gives all governmental institutions the space to work according to the guiding principles of the state as outlined in the OBSS; however, the

69 The Sultan has nominated three ministers in these ministries with the designation of Minister Responsible for Defence, Finance, and Foreign Affairs.

70 Art. 42 of the OBSS.

Sultan always holds the final word. Easily the monarch is the most influential authority in the Omani system, with the power to create or dissolve any governmental institution (judicial, legislative and executive) and to nominate or dismiss any governmental position in any branch. His powers are unlimited according to the Basic Statute and he is the only person who can change or amend it.

According to the Islamic definition, the current ruler may be regarded as just, but overall, Oman operates under an absolute ruling system where all the State's powers are enshrined in one person. Oman does not equal a tyranny due to the Sultan's personal progressive thinking on governance and the interests of his subjects. However this is a risky environment for any future political developments within the succession sphere. The OBSS declares that one of the Sultan's main tasks is to safeguard the rights and freedoms of Omani citizens.[71] This emphasis on rights and freedoms extends to the oath-taking ceremony where the next successor must swear to uphold these principles before taking over the throne.[72] Nevertheless, he can override the Basic Statute itself since there is no constitutional limitation to his power, and which will have direct affects, positively or negatively, over human rights and freedoms based on the new Sultan support or negligence.

In practice, this commitment to safeguarding rights and freedoms is observable in the current Sultan's involvement in judicial verdicts and amendments to the law. This was the case with a recent issue concerning a woman's right to dispute an arranged marriage coordinated by her family without her consent (a practice that still exists in some traditional areas in Oman). The Sultan amended the Judicial Authority Law (R.D. 90/99) with the Royal Decree No. 55/2010 to move the revision of these cases from the Courts of First Instance to the Supreme Court, highest court in the country. Moreover, this

71 Art. 42.
72 Art. 7.

amendment allows women to appeal directly to the Sultan against the Supreme Court's verdict within 30 days. This along with other instances demonstrate that the Sultan is not averse to protecting the rights of vulnerable citizens such as women, even if it means interfering with other branches that are meant to have independence, such as the judiciary. Though highly improbable under the current Sultan, the monarch's influence on the judiciary could also threaten the rights and freedoms of Omani citizens as the OBSS grants this power to future Sultans as well.

3.3.2 The Power of Parliament[73]

Article 58 of the OBSS has contributed to the development of the Omani parliamentary system by establishing a bicameral council though this is a purely consultative body. "The Council of Oman" (*Majlis* Oman) is made up of members of the State Council (*Majlis Ad-Daula*) and the Consultative Council (*Majlis Ash-Shura*). The OBSS leaves the jurisdictions, sessions and procedures of each council up to the discretion of ordinary statute.[74] The only task that the OBSS mentions for the Council of Oman is to witness the oath taken by the new Sultan in a joint session with the Defence Council without any veto or power to disapprove.[75]

The chairman of each council is nominated by the Sultan, and their role in Omani politics constitutes no more than a deliberative function. Both parliamentary houses lack real legislative power, and are limited in their power over governmental branches. In other words, their ability to check and balance the executive is extremely limited.

The legislative powers of both houses are still very weak compared to those of the Council of Ministers (the Cabinet). Parliament

73 Please refer to current developments in this regards in the General Conclusion, Chapter Seven.

74 Art. 58 OBSS.

75 Art. 7.

has the right to review all bills and propose amendments to laws. However, their recommendations should be submitted to the Cabinet without a compulsory review from the other house, which reflects the fact that the Parliament fills no more than an advisory role for the Cabinet.[76]

Legislation in Oman consists of two forms: Primary and secondary legislation. Primary legislation is promulgated by and, is known as, the Royal Decree and is published in the official gazette. Secondary legislation, also published in the official gazette, is issued as a Ministerial Decision and Implementing Regulation based on powers delegated in the Royal Decrees to the concerned executive body or Ministry. Therefore, parliamentary power in both legislations is no more than deliberative.

Although, the powers of the elected *Majlis Ash-Shura* have increased slightly over the last few years, the council cannot address important issues related to national security and defence, foreign policy and relations, the structure of the political system, or the State's monetary system. Therefore, it remains limited to providing consultation and advice in social and economic areas only. The *Ash-Shura* Council is allowed to question government ministers, although it does not have any power to remove them from office. Even the Members' right to question the Minister inside the Parliament is very limited, and the Minister has the right to ignore the requests of the council's members.[77] Thus, Parliament as whole is unable to control the executive and it cannot veto any legislation or executive directives, even those that may violate human rights.

76 Political parties are not allowed to exist in Oman, and the Lower House (*Ash-Shura* Council) is still influenced by the 'tribal' criteria. See Chapter Five for more details on parliament powers and limitations.

77 For more details see Chapter Five (5.4).

3.3.3 Judicial Independence[78]

The principle of separation of power is not explicitly mentioned in the Basic Statute, except in the case of the independence of the judicial branch, which is vested in the Courts.[79] There is a clear separation of tasks between the Judiciary and the Parliament since none of them has any power to interfere with the other.

In line with the provisions of the OBSS, fundamental changes occurred to Oman's legal system in 1999. Royal Decree No. 90/99, which came into force in June 2000, established the levels of courts in Oman as follows: First Instance (Preliminary) Courts; Appeal Courts; and the Supreme Court. Another independent judicial body was established, the Administrative Court, with the power to review all decisions made by governmental bodies. Finally, Royal Decree No. 93/99 established the Supreme Judicial Council.

The Supreme Judicial Council, headed by the Sultan, is the highest judicial body in the country. It is responsible for drawing up general judicial policy. It safeguards the independence of the judiciary and monitors its development. Its legislative authority extends to proposing draft laws on the administration of justice, considering any points that may be raised by the competent authorities concerning such laws, expressing opinions on them as it deems necessary, and expressing opinions on draft judicial co-operation agreements between Oman and other states.

Despite independence on paper, the judiciary is, nonetheless, strongly influenced by the executive branch. The Sultan chairs the council and holds the title of prime minister while the Minister of

78 Although the judicial independence is part of the next section about the rule of law, it was brought forward here to highlight the power of the judicial branch compared to other the branches powers and to examine the principle of the separation of powers. Further analysis and discussion about the judicial independence, the role of the judiciary and the judicial structure will be covered by next section (3.4).

79 Art. 60.

Justice is the deputy Chairman. The Inspector General of Police and Customs also participates, making the Council dominated by members of the executive. The Council makes all judicial appointments and relocations and formulates all judicial policy. This brings under scrutiny its judicial independence, especially when considering that this is the council's main responsibility.[80] The executive control over judicial matters is also observable in the power that the Minister of Justice holds in nominating assistant judges.[81] More broadly, it is also noticeable in the executive committee's power over certain issues, such as the Nationality Committee.[82] Even regulations concerning Parliamentary elections and disputes are handled by the executive branch and are outside the court's control.

3.3.4 Impacts of the Executive Branch

Power over the executive is vested in the Sultan and his Council of Ministers which plays a central role in the state's policies as it extends its reach beyond its own executive mandate to other legislative bodies. Although the Sultan meets with the cabinet occasionally and the Deputy Prime Minister of the Council of Ministers usually presides over cabinet meetings, the Sultan's position as head of the State and head of the government is illustrative of the preponderant power of the executive branch. This is also manifest in the current reality that though the OBSS provides for a Prime Minister under Article 48, the Sultan has not nominated one, coupled with the fact that Parliament does not have the power to accept or veto the nomination of the Prime Minister or any ministerial appointments.

The 29 member Council of Ministers is the executive branch of the government that assists the Sultan in drawing up and implementing general state policy. It is headed by the Sultan and fulfils a number of

80 Art. 3 (R.D. 93/99).

81 Art. 23 (R.D. 90/99).

82 For more details see Chapter Four (4.2.1).

functions (Article 44). In addition to its executive functions, it maintains the power to propose draft laws and decrees and supervises the implementation of the laws, decrees, regulations, decisions, treaties, agreements and court's judgements, which results in some legislative power. The members of the Council of Ministers are responsible to the Sultan. They are collectively responsible for the Council's implementation of the State's general policy, and individually responsible "*... for the manner in which each minister performs his duties and exercises his authority in his respective Ministry or unit*".[83]

There is a harmonised connection between the Council of Ministers and Parliament due to the weakness of the latter, primarily in its limited responsibility to make the Cabinet accountable to the Parliament. The executive branch is further fortified by the Sultan's position as Prime Minister and the Minister of Defence, Finance, and Foreign Affairs. This means that any question directed at the government will be directed to the Sultan where "*His Person is inviolable. Respect of him is a duty and his command must be obeyed*".[84]

However, the establishment of the Administrative Court in 1999 limited, to some extent, the ultimate power of the executive and administrative departments. Although this court does not have the power to override the Sultan's decrees, it provides some protection against administrative decisions in general, which puts the judicial branch in a better position to supervise the actions of the executive.

However, Article 61 of the OBSS criminalises interference in lawsuits or matters of justice. For the sake of judicial protection, Royal Decree No. 75/2005 amended Article 163 of the Penal Law (R.D. 7/1974) to add the punishment of removal from office if any officer refused or intentionally obstructed the implementation of an order issued by a court within two weeks after receiving warning of the implementation. The amendment also requested that the accused person

83 Art. 52 OBSS.
84 Art. 41 OBSS.

present in person before the Court of Misdemeanours at the request of the victim. This amendment opened the possibility to punish officers in court, including officers at the ministerial and under-secretarial level. In terms of the rule of law, this was an important legal development. Thus although the OBSS adopts, in theory, the separation of powers principle of the judicial branch, in reality the executive has significant powers that dominate the government. This domination is obvious in several aspects; one critical example is the Cabinet's interference on the changes and amendments made in the Penal Law, especially the provisions related to the punishment of a public officer who refuses the implementation of a court order.

Since Ministers are only appointed and removed from office by a Royal Decree they are effectively above the law. This was reinforced through the revision of punishment of government officials by R.D. 52/2007. The amendment abolished the punishment of dismissal from office and replaced it with a fine. Essentially the executive's used its power to protect administrators over the best interests of the rule of law and constitutes a significant drawback in terms of government legitimacy.

3.3.5 The Defence Council

Issues related to the safety, security, well-being and the defence of Oman are beyond the jurisdiction of Parliament, the Judicial Courts and the Council of Ministers. Only the Defence Council, which was mentioned for the first time in the OBSS, has this authority. This was established by the Sultan through Royal Decree No. 105/96, thus forming the eight-member Defence Council. The members are chosen on the basis of military and security position and meet by royal command to consider matters related to the tasks outlined in the OBSS. In addition, the council is the ultimate decision-making body for any security or defence issues.

According to the OBSS, the Defence Council's role in the successor system is one of its main tasks; it confirms the appointment of the person designated by the Sultan in his letter to the Ruling Family Council if the latter does not agree with the choice of successor.[85] Furthermore, it witnesses, with the Oman Council, the new Sultan's oath-taking ceremony before he may exercise his authority.[86] Its responsibility also extends to considering matters related to preserving the country's safety and its defence.[87]

It is necessary to distinguish the Defence Council from the National Security Council, although the membership of both Councils is almost identical.[88] The latter was formed by Royal Decree No. 63/2003, which amended the name of the National Security Committee to the National Security Council. The new Council considers all questions related to national security and holds its sessions at the Sultan's direction and under his chairmanship or that of the Minister of the Royal Office.

The National Security Council focuses on internal security issues such as declaring of states of emergency when the State's security or public order is threatened by war, internal disturbance, general crisis or spread of epidemic.[89] It previously played a role in the State's Security Court before it was abolished in 2010.[90] On the other hand, the Defence Council is the body responsible for implementing the General Mobilisation Law (R.D. 76/2008) which authorised the announce-

85 Art. 6.

86 Art. 7.

87 Art. 14.

88 The Defence Council members include: the Sultan (Chairman), the Minister of the Royal Office, the Inspector General of Police and Customs, the Head of the Internal Security Service, the Chief of Staff of the Sultan's Armed Forces, the Commander of the Royal Army of Oman, the Commander of Royal Air Force of Oman, the Commander of the Royal Navy of Oman, and the Commander of the Royal Guard of Oman. The National Security Council comprises of the first five members of the Defence Council and the Head of the Communications and Coordination Department.

89 Art. 1 of R.D. 75/2008 the State of Emergency Law.

90 Check the abolishing of the State's Security Court, section 3.6.4.

ment of mobilisation upon outbreak of war or of its revocation by Royal Orders.

3.3.6 The Ruling Family Council[91]

The Royal Family Council or the Ruling Family Council was formed by the OBSS with one task, "*To determine the successor to the throne*", as stipulated in Article 6.[92] Neither the OBSS nor the law has allocated any other powers or authorities to the council aside from this one. The members of the Council, its role and meetings are still vague due to the absence of any public regulation.

There is no direct connection between this Council and other governmental institutions, including the Cabinet and Parliament. According to the successor system, the Council only has a direct link to the Defence Council in the event that the Ruling Family Council has not agreed upon a successor to the throne. Overall, the Royal Family in Oman does not play an influential role in the country's policies compared to other institutions or compared to other Gulf States, though some members of the Royal Family hold high-ranking positions, such as the Deputy Prime Minister of the Council of Ministers.

However through the Royal Family Council, the Sultan has succeeded in limiting the Royal Family's interference in the country's affairs in order to avoid a conflict of interests or clashes between government institutions. Even the number of Royal Family members working in the Cabinet is fewer than other Gulf States where the most important ministries are headed by a Royal Family member.[93] To some degree, their isolation from national politics has protected the

91 The 'Ruling Family' term used here instead of the Royal Family based on the translated version of OBSS used in this work.

92 As mentioned earlier in Chapter Two (2.3.3).

93 All Gulf States' Prime Ministers, Ministers of Defence, Foreign Affairs, and Interior are from the Royal Families of each state. The case in Oman is slightly different since the Sultan himself heads those positions instead of a member of the Royal Family, but he nominated what is called 'responsible ministers' to run the affairs of these ministries.

Omani Royal Family from direct criticism and allowed for smooth changes in government positions, as ordered by the Sultan.

3.3.7 Other Councils

Article 56 of the OBSS allows for the establishment of specialised Councils where their powers and members are appointed by Royal Decree. Several councils, committees, and authorities concerned with economic, financial, civil service, educational, and governmental developments have been created. Many members of these councils are ministers, government administrators and experts. Usually specialised councils are chaired by the minister whose department is most involved. Some of these councils report directly to the Sultan or to the Council of Ministers for final approval based on the Royal Decree that established it. Other councils are chaired by the Sultan himself and are neither subject to the Council of Ministers, the Council of Oman nor the Courts. The most notable examples include the Monetary Governors Council, and the Financial Affairs and Energy Resources Council.

3.4 The Rule of Law

> *"Judicial independence is a pre-requisite to the rule of law and a fundamental guarantee of a fair trial. A judge shall therefore uphold and exemplify judicial independence in both its individual and institutional aspects".*[94]

It is commonly agreed that judicial independence is one of the principal building blocks of the rule of law. Such independence is also necessary in order to achieve the principles of impartially, equality before the law, and to ensure the application of proper justice. The Judicial as an institution is reflected by the independence of its adminis-

94 The Bangalore Principles of Judicial Conduct (2002) downloadable from: <http://www.unodc.org/pdf/crime/corruption/judicial_group/Bangalore_principles.pdf>

tration, financial, and decision-making powers and processes. This can be noted from the existence of a Supreme Judicial Council, and a clear judicial system that regulates the courts and the judicial staff members, and that the judiciary is free from interference.

The independence of the judiciary also requires several substantive principles and procedural safeguards, such as the existence of independent, competent and impartial tribunal with public trial, the recognition of the individual before the law, the right of access to a court, the presumption of innocence, the right to an appeal to a higher tribunal, the prohibition to be tried more than once for the same offence after final judgment, and trial without undue delay and within a reasonable time; Most of which have been recognised by Articles 18 to 25 of the OBSS.

The international community has paid a great attention about the independence of judiciary and its basic principles enshrined in different treaties and conventions, such as the preambles of the UN Charter and the Declaration of Human Rights, article 38 (1) (b) and (c) of the Statute of the International Court of Justice.[95] Furthermore, it has also been seen as "an absolute right that is not subject to any exception" for the requirement of "independence of a tribunal" established in article 14, paragraph 1, of the ICCPR.[96]

In 1978, the efforts of the International Commission Jurists have succeeded on the establishment of the Centre for the Independence of Judges and Lawyers, which developed the principles of independence in accordance with international standards.[97]

---

95 (A/HRC/11/41) Promotion and Protection of All Human Rights, Civil, Political, Economic, Social and Cultural Rights, Including the Right to Development – Report of the Special Rapporteur on the independence of judges and lawyers (24 March 2009).

96 Stated by the Human Rights Committee in its general comment No. 32. (Art. 14: Right to equality before courts and tribunals and to a fair trial, CCPR/C/GC/32, para. 19); see also communication No. 263/1987, Gonzalez del Rio v. Peru, para. 5.2.

97 History of the International Commission of Jurists. See <http://www.icj.org/default.asp?langage=1&nodeID=340>

The UN Commission for Human Rights and the United Nations Congress on the Prevention of Crime and the Treatment of Offenders efforts have carried out excellent outcome in this respect, culminated by the adoption of the Basic Principles on the Independence of the Judiciary in 1985.[98]

The rule of law, in its most basic sense, is a principle that stresses the fact that no one is above or immune to the law and all persons are entitled to equal protection before it, as well as the fact both the government and the governed should keep to the general rules of law.[99] In 2004, the then Secretary-General of the United Nations defined the rule of law thus:

> *"... a principle of governance in which all persons, institutions and entities, public and private, including the State itself, are accountable to laws that are publicly promulgated, equally enforced and independently adjudicated, and which are consistent with international human rights norms and standards. It requires, as well, measures to ensure adherence to the principles of supremacy of law, equality before the law, accountability to the law, fairness in the application of the law, separation of powers, participation in decision-making, legal certainty, avoidance of arbitrariness and procedural and legal transparency".*[100]

Making the government itself subject to the law may be regarded as the first guarantee for rights' protection. The OBSS makes the same indication in Article 59 stating that:

> *"The sovereignty of the law is the basis of governance in the state.*

98 Basic Principles on the Independence of the Judiciary. See http://www2.ohchr.org/english/law/indjudiciary.htm, and the Basic Principles on the Role of Lawyers <http://www.advocatenvooradvocaten.nl/basic-principles/>

99 Alder, J (2007), p. 149.

100 Secretary-General, R. o. (23 August 2004). The Rule of Law and Transitional Justice in Conflict and Post-Conflict Societies. Retrieved 21 January 2011, from United Nations: <http://www.unrol.org/files/2004%20report.pdf>

Rights and freedoms are guaranteed by the dignity of the judiciary and the probity and impartiality of the judges".

The following sections aim to describe the judicial system in Oman and explore to what extent the OBSS has developed the judiciary branch in a way that will protect the rights and freedoms of its citizens. In a basic sense, the Constitutional and Administrative Courts are guardians of the rule of law and are best placed to offer judicial remedies for any human rights violation. Hence, the aim is to provide an overview of their hierarchy and powers, highlight limitations and suggest remedial solutions.

3.4.1 Historical Background of the Judicial System in Oman[101]

Prior to Sultan Qaboos' rule, the judicial system in Oman was unfamiliar with the laws and legislation as they currently stand. The courts and judicial systems were simple; there were no formal courts with varying degrees of jurisdiction. Often, the judge and notary sat within the State's governor's office. The *Shariʿa* Courts were based on Islamic law, mostly of the *Ibadi* doctrine, and they had the jurisdiction to decide on civil and criminal matters, including matters of personal status. Customs and tribal traditions also played a role in reconciling disputes. In addition, some tribal and international treaties played a role in determining the judiciary's parameters during that era.[102]

The first development of the contemporary judicial system took place with the establishment of the Ministry of Justice in 1970.[103] This occurred after several decrees were issued to regulate different as-

101 Al Abri, I. (2010). *The judicial system in the Sultanate of Oman (in Arabic)*. Retrieved 13 January 2011, from Ministry of Justice website: <http://www.moj.gov.om/HostedPages?c=&PageId=3>

102 Such as the case with the agreement with British Empire in 19th century to prevent Slave Trade. See Chapter Two (2.1.2).

103 1970 with the Ministries of Interior, Health and Knowledge (education), see Ministry of Justice website.

pects of the country's development including the Labour Law,[104] the Law of the Distribution of Fertile Land,[105] the Land Regulation Law,[106] the Lands Law,[107] the Commercial Registration Law,[108] the Foreign Crafts Law,[109] the Omani Penal Law,[110] and the Commercial Law.[111]

The issuing of such legislation and of the subsequent regulations that followed resulted in the creation of specialised courts and quasi-judicial committees such as the Police Criminal Court,[112] and later became the Criminal Court.[113] Jurisdiction to reconcile disputes in commercial matters was initially vested in a committee called 'The Authority for the Settlement of Commercial Disputes',[114] which later became 'the Commercial Court'.[115] In the same framework, specialised judicial committees and courts were established for different purposes, such as the Land Affairs Committee[116] in accordance with the Law of Land Affairs and the Rental Disputes Resolution Committees.[117]

However, there was no single body charged with regulating or supervising these various courts (legal, penal, commercial). Most *Shariʿa* courts followed the Ministry of Justice's guidelines, while the Commercial Court though independent were supervised by the Minister of Justice. The Criminal Tribunal was under the supervision of the State Advisor for Criminal Affairs, the specialised legal commit-

104 R.D. 34/73.
105 R.D. 4/72.
106 R.D. 6/72.
107 R.D. 5/80.
108 R.D. 3/74.
109 R.D. 4/74.
110 R.D. 7/74.
111 R.D. 55/90.
112 which was established by Royal Decree no. 7/74.
113 R.D. 25/84.
114 R.D. 79/81.
115 R.D. 13/97.
116 R.D. 6/72.
117 R.D. 4/73.

tees for land disputes were under the Ministry of Housing, and those responsible for hearing lease and rental disputes were under the respective municipality based on the region.[118] In addition, several judicial committees existed, such as the Grievance Committee,[119] the Committee of Incest[120] and the Committee of Legal Instruments.[121]

It can be concluded that during this period in Oman, there was an absence of a single reference for judicial issues since the creation of different courts and judicial bodies was based on social and economic development without a clear plan, and the *Shariʿa* judges, in particular, were not familiar with the concept of international standards.

3.4.2 The Legal System after the Basic Statute

The unity of the judiciary is an important pillar for achieving an effective judiciary system. After 26 years of the Sultan's rule, it was deemed necessary to make changes to the old fragmented judicial system via a new constitution. The legal order of Oman was largely codified in the OBSS, which enshrines a chapter dealing with the judiciary that confirm its independence and affirms the principle of the rule of law was the basis of the State's governance.[122]

The OBSS lists several judicial guarantees and principles in this regard, such as honouring the judiciary's integrity and impartiality as it safeguards the rights and liberties of Omani citizens.[123] It also addresses the unification of judicial authorities and the independence of the judiciary, which was uncertain prior to the OBSS promulgation.[124] Moreover, it states explicitly that it holds no power over judges in

118 Such as the Ministry of Regional Municipalities, or Muscat Municipality, or Dhofar Municipality.

119 Minister of Justice Decision 3/78.

120 Royal Orders understanding from the letter of the Minister of Justice, Awqaf and Islamic Affairs, No. (JAIA/MO/29/1106/90).

121 Decision of the Minister of Justice, Awqaf and Islamic Affairs No. (252/85).

122 Chapter 6 in the OBSS.

123 Art. 59.

124 Articles 60, 62 and 66.

their rulings except in accordance with the law and that they cannot be removed unless in cases specified by law. Furthermore, it criminalises interference by officials in lawsuits or matters of justice.[125] Finally, the State guarantees the approximation of judicial bodies to litigants and the speedy settlement of cases.[126]

It should be noted that the OBSS defined the future plan of the judiciary, but did not put forward particulars. It set forth the general principles of the judicial authority and determines the trends in establishing legal courts, their levels and their terms of reference. Elaborations upon these guidelines originated from other statutes, such as the Judicial Authority and Procedures Laws. The Judicial Authority Law (R.D. 90/99) is the most significant judicial development after the OBSS. It unites the ordinary litigation bodies into courts with specialised departments, and mentioned the possibility of establishing specialised courts.[127] With the subsequent issuing of relevant laws, the new comprehensive legal system has shaped Oman.

Afterwards, it was necessary to translate these principles into mechanisms that could be implemented. This process subsumed all ordinary judicial bodies into one single institution, and organised all judges and public prosecutors affairs.[128] Moreover, it succeeded in subjecting the judiciary to one central authority at the top of the judicial hierarchy, namely the Supreme Judicial Council. In particular, this law has granted the council the power to ensure judicial independence and to achieve the most recent developments in this area, which include the following tasks:

- Supervising the proper functioning of the courts and prosecutors.

125 Art. 61.

126 Art. 25.

127 Articles 62 and 67 of the Judicial Authority Law (R.D. 90/99).

128 This is in relation to the appointment, promotion, transfer and delegation of judges, and their professional affairs including guarantees and assigns them to their respective jurisdictions.

- Pursuing the courts' development and approximation of judicial bodies to litigants and speedy settlement of cases.
- Considering nominations for appointment or promotion in judicial office.
- Proposing draft laws and reviewing legislation related to the judiciary.
- Expressing opinions on draft agreements for judicial cooperation between Oman and other countries.
- Other judiciary matters that the law provides for.
- Expressing opinions on any other topics the Sultan may present to the Council.

3.4.3 The Court System in Oman

In Oman today, the court system comprises three types of judicial bodies: a) ordinary courts, which deal with criminal, labour, social, tax, rent, personal, patent law and most civil cases; b) specialised courts that hear cases related to administrative, national security or other special areas based on the statute that establishes such courts; and c) 'The Authority on Conflicts of Jurisdictions and Rules' (hereinafter referred to as the ACJR), which has some constitutional power since no Constitutional Court currently exists. The ACJR is responsible for Conflict of Laws, Conflict of Jurisdiction, judicial review and constitutional interpretation to some extent. In addition, the military courts, as mentioned in the OBSS, "*... deal solely with military offences committed by members of the armed and security forces. Its jurisdiction cannot be extended to others except in the case of martial law and within the limits prescribed by the Law*".[129]

All Gulf States today, including Oman, follow in part elements of the Civil Law system, although most were formerly under the British protectorates. The Judicial Authority Law establishes three levels of ordinary courts: The Supreme Court, Appeal Courts and First In-

129 Art. 62.

stance Courts. The latter two are trial courts, while the Supreme Court is an appellate court, which also operates as the High Court of Justice.

According to Article 20 of the Judicial Authority Law, the ranking of judges with judicial functions are listed from higher to lower as follows: Chairman of the Supreme Court, Deputy-Chairman of the Supreme Court, Supreme Court Judge, Appeals Court Judge, First Judge of the First Instance Court, Second Judge of the First Instance Court, Judge, Associate Judge.

The hierarchy of the ordinary courts is explained below starting with those of the lowest jurisdiction to those of the highest jurisdiction.

The Courts of First Instance are, essentially, basic trial courts. All civil and commercial litigations, requests for arbitration, personal status cases and public, labour, tax and rent cases and other disputes are brought before this court in the first instance, unless otherwise stipulated by a special provision in the law.[130]

Appeal Courts are the second level courts in the Omani judiciary. They have jurisdiction over appeals against judgments issued by Courts of First Instance. However, these courts will not hear disputes that are presented for the first time.[131]

The Supreme Court is at the top of the judicial hierarchy in Oman, and there is one Supreme Court located in the capital, Muscat. Its jurisdiction extends to hearing appeals from Appeal Court judgements, overseeing the correct application of the law before all courts and monitoring judges' adjudications. The Court can confirm a judgment

130 Generally, a single judge presides over each case, but there are other divisions where the case may be heard by a panel of three judges. There are forty-two First Instance Courts throughout Oman.

131 Thirteen Appeal Courts current exist in Oman. Their quarters and jurisdictions are determined by the Minister of Justice Decisions. Each court consists of a chairman and a sufficient number of judges, and each court has as many departments as is necessary. Each department is headed by the chairman or the senior judge of the department, and the judgments are issued by three judges.

if it conforms to the law, it can invalidate rulings and return them back to the same judge, or send it to others if it violates the law, has an error in application or interpretation, or if the procedures were invalid and impacted the ruling.[132]

Some cases may be automatically considered as matters for the Supreme Court if the punishment allotted by the State Security Court is death or imprisonment of 15 years or more.[133] Additionally, the Supreme Court may act as a trial court if there is an appeal against the ruling of a lower court where the case was assigned by the Supreme Court.[134]

3.4.4 The Constitutional Court

A concrete way to enhance human rights protection is to challenge the state and relevant constitutional issues through the courts.[135] Thus, the Constitutional Court is one of the most effective mechanisms for protecting rights and freedoms of citizens, within the framework of constitutional rights. The creation of a Constitutional Court as the supreme judicial institution that deals primarily with constitutional law is crucial. This court's authority in protection and enforcement of the provisions laid out in the constitution, including the protection of fundamental rights and freedoms is entrenched in Chapter Three of the OBSS.[136]

---

132 The Supreme Court consists of the chairman and an adequate number of judges and deputy chairmen. It also contains departments that decide on current contestations. Each department is headed by the chairman or one of his deputies, and its judgments are issued by five judges.

133 Art. 17 of the State Security Court Law (R.D. 64/2003).

134 Article 246 of the Criminal Procedures Law (R.D. 97/99).

135 Brand, D. (2005). Introduction to socio-economic rights in the South African Constitution. *Socio-economic Rights in South Africa.* pp. 38-39.

136 Wihelm Karl Geck has listed several pre-requisites for determining the constitutionality of legislation: The written constitution must be the supreme law of the land; the judiciary must be independent and the constitution should not prevent or, ideally, provide for the establishment of a judicial review of the constitutionality of legislation. An examination of these pre-requisites in the context of the

The OBSS does not directly mention the Constitutional Court. The only article that refers to such an institution is Article 70, which provides a statute to define the judicial body "*entrusted with the settlement of disputes pertaining to the extent of conformity of laws and regulations with the Basic Statute of the State and that the said laws and regulations do not contradict with its provisions*". Nevertheless, specifically mentioning such a body in a constitutional text gives it more legitimacy and power than leaving it to an ordinary statute. Four years after the promulgation of the OBSS, the Judicial Authority Law came into effect and referred to the establishment of a panel within the Supreme Court, naming it the 'Authority on Conflicts of Jurisdictions and Rules' or (ACJR).[137] Article 11 of the Judicial Authority Law makes explicit reference to the function of reviewed cases related to the constitutionality of legislation by the same body responsible for the Conflicts of Jurisdictions and Rules.[138] However, the ACJR did not have the opportunity to practice its functions for almost 10 years, as the relevant statute that should clarify the competence of this institution and its procedures was not declared until 2008.[139]

So far, the ACJR has not reviewed a single case related to the con-

---

Omani system shows that they are fulfilled to some extent. See Geck, W. (1966). Judicial Review of Statutes; A comparative institutions and practices. *Cornell Law Quarterly*, 51, p. 252.

137 ACJR consists of eleven of the highest ranking, senior judges from the Supreme and Administrative Courts. six members are from the Supreme Court, and five members from the Administrative Court, and the panel is headed by the chairman of the Supreme Court or in case of his absence the senior judge on the panel. The decision has to be made with the majority votes of at least seven votes.

138 Article 11 of the Judicial Authority Law states that: "*To settle negative or positive disputes on jurisdiction among courts in ordinary courts, administrative courts, and other courts and judicial bodies. The Authority is also authorized to settle disputes of conformity to the laws and regulations of the basic system of the state and not breaching its judgments*".

139 Article 11 of the Judicial Authority Law, and the Authority on Conflicts of Jurisdictions and Rules Law (R.D. 88/2008) came to clarify the competence and procedure of the Authority.

stitutionality of legislation or confirmed any law or regulation with the OBSS. This is due to the lack of relevant terms of reference for the constitutional body. The ACJR Law (R.D. 88/2008), the main legislation in this area, and neglects to refer to it. The delay in establishing a Constitutional Court or declaring this body's terms of reference still leaves Omani rights and freedoms unprotected, as neither the OBSS, nor the Royal Decrees nor the Judicial Authority Law have given power to this panel to declare legislation unconstitutional. Thus, it is not realistic to refer to an existing Constitutional Court in Oman or to a body that can act on that level.

Rectifying the absence of this court is a crucial necessity; however, the ACJR is still lacking the power and appearance of the Constitutional Court due to its ad hoc existence, as the law itself refers such a body based on '*the necessity and needs*'.[140] The membership of this panel confirms the ad hoc status of the body; it consists of judges from different courts. Additionally, the organisation of the ACJR is rather vague as it has interlinked tasks with the Judicial Authority Law and the Authority on Conflicts of Jurisdictions and Rules Law. The latter has specified only two areas of jurisdictions for the Panel, none of which are related to constitutional review.[141]

The importance of the Constitutional Court in protecting civil liberties can be deduced from the Kuwaiti model where a Constitutional Court ruling 1 May 2006 declared the Articles 1 and 4 of the decree known as Law No. 65 of 1979 unconstitutional based on the organisation of meetings and public processions. Within the same law, the court also decided the unconstitutionality of Articles 2-3, 5-6, 8-

140 Art. 10 (R.D. 90/99).

141 The Authority on Conflicts of Jurisdictions and Rules (R.D. 88/2008) has specified only two areas of jurisdiction for the Authority; the settlement on the positive or negative conflict of jurisdictions between the courts, and the settlement on conflict of adjudications.

11, and 16-20, which forced legislators to create a new statute that could effectively regulate processions.[142]

The last Chapter of the OBSS clearly highlights the supremacy of the Basic Statute over other laws and regulations from different aspects. It prevents the suspension of any constitutional provision except during periods of Martial Law and within the limits prescribed by law.[143] Moreover, it requests that the competent authorities issue non-existing laws necessitated by the OBSS within two years from the date of its coming into force.[144] It also prevents any State authority from issuing rules, regulations, decisions or directives "*... which contradict the provisions of the applicable laws and decrees, or international treaties and agreements which are part of the Law of the Land*".[145] In this regard, Article 79 emphasises that any law or regulation should be in line with the provisions of the OBSS; such emphasis confirms the supremacy of the OBSS over other laws in Oman.

Hence, there is a need for a judicial review of the constitutionality of the laws in order to ensure that all existing and forthcoming laws are in line with the provisions of the OBSS. This necessitates the existence of a judicial body that can interpret the constitutional texts

142 Alqabas Newspaper (21. April 2009). Government Backtracked the Decrees on Assemblies and Dual Nationality (in Arabic). Retrieved 3rd August 2009, from <http://www.alqabas.com.kw/Article.aspx?id=492109> An example of human rights violation in Oman can be deduced from the OBSS itself, as it gives legislators the right to restrict the rights and freedoms embodied in its provisions by issuing or amending statutes and regulations without limitation. (Based on Art. 81 OBSS) the Law of Civil Association (R.D. 14/2000), issued 4 years after the OBSS, vitally contradicts the right of association protected by the constitutional provision (Art.33). Check the Freedom of Associations Chapter Six.

143 Art. 73 of the OBSS. There is no Martial Law as a name under the Omani System yet, and this Article might be applicable to 'a State of Emergency Law' R.D. 75/2008 which has the impact of Martial Law, as it limits people's rights and freedoms in state of emergency in different aspects, such as the freedoms of movement and assembly and many of procedural safeguards and other freedoms and rights as stipulated under Articles 4-7.

144 Art. 78.

145 Art. 80.

and determine the validity of laws and regulations. Article 77 states that any applicable laws, regulations, decrees, orders and decisions in force shall remain in force only if they are not in conflict with any of the OBSS's provisions.[146]

Several laws issued prior to the promulgation of the OBSS directly violate it, such as the Law on the Organisation of the Omani Nationality (RD 3/83) and the Press and Publications Law (R.D. 49/84). However, these conflicts also occur in legislations issued since the promulgation of the OBSS, such the Law of Civil Association (R.D. 14/2000).

The constitutionality of a law can be examined before its declaration, such as in France, by a political institution or after the enactment of the legislation by courts. The latter examination includes two different forms of judicial review: a) A decentralised system, which gives courts the power to disregard any ordinary law in case of conflict with the constitution, as is the case in the American system; b) A centralised system where the power to examine the constitutionality of legislation is exercised by a single judicial body such as a Constitutional Court or a special body. The latter is most common in Gulf States, and is stipulated by the OBSS and the Judicial Authority Law. Since the Omani system still lacks such a constitutional judicial body in practice,[147] conflicts between the OBSS and other laws are expected. The continuation of such conflicts without a clear solution endangers the rights and freedoms of Omani citizens. Therefore, an appropriate solution may be to follow a decentralised system where judges can refrain from applying ordinary law if it is in conflict with text in the OBSS. Such a practice will protect Omani rights and freedoms until the ACJR has the authority to rule over such cases.

With this in mind, the First Instance Administrative Court in Muscat tried to implement such a decentralised system when it reviewed a case and declared the unconstitutionality of an article within an or-

146 Art. 77.

147 Although legislations still refer to its existence.

dinary law based on its conflict with the OBSS.[148] However, the Appeal Department of the Administrative Court overruled the First Instance Court's ruling based on the fact that:[149]

> *"... the legislator has entrusted the power to review the compatibility of ordinary laws with the Basic Statute exclusively to the Judicial Body, as provided in Article 10 of the Judicial Authority Law; hence, all courts of different types and levels do not have the jurisdiction to review the constitutionality of the law or to abstain from its application".*[150]

The Appeal Court's ruling was criticised by some jurists for several reasons. Al-Busaidi points out some of these reasons:[151]

1. The Court's ruling is in violation of the principle of the rule of law and supremacy of the Constitution, as Article 77 of the OBSS refers to the validity of existing laws if they are consistent with its provisions. Article 7 of the law referred to in that case violates a provision of the OBSS, thus, to refrain from applying the law is the right practice until the declaration of the procedures of the competent authority (the ACJR).
2. The Independence of the judiciary from other authorities requires that it not act in agreement with them, especially when the case is related to the disrupting the provisions of the OBSS. Furthermore, the OBSS stresses the importance of issuing related laws within two years after the promulgation of the OBSS,[152] which had not

148 First Instance Court Case No. (22) for the year (1 J) (20 February 2002) before the First Instance Administrative Court, which disregarded Article 7 of the Law of 'After Service Wages and Rewards in Royal Oman Police'.

149 The Administrative Court. (2003). *Set of Legal Principles Established by the Court for years I and II (2001-2002).* Muscat: The Technical Office.

150 The Appeal Administrative Court Decision No. (5) of the year (2 QS) (11 May 2002).

151 Al Busaidi, T. (2008). Organising the Constitutional Review in the Sultanate of Oman (in Arabic). *Journal of Law,* University of Bahrain 293-361.

152 Art. 78.

yet occurred when the court made its ruling, and has not happened until today.

3. Until the completion of a centralised system in the form of a court or a constitutional body in Oman, the rule of law requires the application of an abstention doctrine and the use of a decentralised system. Otherwise, the pending formation of the body or its terms of references will violate the rule of law, which will threaten the rights and freedoms of Omani citizens.
4. The Appeal Department's ruling has intervened in the authority of other courts that are beyond its competence. The court has banned other courts from declaring the constitutionality of legislation, while such decision is accepted if announced by the Supreme Court.
5. The ruling has left any constitutional dispute or claim without a remedy while waiting for the terms of reference of the Authority on Conflicts of Jurisdictions and Rules. Hence, the Appeals Court made the constitutional review issue more vague and ambiguous.

Overall, it seems that the legislator's reference to the Authority on Conflicts of Jurisdictions and Rules as a body responsible for constitutional review remains meaningless until the judiciary can reach a satisfactory stage where its full independence achieved. Then, a Constitutional Court can be instituted, either permanently or temporarily.[153]

It is not appropriate to leave open such a crucial judicial gap for such a long period without promulgating the necessary statute, especially if the gap is concerned with cases of crisis and emergency. Therefore, opening the opportunity for the courts to refrain from applying unconstitutional laws and regulations is the best method to so-

153 Bearing in mind that it was the Sultan's priority to establish a Constitutional Court after the promulgation of the OBSS: it is "*The guardians of the law, without that you cannot have a proper government, they are the ones to say what is right and wrong*". See Miller, J. (1997) p. 16.

lidify the rule of law in Oman until a body with central jurisdiction over constitutional disputes can be established.

The main difficulty that will face any authority or constitutional body in Oman is that the ultimate legislator is the Sultan holding that position with the assistance of the Cabinet and consultancy from the Parliament. Therefore, any legislation declared unconstitutional is likely to clash with the monarchical power of the Sultan who is hierarchically above the Constitutional Court. The existence of a legislative parliament can contribute to the protection of rights and freedoms, especially, if the parliamentary members represent diverse groups within the country and can participate in drafting bills according to the constitution. It may be more appropriate for Oman to follow a mixed model of constitutional review, by adopting the prior-examination of the draft law before its declaration (Civil system) in addition to the centralised model where a Constitutional Court or body reviews the law after its promulgation; this will add to the protection of individual rights and freedoms.[154]

3.4.5 The Administrative Court

Judicial review and putting particular legal issues in the hands of administrative courts is a growing trend in many legal systems; indeed, it is one of the main aspects of the rule of law. After the promulgation of the OBSS in Oman, the whole legal system was reshaped and the country adopted a new judicial system where the administrative courts existed in line with the ordinary courts. This changed the interrelationship between public bodies and citizens by creating a new level of judicial review.

Prior to the existence of the Administrative Court, executive decisions were immune to judicial review. Ordinary courts did not have any jurisdiction over administrative disputes with the exception of the old Commercial Court, which has the right to review contracts

154 Such system has been followed by the Constitutional Court in Bahrain.

where the government is a party. The right to appeal an administrative decision usually followed the method of a petition to the responsible Minister, who maintains the ultimate power to review or ignore a case, and in certain cases, the appeal may reach the Sultan who can form a panel of ministers or administrators to review the complaint. Hence, the risk of violating an individual's rights is high without any judicial review or protection.

Article 67 of the OBSS provides for the formation of a panel or a special court responsible for examining and controlling the legality of administrative actions as an additional guarantee to maintain basic human rights. Hence, the Judicial Authority Law refers to the establishment of this judicial body as the Administrative Court,[155] followed by the Administrative Court Law (R.D. 91/99), which clearly defines the terms of references and the jurisdiction of the court.

Initially, the Administrative Court Law was formed to fill the gap between protecting public personnel and administration abuses.[156] This task was filled by the jurisdiction of the Court and its supervision of authority. The law stipulates three tasks for the court related to examining the disputes between public services' employees and administration decisions.[157] Moreover, by making the Minister of Diwan Royal Court directly responsible, the legislator has avoided the situation where the judicial court belongs to the Ministry of Justice, as is the case with other ordinary courts. The supervision of the Minister of Diwan Royal Court may be regarded as part of the court's independence.[158] However, such independence can exist under the Minister of Justice similar to the ordinary courts, and the supervision of

155 Art. 4.

156 This asserts the concept that human rights in Oman cannot sustain without the legislative and the judicial protection.

157 Articles 6.1, 6.2, and 6.3.

158 Alroya Newspaper (20 January 2011). *The Administrative Court: 11 Years in Judicial Service Report (in Arabic).* Retrieved January 2011, from <http://www.alroya.info/ar/alroya-newspaper/internal/13165----11------->

the Minister of Diwan Royal Court is linked to his position as the chairman of the Civil Services Council within which most of the personnel disputes fall.

Articles 6.4 and 6.5 give the court the right to review cases of direct interest to individuals against administration decisions either from executives or committees. In particular, the law gives the Court the power to directly abolish administrative decisions and to decide whether they are legitimate. Overall, this has resulted in new avenues to protect individuals.[159] The Court may comments on legislation and regulations that are not in line with the OBSS, and suggests amendments and changes. Although the suggestions are not compulsory it has often succeeded in changing some laws and regulations in the interest of the rights of the individual. Such was the case in granting women the right to own residential plots, making them equal to a man's right without discrimination.[160]

The First Instance Court also tried to take responsibility for constitutional review. Indeed, this is a necessary step, especially in the context of an absent Constitutional Court that would make a great impact on judicial review and the rule of law in Oman. Nevertheless, the Appeals Court has repealed the ruling of the First Instance Court.[161]

Royal Decree No. 3/2009 amended the Administrative Court Law which has widened the court's scope to include more individual disputes against the state which were not part of the original law. Article 6.5 gives the individual the right to compensation as a result of wrong administrative decision, and Article 6.7 gives the Court the

159 The court cannot examine or rule on any legislative provision, even if it violates the Basic Statute, as its power is merely over executive orders and regulations (a direct question to the court's judges on the court's conference, Sur-Oman 11/06/08).

160 The Original statute which was declared in 1983 has a clear discrimination issue, as to be entitled to receive a plot from the government you need to be a male citizen over the age of 21 years. The law has been changed by the one which invalidate such provision according to (R.D. 125/2008).

161 Refer to section 3.4.4 for more details.

right to review a refusal or abstention of any administrative institution, where the law or regulation requires the administrative body to take an action and make a decision. These new amendments are linked to individual and public rights as protections against the state. This stands in contrast to the original law, which was concerned with staff complaints against an administrative body.

However, Article 7 of the Law still stipulates exceptions in the Administrative Court's jurisdictions that constrain its ability to protect the rights and freedoms of Omani citizens.[162] These limitations have wide-ranging effects including the Court's inability to review complaints related to security and military matters apart from those of public relations and affairs. The significance of these limitations is the Court's lack of jurisdiction over all Royal Decrees, Royal orders and Sovereignty affairs. This exemption prevents the Court from reviewing the broad array of laws and closes the door on possibility to take an action in this regard.[163] Exemptions extend to include areas such as the right to nationality, which is the first individual right stipulated in the OBSS.[164] These amendments exempt all nationality and tribal affairs from the judicial review of the Court[165] and have a direct impact on personal rights, such as the rights related to name and identity. A number of cases have been presented before the court without any successful remedy to prevent administrative abuses on individual's right.[166]

---

162 R.D. 3/2009.

163 As the First instance Court has tried in the First Instance Court Case No. (22) for the year (1 J).

164 Art. 15 OBSS, see Chapter Four.

165 Art 7.3 of the R.D. 3/2009.

166 Such as the Appeal Administrative Court Decision No. (265) of the year (8 JS). The court decided that the decision of Ministry of Interior to change the Tribe name is a tribal affair which is part of the Sovereignty affairs exempted from the court's jurisdiction. The decision has been made based on the original Law (91/99) and before the declaration of the new amendments which is clearly defined the tribal affairs as exemption in addition to all Sovereignty affairs.

Although, the Administrative judicial review is relatively new in Oman, it has succeeded in creating new avenues for redress.[167] However, the power of Parliament and the absence of a Constitutional Court both threaten human rights in Oman, thus, the Administrative Court is the most obvious and influential guardian of the system today.[168] On one hand, the Council of Ministers is only constitutionally responsible before the Sultan, and Parliament does not have a vote of confidence over the Cabinet or any individual Minister. On the other hand, the non-activation of the constitutional body has left a wide area without judicial review. A more nuanced judicial mandate is needed. Justice Ali Shehata states:

> *"If the Basic Statute has given great importance to citizens' rights and freedoms, the establishment of the Administrative Court was a basic guarantee of these rights and freedoms and the embodiment of the principle of legality. Which means the rule of law and the subjection of the executive to its requirements, so that the actions of positive and negative in a circle and within the legal system of the state. However, undergo the administration to the law does not mean preventing the public authorities from its discretionary power within the scope of the public interest".*[169]

167 It follows the same approach as the Administrative Courts in France and Egypt, and expressly alleges the invalidity of an administrative decision based on any defect accompanied with the decision, which protects people's rights to some extent.

168 For instance, the Administrative Court has decided that the expulsion decision taken by the Public Prosecution for the accused is an administrative decision which is subject to the jurisdiction of the Administrative Court and it is not considered an exercise of judicial function entrusted to the Public Prosecution. See Appeal Administrative Court Case No. (3) of the year (11 QS).

169 Shehata, A. (October 2003). *A Guide to the Administrative Court in Oman.* Muscat: Administrative Court.

3.5 Human Rights Treaties and Reports

National legal and constitutional guarantees are not the only protections available for rights and freedoms, though they are the most efficient. International conventions and treaties can play an important role too, especially if these treaties are part of international human rights instruments as well as the national legal system. Human rights reports are influential in guiding the state to violations and weakness from third party overview.

The Vienna Convention on the Law of Treaties determined that international law will apply to a state regardless of its domestic law and the state cannot plead its own domestic law or constitution as an excuse for breaches of international obligations.[170] The OBSS implements a *monist* system for the relationship between international law and national law, which assumes that domestic and international legal systems form one system of law, and international law, can be applied directly without transformation and without the need to enact domestic legislation.[171]

The OBSS recognises international law and international treaties as part of the law of the land. This is obvious under several articles: Article 72 gives ratified treaties and agreements supremacy over other statutes and regulations, even over the OBSS itself. It states that the application of the Basic Statute "*shall not prejudice treaties and agreements the Sultanate has entered into with other countries, international institutions and organisations*", and ratified treaties and agreements "*shall have the force of law*".[172] Furthermore, "*adherence to the international and regional charters and treaties and the generally recog-*

170 Article 27 of the Vienna Convention. Oman has joined the convention on 18 October 1990.

171 It is different than the dualists' theory where the international law is inferior and can only become part of domestic law by being incorporated into it by domestic legislation, such as the UK system.

172 The only exception by the OBSS if the "*treaties and agreements have secret terms contradicting their declared ones*" Art. 76.

nised norms of international Law" is one of the political principles guiding State policy.[173] Article 80 prevents any authority in the State from issuing regulations, statutes, decisions or directives that contradict the provisions of international treaties and agreements that are part of the Law of the Land. Though the Sultan is the only person capable of "*signing international treaties and agreements according to the provisions of the Law or authorizing their signature and issuing Decrees ratifying the same*",[174] the Council of Ministers is tasked to supervise the implementation of treaties and agreements.[175]

The influence of international agreements on the Omani legal system is observable in the case of the US-Oman Free Trade Agreement (OFTA). This agreement encourages the Omani government to recognise the existence of trade unions and protect them, which was not the case before. Even the freedoms granted for trade unions are more than those granted for other associations and NGOs. This shows the power of mutual agreements to provide and enhance the protection of rights and freedoms.[176] Thus, international treaties and agreements may serve as a pillar of human rights safeguards in Oman, especially international and regional human rights conventions and agreements.

3.5.1 Human Rights Treaties

The Gulf States have signed several international human rights treaties and conventions. However, the legal impact of the ICCPR and ICESCR is particularly important since, together with the Universal Declaration of Human Rights, they form the International Bill of Rights. It is notable that several Gulf States, Oman, Qatar, Saudi Arabia and the UAE, have not yet signed these instruments.

Oman has ratified four of seven core international human rightstreaties; in 1996, it ratified the Convention on the Rights of the Child

173 Art. 10.
174 Art. 42.
175 Art. 44.
176 Check Chapter Six, the Role of Labour Unions as Associations in Oman (6.3).

Table 4: Gulf States and Human Rights Instruments

			Oman	Bahrain	Kuwait	Qatar	Saudi Arabia	UAE
			Ratified/ Joined	Ratified/ Joined	Ratified/ Joined	Ratified/ Joined	Ratified/ Joined	Ratified/ Joined
International Human Rights Treaties and Agreements*								
ICCPR		International Covenant on Civil and Political Rights		20-Sep-06	21-May-96			
	Protocol 1	International Covenant on Civil and Political Rights Concerning communications from individuals claiming to be victims of violations						
	Protocol 2	Second Optional Protocol to the International Covenant on Civil and Political Rights						
ICESCR		International Covenant on Economic, Social & Cultural Rights		27-Sep-07	21-May-96			
	Optional	Optional Protocol to the International Covenant on Economic, Social & Cultural Rights						
ICERD		Convention on the Elimination of All Forms of Racial Discrimination	2-Jan-03	27-Mar-90	15-Oct-68	22-Jul-76	22-Sep-97	20-Jun-74
CEDAW		Convention on the Elimination of All Forms of Discrimination Against Women	7-Feb-06	18-Jun-02	2-Sep-94	29-Apr-09	7-Sep-00	10-Jun-04
	Optional	Optional Protocol to the Convention on the Elimination of Discrimination against Women						
CRC		Convention on the Rights of the Child	09-Dec-96	13-Feb-92	21-Oct-91	3-Apr-95	26-Jan-96	3-Jan-97
	Optional 1	Optional Protocol to the Convention on the Rights of the Child on the Involvement of Children in Armed Conflict	17-Sep-04	21-Sep-04	26-Aug-04	25-Jul-02		
	Optional 2	Optional Protocol to the Convention on the Rights of the Child, Sale of Children, Child Prostitution & Child Pornography	17-Sep-04	21-Sep-04	26-Aug-04	14-Dec-01		
CAT		Convention against Torture and Other Cruel, Inhuman or Degrading Treatment or Punishment		06-Mar-98	08-Mar-96	11-Jan-00	23-Sep-97	
	Optional	Optional Protocol to the Convention against Torture & Other Cruel, Inhuman or Degrading Treatment or Punishment						
CRPD		Convention on the Rights of Persons with Disabilities	6-Jan-09	25-Jun-07			24-Jun-08	19-Mar-10
	Optional	Optional Protocol to the Convention against Torture & Other Cruel, Inhuman or Degrading Treatment or Punishment					24-Jun-08	12-Feb-08
CPPCG		Convention on the Prevention and Punishment of the Crime of Genocide		27-Mar-90	07-Mar-95		13-Jul-50	11-Nov-05

ICSPCA		International Convention on the Suppression and Punishment of the Crime of Apartheid	22-Aug-91	27-Mar-90	23-Feb-77	19-Mar-75		15-Oct-75
CRSR		Convention relating to the Status of Refugees						
	Protocol	Protocol relating to the Status of Refugees						
MWC		Convention on the Protection of the Rights of All Migrant Workers and Members of their Families						
ICPAPED		International Convention for the Protection of All Persons from Enforced Disappearance						
CTOC		Convention against Transnational Organized Crime						
	Protocol 1	Protocol to Prevent, Suppress and Punish Trafficking in Persons, Especially Women and Children	13-May-05	7-Jun-04	12-May-06	29-May-09	20-Jul-07	21-Jan-09
	Protocol 2	Protocol against the Smuggling of Migrants by Land, Sea & Air	13-May-05	7-Jun-04	12-May-06		20-Jul-07	
Regional Human Rights Conventions**								
ACHR		Arab Charter of Human Rights	May 2004	May 2004	May 2004	May 2004	May 2004	May 2004
CDHRI		Cairo Declaration on Human Rights in Islam						
International Labour Organization Conventions***								
C.87		Freedom of Association and Protection of the Right to Organise Convention			21-Sep-61			
C.98		Right to Organise and Collective Bargaining Convention			9-Aug-07			
C.29		Forced Labour Convention	30-Oct-98	22-Jun-81	23-Sep-68	12-Mar-98	15-Jun-78	27-May-82
C.105		Abolition of Forced Labour Convention	21-Jul-05	14-Jul-98	21-Sep-61	2-Feb-07	15-Jun-78	14-Dec-00
C.100		Equal Remuneration for Men and Women Workers for Work of Equal Value					15-Jun-78	24-Feb-97
C.111		Discrimination Employment and Occupation Convention		26-Sep-00	01-Dec-66	18-Aug-76	15-Jun-78	28-Jun-01
C.138		Convention concerning Minimum Age for Admission to Employment	21-Jul-05		15-Nov-99	3-Jan-06		02-Oct-98
C.182		Convention concerning the Prohibition and Immediate Action for the Elimination of the Worst Forms of Child Labour	11-Jun-01	23-Mar-01	15-Aug-00	30-May-00	08-Oct-01	28-Jun-01
	*	United Nations Treaty Collection website	http://treaties.un.org/Pages/Treaties.aspx?id=4&subid=A&lang=en					
	**	Arab Human Rights Index website	http://www.arabhumanrights.org/en/countries/country.aspx?cid=1					
	***	International Labor Organization website	http://www.ilo.org/public/english/region					

(CRC) and two of its optional protocols.[177] It ratified the International Convention on the Elimination of All Forms of Racial Discrimination (ICERD) in 2003, the Convention on the Elimination of All Forms of Discrimination against Women (CEDAW) in 2006 and the Convention on the Rights of Persons with Disabilities (CRPD) in 2009. Oman acceded to the Arab Charter on Human Rights in 2004 but did not ratify it, like most Arab States. It agreed to the guiding document titled, 'Cairo Declaration on Human Rights in Islam' in 1990, which does not require ratification.[178] (This is set out in Table 4 above).

Oman has ratified four out of the eight core International Labour Organization (ILO) conventions connected to human rights. This includes the C29 'Forced Labour Convention, 1930', C105 'Abolition of Forced Labour Convention, 1957', C138 on 'Minimum Age Convention, 1973' and C182 on 'Worst Forms of Child Labour Convention, 1999'.[179] However, other important conventions connected to human rights have not yet been ratified, such as C87 on 'Freedom of Association and Protection of the Right to Organise Convention, 1948' and C98 on the 'Right to Organise and Collective Bargaining Convention, 1949'.[180]

Similar to other Gulf States, Oman usually has reservations about general provisions in conventions that it accedes to, based on the ground that it is not consistently with Islamic law or not enforceable under Omani law; such as the reservations on the general provisions of CEDAW, and the provision on the child's right to freedom of reli-

---

177 In 2004.

178 The Arab Human Rights Index (UNDP) (n.d.). *Oman: Human Rights Profile.* Retrieved 3 February 2011, from <http://www.arabhumanrights.org/en/countries/country.aspx?cid=13>

179 Ratified in 1998, 2005, 2005 and 2001 respectively. See ILO website <www.ilo.org>

180 The Government indicated that ratification of C.87 and C.98 are under consideration. See ILO (2008). Country Baselines under the 1998 ILO Declaration Annual Review (2000-2008): Oman. Retrieved 11 January 2011, from: <www.ilo.org/wcmsp5/ groups/public/---ed_norm/--declaration/documents/publication/wcms_decl_facb_omn.pdf>

gion.[181] Other reservations are related to nationality rights, such as Article 7 of the Rights of Child and Article 9.2 of CEDAW.

Ratification of other core international human rights instruments, such as the ICCPR, and the ICESCR will grant jurisdiction the Omani courts to determine any human rights violations where the judges can directly apply international law even if it does not conform to domestic law. In this way, Oman will also be subject to international law violations. Therefore, Oman was reluctant to sign the ICCPR and the ICESCR, which cover most important rights and freedoms recognised today. Recently, Oman has committed to consider acceding to both human rights instruments as an outcome of the Human Rights Council for the Universal Periodic Review (UPR).[182]

There are several recommendations by different human rights bodies and reports to adopt other UN conventions, such as the International Convention on the Protection of the Rights of All Migrant Workers and Members of Their Families, and other (ILO) Conven-

181 Article 14 of the Rights of Child Convention.

182 Several human rights treaty body concluding observations regarding Oman has recommended the accession to the ICCPR and the ICESCR; such as Convention on the Rights of the Child document CRC/C/OMN/CO/2 about the Consideration of Reports Submitted by States Parties under Article 44 of the Convention, Concluding observations: OMAN (29 September 2006), and CEDAW document CEDAW/C/OMN/CO/1 about Concluding observations of the Committee on the Elimination of Discrimination against Women: Oman (21 October 2011). It was also one of the Omani Society for Writers and Literati in Oman recommendations, which was supported by several delegations during the Universal Periodic Review and has got the Oman's commitment to consider accession to the ICCPR and the ICESCR. For more information check the following documents about Oman from the Universal Periodic Review website: <http://www.upr-info.org/-Oman-.html>; A/HRC/WG.6/10/OMN/3 'Summary prepared by the Office of the High Commissioner for Human Rights in accordance with paragraph 15 (c) of the annex to Human Rights Council resolution 5/1' (08/11/2010), Final Report: A/HRC/17/7 'Report of the Working Group on the Universal Periodic Review: Oman' (24 March 2011), Addendum: A/HRC/17/7/Add.1 'Views on conclusions and/or recommendations, voluntary commitments and replies presented by the State under review' (3 June 2011).

tions, such as C87 on the Freedom of Association and Protection of the Right to Organize '1948', C97 on Migration for Employment '1949', C98 on the Right to Organize and Collective Bargaining '1949', C100 on the Equal Remuneration Convention '1951', C111 on the Discrimination (Employment and Occupation) Convention '1958', and C143 concerning Migrations in Abusive Conditions and the Promotion of Equality of Opportunity and Treatment of Migrant Workers '1975'.[183]

3.5.2 Human Rights Reports

Human Rights reports may be drafted by individuals, local institutions or by international organisations. Coverage and accuracy of the report plays an influential role in human rights protection.[184] However since the government tightly controls issues related to forming associations, there is no international or non-governmental human rights organisation that exists in Oman. NGOs face a great deal of bureaucratic documentation and procedures, and limitations exist on the kind of associations that are officially approved by the government.[185]

The media and human rights defenders have influential roles with regards to human rights reporting. Such as being as watchdogs, either by raising awareness on rights and freedoms issues via publicising the news and analysis, or by creating pressure on decision makers or law enforcers. They are like voice of the voiceless. However, both of

183 CEDAW/C/OMN/CO/1 Concluding observations of the Committee on the Elimination of Discrimination against Women: Oman (21 October 2011), and Human Rights Council document A/HRC/4/23/Add.2 Implementation of General Assembly Resolution 60/251 (15 March 2006).

184 The Office of the United Nations High Commissioner for Refugees is a good source of reports as it has collected several reports from different sources and partners, and the reader can check the following link to find list of reports about Oman from different Organisations: <http://www.unhcr.org/cgi-bin/texis/vtx/refworld/rwmain?page=country&skip=0&coi=OMN&x=11&y=11>

185 See Chapter Six about the Freedom of Association.

them are subject to many of the restrictions and limitations in Oman and journalists must practice self-censorship to avoid government penalties.

Over the last few years, the spreading of internet usage inside Oman has led scrutiny by human rights activists and individuals in reporting human rights violations. Activists usually share their thoughts and report incidents through online blogs and forums, which has expanded freedom of expression in the country, albeit the Internet is monitored and controversial websites are blocked.[186] This development has changed the way individuals send messages to the outside world and communicate with international organisations such as the Amnesty International and Freedom House, or with regional organisations such as the Arabic Network for Human Rights Information and the Arab Commission for Human Rights. Thus, the few local organisations do succeed in reporting violations to the public through their own websites and other public media, though such reports usually take the form of an announcement with a friendly tone to ask that the government review certain issues.[187] The only national human rights body that exists in Oman is a governmental one called the 'National Human Rights Commission' that was established in 2008. It has not reported or announced Oman's current human rights status, and is expected to release its first periodical report in late 2011.

At the international level, the governments' restrictions on the press and media have an impact on the shortage of reports about the

---

186 The most famous forums and blogs are: *Sablat Alarab* which has been closed permanently in 2005 followed by *Farrq in 2010*, and today *Sablat Oman and Alharah AlOmania* are the most famous. Recently, Facebook and Twitter have helped the spread of information especially between young generations.

187 The most active association in this regards is the Omani Society for Authors and Writers. The example of the way of demanding can be noticed form the announcement by the association on 1st of March 2011 after the assembly dispersion in Sohar State. Retrieved on 11 March 2011, from Sablat Oman: <http://Portal.s-oman.net/articles/201103/7219.htm>

country and few reports can be found. The difficulty of covering violations of rights and freedoms in Oman has led some well-known human rights organisations, such as Human Rights Watch, to publish only a few reports about the human rights status of the country, compared to other countries in the region.[188] Few comprehensive reports about Oman can be obtained from the Annual Human Rights Reports, International Religious Freedom reports and Trafficking in Persons (TIP) Reports. All of these are issued by the U.S. State Department.[189] The U.S. Embassy in Oman has successfully routinely reported on the latest developments in the country using information to which local citizens do not have access.[190]

Today, the only official reports published about Oman's current human rights status are those based on the requirements of international treaties and United Nations conventions. Oman reported to the Committee on the Rights of the Child (CRC) in 2001 and 2006 as well as the two Optional Protocols in 2009 and the Committee on the Elimination of Racial Discrimination (CERD) in 2006. It also reported to the Committee on the Elimination of All Forms of Discrimination against Women in 2009[191] as well as its regular reporting to the ILO.[192]

Human rights reports play an influential role in Oman as the government carefully reviews most reports published and sometimes re-

---

188 Until July 2011, there are only 2 reports about Human Rights in Oman during the period from July 2005 to March 2011. Check <http://www.hrw.org/ar/search/apachesolr_search/Oman>

189 'Bureau of Democracy, Human Rights, and Labor'.

190 Such as the case with their last report (2010) about the corruption in the Royal Oman Police. See Bureau of Democracy, Human Rights, and Labor. (2010). 2009 *Human Rights Report: Oman.* Retrieved 12 October 2010, from <www.state.gov/g/drl/rls/hrrpt/2009/nea/136077.htm>

191 The Arab Human Rights Index (UNDP) (n.d.). *Oman: Human Rights Profile.* Retrieved 3 February 2011, from <http://www.arabhumanrights.org/en/countries/reports.aspx?cid=13>

192 Oman has started reporting to ILO in accordance to the conventions ratified from 2003. ILO (2010). Oman Observation(s). Retrieved 11 January 2011 from <http://www.ilo.org/ilolex/cgi-lex/commentplus.pl?Oman@ref >

quests that different governmental bodies send their comments and responses. The importance of these reports can be derived from the 2007 U.S. State Department's Report on Human Trafficking when the report cited Oman for the second year among countries that have made no efforts to fight this global issue.[193] Oman rejected and protested the report in *Ash-Shura Council* and Cabinet to the media and citizenry. However the result of this report was immediate and impressive and resulted in the Law of Combating Human Trafficking (R.D. 126/2008). In addition, this report also led to the formation of the National Committee for Combating Human Trafficking according to Articles 22 and 23 of the same Law, followed by several amendments and changes on the Omani Labour Law via R.D. 63/2009.

The most recent national report was submitted by the government to the Human Rights Council for the Universal Periodic Review (UPR) on 26 January 2011. It was the first comprehensive national report about human rights issues in the country with participation from the Ministry of Foreign Affairs, Ministry of Social Development, the Omani National Human Rights Commission and NGOs and associations in the UPR process who shared their perspectives.[194]

There were several positive outcomes from the Review, as Oman's government has voluntary pledges to consider entering into the ICESCR and ICCPR, as well reviewing a number of ILO-related human rights treaties with the view to ratifying them, including Convention No. 87 on the Freedom of Association and Protection of the

193 Bureau of Democracy, Human Rights, and Labor (2008). *2007 Human Rights Report: Oman.* Retrieved 8 June 2009, from U.S. Department of State: <http://www.state.gov/g/drl/rls/hrrpt/2007/100603.htm>

194 The report A/HRC/WG.6/10/OMN/1 (18 November 2010) is required in accordance with paragraph 15 (a) of the annex to HRC resolution 5/1, as the Universal Periodic Review (UPR) is a new and unique human rights mechanism of the United Nations (UN) Human Rights Council aiming at improving the human rights situation – check Oman Report *National report submitted in accordance with paragraph 15 (a').* Retrieved 6 February 2011, from UN Human Rights Council – Tenth Session: <http://www.un.org/webcast/unhrc/archive.asp?go=110126>

Right to Organize (1948) and Convention No. 98 on the Right to Organize and Collective Bargaining (1949).

Also, it will undertake a periodic review of its reservations to other international human rights treaties and advance its National Human Rights Commission in a manner consistent with the Paris Principles. In addition, it will continue its work on the promotion and protection of human rights and strengthening the environment within which civil society operates and will specifically consider amending its Law on National Associations (promulgated by Royal Decree 14/2000) whenever necessary, ensure bringing into force the Omani Law of the Child in pursuit of its national strategy on children and in line with its CRC obligations, and continue the integration of human rights education in the remaining grades in schools.[195]

3.6 Human Rights Developments

During the last few years several steps have been implemented in favour of human rights protections. The following section elaborates substantial milestones to show the developments that have occurred in the last decade.

3.6.1 Women's Rights

In comparison to other Gulf States, Oman has succeeded in a principled stance and practical enunciation promoting women and children's rights. Oman is a State Party to most international instruments

195 The government will establish a follow up committee to review all recommendations made during the review process with a view to forming a national plan of action for the next four years. For more details, please refer to the 'National report submitted in accordance with paragraph 15 (a) of the annex to Human Rights Council resolution 5/1: Oman' - A/HRC/WG.6/10/OMN/1 (18 November 2010), and Addendum: A/HRC/17/7/Add.1 (3 June 2011) 'Views on conclusions and/or recommendations, voluntary commitments and replies presented by the State under review'. downloadable from the Universal Periodic Review website: <http://www.upr-info.org/-Oman-.html>

concerning women and children.[196] Today, women have the right to vote and to be elected into government and several women serve as ministers (two are full cabinet members) while 15 women serve on the State Council. Forming a women's association is permitted without the need for Cabinet's approval, a requirement for any other association. Furthermore, NGO's dealing with women and children receive financial and moral support from the government. As well Royal Decree No. 125/2008 amended the System of Entitlement to Government Land, which directed the Ministry of Housing to include women in government land grants and to treat them equally to men.

Furthermore, several statutes were amended to give the women equal rights. Article 12 of the Omani Passports Law (R.D. 69/97) by Royal Decree No. 11/2010 permits a woman to obtain a passport without requiring her husband's approval,[197] and R.D. 35/2003 on labour law stipulates provisions that ensure the protection of women by prohibiting their dismissal from employment for reasons of sickness, pregnancy or childbirth. It is significant that in some instance the Sultan himself has personally intervened to guarantee and protect women's rights. This was reflected in his amendment to the Judicial

196 Oman has not signed, yet, the Optional Protocol to the Convention on the Elimination of All Forms of Discrimination against Women, hence it does not provide a communications procedure which allows either individuals or groups of individuals to submit individual complaints to the Committee. Oman showed its consideration of its possible accession to the Optional Protocol of the Convention. See the 'Concluding observations of the Committee on the Elimination of Discrimination against Women: Oman' 3–21 October 2011 (CEDAW/C/OMN/CO/1). Recently, Oman has withdrawn all reservations it has made on the Convention on the Rights of the Child, but without withdrawing the reservation on Article 14 on the right of choice of religion. See Appendix 3 for more information.

197 On 10/20/2009, The Kuwaiti Constitutional Court decision granted a woman the right to obtain passport and the right to travel without the prior consent of her husband. It abolished a provision in immigration law, which dates back to 1962. See Ensaf (2009) Final verdict: the Kuwaiti woman can travel without the consent of her husband; <http://www.ensaf.org/articles/index.php?news=178>

Authority Law (R.D. 90/99) by R.D. 55/2010, which gave women the right to dispute, and even take cases to the Sultan's office, against arranged marriages that are usually organised by family without the individual's consent.[198]

These amendments and developments show that the state and the Sultan are willing to support women and encourage them to contribute to the country's development. However, there remain ample issues to be addressed and a great deal of work to be done in the protection of rights and freedoms for both women and children; in particular, women's rights to nationality and other personal issues require further attention.[199]

3.6.2 Human Rights Commission

Local independent and non-governmental human rights organisations are powerful tools that can supervise and observe violations; they are a very valuable source of information as their observations from inside the country can be more accurate and substantial than external reports. However, under the law of civil association, there are many restrictions for establishing non-governmental human rights organisation without permission.

The Sultan issued Royal Decree No. 124/2008 to establish the first human rights organisation in the country, the 'National Human Rights Commission'.[200] Although it is a governmental organisation;

198 See section 3.3.1)

199 Such as the discrimination over the Payment of Pension Fund in the case of death according to the Public Authority for Social Insurance regulation which is governed by the Omani Social Insurance system was established by Royal Decree No. 72/1991. According to the Concluding observations of the Committee on the Elimination of Discrimination against Women Report about Oman CEDAW/C/OMN/CO/1(21 October 2011) that equality between women and men is limited to the public rights and does not extend to the private sphere relations of family and marriage.

200 Oman is the last of the six Gulf States to form a human rights body to do this.

and its independence and compliance with the Paris Principles,[201] was one of the main concerns of the Committee on the Elimination of Discrimination against Women;[202] this was an important step in acknowledging human rights organisations in Oman. The commission is affiliated with the State Council '*Majlis Ad-Daula*', the upper house, but it exercises its functions independently.[203]

It is not clear to what extent this commission will develop the perspective on human rights in Oman, as its first annual report, required by Royal Decree, is not yet published. However, its inquiries and comments directed at different governmental institutions have sent a strong message to the Omani authorities concerning its role in the country. The commission commenced operations in 2010.[204] During its first year it participated in drafting the national report for the Universal Periodic Review (UPR) as required by the United Nations Human Rights Council (UNHRC). It also conducted several official visits

---

201 The High Commissioner for Human Rights congratulated Oman for its recent establishment of national human rights institution during her visit to Oman in April 2010, and from 30 October to 3 November 2010, the Office of the High Commissioner for Human Rights organised in Muscat a workshop on the Paris Principles for members of the Oman Human Rights Committee. It provided advice and assistance on strengthening NHRIs in Oman and other Gulf States. See the A/HRC/16/76, 'Summary of the Secretary-General's Report' about National institutions for the promotion and protection of human rights, Human Rights Council (7 February 2011). Downloadable from: <http://www.ohchr.org/Documents/Countries/NHRI/A-HRC-16-76.pdf>

202 In addition to its lack of any comprehensive and effective complaints mechanism, accessible especially to women including women migrant workers. Check the report CEDAW/C/OMN/CO/1: 'Concluding observations of the Committee on the Elimination of Discrimination against Women: Oman' Fiftieth session, Geneva, 3–21 October 2011.

203 The commission's membership is determined by the Sultan's nomination via a Royal Decree no. 124/2008, and almost half of its 14 members are from NGOs. It is chaired by a Member of the State Council and includes representatives from a range of civil society institutions such as the General Federation of Oman Trade Unions, NGOs, lawyers and representatives from government authorities.

204 R.D. 10/2010.

and observations and began receiving complaints about human rights violations. However, its operations will need some time to achieve their full potential.

Nevertheless, it is important that the government allows the existence of other human rights NGOs since these organisations are not limited or restricted by governmental nominations and operations.

3.6.3 Anti-trafficking Law

The issuance of the Law of Combating Human Trafficking (R.D. 126/2008) was subsequently passed and prescribes punishment ranging from 3 to 15 years' imprisonment. This has enhanced the public's and authority's awareness about the seriousness of human trafficking. This was the result of the US State Department's Report on Human Trafficking 2007,[205] which cited Oman among the weakest level (Tier 3) countries for a second year after being under the Tier 2 Watch List the year before.[206]

As can be seen, though the government did not agree with the outcome of the report which accused Oman of being a destination and transit country, primarily from North Asia, some of whom are

205 Although the UN human rights Report of the 'Special Rapporteur on trafficking in persons, especially women and children' has recognised Oman as one of the countries of destination for trafficking in persons for forced labour and sexual exploitation in 2007, but this report was not influential as much as the US State Department's Report on Human Trafficking 2007. See Human Rights Council's document A/HRC/4/23/Add. 2 (25 April 2007) Human Rights Council-Implementation of General Assembly Resolution 60/251 of 15 March 2006 Entitled "Human Rights Council", Report of the Special Rapporteur on trafficking in persons, especially women and children, Sigma Huda Addendum MISSION TO BAHRAIN, OMAN AND QATAR.

206 The U.S. Department of State has categorised the countries based on Tier system, which list the countries based on their fulfilment with the Trafficking Victims Protection Act's (TVPA) minimum standards, ranking the best as TIER 1 and the weakest is TIER 3. Office to Monitor and Combat Trafficking in Persons. (2010). *Tier Placements: Trafficking in Persons.* Retrieved 13 January 2011, from the U.S. State Department: <http://www.state.gov/g/tip rls/tiprpt/2010/142755.htm>

engaged in trafficking persons, specifically in conditions indicative of forced labour. Regardless of the validity of the report, Oman took the report seriously by issuing the new law combating human trafficking, followed by the establishment of a National Committee for Combating Human Trafficking, and amending several legislations and regulations; such as amending the Omani Labour Law by R.D. 63/2009.

Prior to the promulgation of the Law of Combating Human Trafficking, Oman used several articles of the Penal Law (R.D. 7/1974) to criminalise trafficking activity, mainly by using Articles 260, 261 and 218. However, these articles do not cover most forms of human trafficking, which leaves the area of trafficking open; for example, illegally using child jockeys from north Asia in camel racing, where they are subjected also to physical and sexual abuse.[207]

In 2005, government agencies took steps to issue legislation banning the commercial exploitation of children as camel jockeys to ensure that only Omani nationals were recruited as camel jockeys with a minimum age of 15 years.[208] Few have accepted and responded to the decision and the finding of some fraud cases in the matter has led the government to increase the age for camel jockeys to 18 years and to prohibit any children in camel racing.

The courts also acted immediately in implementing the new legislation by convicting several persons. Although the latest U.S. Department's Report on Human Trafficking 2010 referred to the government's progress as 'significant' albeit noted the lack of formal procedures to proactively identify victims of trafficking among other vulner-

---

207 Major forms of human trafficking include: forced labour, sex trafficking, bonded labour, debt bondage among migrant labourers, involuntary domestic servitude, forced child labour, child soldiers, and child sex trafficking.

208 UN Human Rights Council – Tenth session (January 2011). *Unicef Inputs and Report on the Universal Periodic Review: Oman.* Retrieved 6 February 2011, from: <http://lib.ohchr.org/HRBodies/UPR/Documents/Session10/OM/UNICEF_United NationsChildren%27sFund_eng.pdf>

able groups. This said it classified Oman several rungs up in its index.[209]

3.6.4 Abolishing the State Security Court

The State Security Court was established in 2003, by Royal Decree No. 21/2003. It is a specialised court that does not fall under the ordinary courts system of the Judicial Authority Law. The Judges are a mix of the Supreme Court judges, Appeals Court judges and Security and Military Officers.[210] The Court's jurisdiction covers the crimes mentioned under Articles 123-153 of the Penal Law, which covers attacks on the State's internal and external security, and any other cases forwarded from the Sultan to the court. Attacks on the State's internal security include various situations such as an attack on the Sultan, overthrow of the government, disobedience, civil war, terrorist acts, aircraft hijacking, insulting the national flag, carrying unlicensed weapons and riot assemblies. Subsequently, an attack on the State's external security includes acts such as treason, spying, insulting foreign flags and attacks on foreign heads of state and their representatives.

Although the court serves as a specialised court, the high involvement of the National Security Council can affect its impartiality and can violate the rights and freedoms of the person, as the Council is the most influential authority in the hierarchy of this court. It is this body that suggests judges from other security and military bodies and it can refer other cases to the Sultan and even nominate security officers as prosecutors in some cases. Moreover, the mixture of judges

209 Office to Monitor and Combat Trafficking in Persons (2010). *Trafficking in Persons Report 2010: Oman.* Retrieved 15 February 2011, from U.S. State Department: >http://www.state.gov/documents/organization/143188.pdf>

210 Establishing the Court in 2003 was part of the country precautionary steps towards regional political developments, especially in terms of the war on terror. The most famous case handled by the Court was in May 2005 when it distributed jail sentences between one and 20 years to 31 Islamists accused of being part of a banned organisation that was plotting to overthrow the government.

from military and security backgrounds draws attention to this court's ability to protect the citizen's rights and freedoms.

For example, it is possible to violate the freedom of assembly by treating public assemblies as riots under Article 137 of the Penal Law, which is governed by the State Security Court system. Another example is that Article 12 of the State Security Court Law (R.D. 64/2003) has given an investigating body the right to allow or deny the alleged perpetrator's right to have a lawyer.

In 2010, the Sultan repealed the court and its law through Royal Decree No. 102/2010, a significant step toward the real protection of human rights in Oman.[211] This means that security issues are now under the jurisdiction of ordinary courts where human rights are better defined and protected.

3.6.5 The independence of the Public Prosecutor

Prior to the promulgation of the OBSS, the Office of the Public Prosecutor (hereinafter referred to as OPP) was fully part of Royal Oman Police as a Directorate General of Criminal Prosecution.

Article 64 of the OBSS enshrines the establishment of independence Public Prosecution who:

> *"... shall conduct criminal proceedings on behalf of the society, supervise criminal investigation, and attend to the enforcement of criminal law, pursuit of the guilty and execution of judgements".*[212]

In 1999, Royal Decree No. 92/99 created the OPP as an independent institution. However, the office is affiliated administratively to the Inspector General of Police and Customs Office who supervises its work in the interim until it manages to build its judicial cadres and

211 The new Royal Decree cancels R.D. 21/2003 Establishing the State Security Court and Appointing Its Chairman, the State Security Court Law issued by the R.D. 64/2003 and the R.D. 89/2004 amending some provisions of the aforesaid State Security Court.

212 Article 64 OBSS and Article 1 of the Public Prosecution Law (R.D. 92/99).

has worked to extend its services to the various regions in the country according to Article 1 of the Decree.

The difficulty of the Public Prosecutor Law and its affiliation to the Inspector General of Police and Customs can be derived mainly from the clear interference of the Inspector General in almost every aspect of the public prosecutor's work. Most of the staff who were working in the Directorate General of Criminal Prosecution in the Royal Oman Police were transferred to the new institution. A crucial issue is their security background, as well as the fact that some of them lack the legal education required to conduct the public prosecution. This influences the way public prosecution works in Oman, though the new judges who have joined the Public Prosecution in the last few years have mitigated the impact of old generation. The Law itself grants the Inspector General wide jurisdiction interfering with the independence required for public prosecution. For instance, the Inspector General can delegate some criminal cases to police officers rather than prosecutors,[213] can instruct all public prosecutors,[214] can propose nominations for all prosecutor offices with the power to appoint an Associate General Prosecutor,[215] can promote and appraise the prosecutors,[216] and can issue the prosecutor's inspection by-law.[217]

In March 2011, the Sultan issued the R.D. 25/2011 which seeks to solidify the independence of the Office of Public Prosecution. It grants the Public Prosecutor authority to exercise all of the powers of the Inspector General of Police and Customs as mandated in the Public Prosecution Law. This move is initial positive step towards the judiciary independence and fair trial.

213 Art. 3.
214 Art. 6.
215 Art. 7.
216 Art. 8.
217 Art. 14.

3.6.6 Legislative and Audit Powers for the Council of Oman

In early 2011, most sit-ins and demonstrations that erupted across Oman focused on economic developments and the needs of unemployed and low income workers agitating for better life conditions. Later, they developed to be demands for changing certain cabinet members and anti-corruption. Small group of human rights actives, lawyers and individuals had put their request for a contractual constitution voted through a referendum.[218] Following this some impressive steps have recently been adopted in Oman after weeks of sit-ins and demonstrations. At the beginning of March 2011, the Sultan issued Royal Decree No. 39/2011 granting legislative and audit powers to the Council of Oman. This is a major issue that can help Oman move toward a constitutional monarchy and maybe a full democracy in the future.

The Sultan's step was not expected to happen so fast, as he changed almost half of the Cabinet members and issued several remarkable Royal Decrees and Orders to employees within a few days. He increased income and gave more freedoms and rights to the people. He ordered the security forces not to interfere or break up the sit-ins since they were practiced peacefully; this was not the case previously. He also nominated five members from the *Ash-Shura* Council (elected house) in the new Cabinet formation,[219] which is another big step for democracy in Oman.

The Royal Decree provides for the establishment of a technical committee of experts which shall be constituted to develop the draft amendment of the Basic Statute of the State to be in line with the provision of Legislative and Audit Powers. It is not clear to what extent the legislative powers will be granted to the Council of Oman as the

218 See section 2.5.

219 The Sultan also has nominated another 2 members from *Ash-Shura Council* at ministerial level as chairpersons for the State Audit Institution and the Tender Board.

technical committee has not been announced publicly yet. The announcement of the committee members can give an indication about their background and their expected formation.

From another perspective, it is expected that any legislative power granted to the Council of Oman which comprises both houses of the parliament will be limited to the final approval of the Sultan, as it is the case of Kuwait and Bahrain. Overall, it is expected that the committee will be directed by the Sultan in the general framework where the changes might be covered. From the Decree it is clear that the committee will only have the right to review articles related to the legislative and auditing powers as suggested. Hence, it will not be possible for the committee to change the royal successor system or any human rights and freedoms' articles. Most interestingly is to see if the committee will suggest changes to the last Article of the OBSS, which allows the Sultan to change and amend part or in full the OBSS. The committee is also limited by sending the report to the Sultan who can approve or reject their suggestions as a final word. Nevertheless, issuing the R.D. 39/2011 is a remarkable development.

3.7 Conclusion

The Omani Basic Statute indeed provides for many basic rights and freedoms, and some third generation solidarity rights, stipulated under international human rights instruments through having constitutional references. However, other rights and freedoms are not mentioned under the Basic Statute for one of two reasons; either because they are protected by several ordinary statutes and regulations, such as for women, children, family, and other procedural rights and freedoms; or due to their contradiction with overall State's policies and cautions, such as the right of life which does not fit with capital punishment under the current laws, and political rights which are not guaranteed due to the current governmental system.

Some rights and freedoms are provided in an uncertain way that gives the legislator full discretion to regulate and control based on expressions such as 'within the law limits' or 'in accordance with the law'; where fundamental rights and freedoms should be controlled and limited by the constitution itself, by setting up some general terms. Additionally, the Basic Statute still omitted the universal aspect of rights and freedoms, since the enjoyment of most of these rights is for Omani citizens rather than others who are resident in Oman.

The principle of separation of powers, for example, cannot exist with the absolute monarchy system, where the executive branch is still dominant amongst other branches and where the parliament is an icon for consultation with no power to legislate or to check upon the executive. Moreover, the judiciary, although independent to some extent, lacks full independence as the jurisdiction granted to the courts does not cover areas relating to civil rights, such as nationality and freedom of assembly.

A court responsible for examining constitutionality of legislations is one of the most important guarantees still missing in Oman, although the law established 'The Authority on Conflicts of Jurisdictions and Rules' as a panel to take some of the court's tasks, but has not reviewed cases yet due to the lack of its terms of references. An effective protection for citizen's rights and freedoms can be done by amending the Basic Statute to establish such a court, or giving this jurisdiction to the panel or even to other ordinary courts.

Currently, there is a judicial control of the executive by the Administrative Court which succeeded to some extent in protecting some rights and freedoms where such protection was not possible before the promulgation of the Basic Statute. But it is still inadequate, since some legislation exempted the executive actions and decisions from the court's jurisdiction. This includes the nationality right, and other national supremacy issues.[220]

220 Such as the tribal, borders, and regional issues.

The effectiveness of international treaties and reports in promoting rights and freedoms in Oman can be noticed, such as issuing the Juveniles Accountability Law (R.D. 30/2008) based on the Convention on the Rights of the Child,[221] and the Law of Combating Human Trafficking (R.D. 126/2008). Further progress that is postulated can be achieved by Oman signing and ratifying the core human rights' treaties in particular the International Covenant on Civil and Political Rights (ICCPR), and the International Covenant on Economic, Social and Cultural Rights (ICESCR).[222]

221 Committee on the Rights of the Child (2006). *Meeting of the 43rd Session (Geneva, 11 September–29 September 2006): Oman (second periodic report).* Retrieved 11 March 2011, from <http://olddoc.ishr.ch/hrm/tmb/treaty/crc/reports/crc_43/crc_43_oman.pdf>

222 Where Oman expressed its own commitment to consider accession to both. Refer to section 3.5

Part II:
Human Rights Case Studies: Nationality, Shura, and Freedom of Association

4 Omani Nationality and Human Rights

4.1 Introduction

Nationality may be considered one of the most important rights in the Gulf States, given that the rights and freedoms granted to citizens, depend on it. In addition, the absence of human rights legislation and practices for the protection of non-citizens and the fact that most international human rights instruments have not been signed or ratified by most of these states, makes the constitution the main source of protection. All Gulf States have asserted nationality as one of the main rights stipulated under their constitutions, and it is of fundamental significance when the constitution itself connects the granting or depriving of other rights and freedoms with the person's nationality, such as is the case under the Omani Basic Statute.[1] Although there is a distinction between nationality and citizenship under some systems,[2] such as in the UK and the USA,[3] the Omani legal system makes no distinction between them.

1 Art. 17.

2 According to the Britannica Concise Encyclopaedia "Nationality is inferior to citizenship, insofar as the latter implies a full set of political privileges and the former does not"; "Nationality". Encyclopaedia Britannica, Inc. (2006). Retrieved 01 May 2009 from <http://www.britannica.com>

3 Not all U.S. nationals are U.S. citizens; all U.S. citizens are U.S. nationals, according to Title 8 of the United States Code § 1408, it is possible to be a U.S. national without being a U.S. citizen, A person whose only connection to the U.S. is through birth in an outlying possession or through descent from a person so born acquires U.S. nationality but not U.S. citizenship. See Legal Information Institute website, Cornell University, Law School website. § 1408. Nationals but not citizens of the United States at birth. Retrieved 1 May 2009, from <http://www.law.cornell.edu/uscode/8/1408.html> Also, British citizenship is one of the six different forms of British nationality including British citizenship; British overseas citizenship; British overseas territories citizenship; British national (overseas); British protected person; and British subject. For more details see UK Border Agency website. What is British citizenship? Retrieved 1 May 2009, from <http://www.ukba.homeoffice.gov.uk/britishcitizenship/aboutcitizenship>

Thus, anyone obtaining nationality either by law or by naturalisation will be a citizen, and will enjoy all the citizen's rights mentioned explicitly by the Basic Statute or by other laws and regulations.

In addition to historical, religious and traditional homogeneity amongst the Gulf States, there are different areas where they have adopted similar policies and regulations, such as women's and children's rights to nationality or the need for permission for mixed marriages. Their similarities in matters of nationality, usually at the level of practices rather than systems, arise from two influential factors.

The first is that rapid economic development in these states with small populations has led them to import workers on a large scale over the last fifty years. The immigration policies of all six Gulf States have permitted the massive entry of foreign workers. This has meant a growing demographic imbalance, with the number of foreign workers exceeding the native population in some Gulf States, leading the authorities to change or restrict their nationality policies. This has created three levels of social hierarchy, with citizens at the top, enjoying full rights and freedoms, foreigners at the second level with restrictions on movement and work, and finally the stateless, with few rights and freedoms.

Secondly, the Gulf Cooperation Council (GCC), comprised of the Arab States of the Gulf plays an influential role in unifying legislation and regulations amongst its members. In its attempts to promote unity between all the Gulf States, it has a direct influence over several treaties and pieces of legislation which cover the whole region. For instance, according to the GCC treaties, every person holding the nationality of any Gulf State is a citizen of the GCC and as such has the right to move freely, reside, and own property within the member states.[4] Thus, the nationality strategy of each indi-

4 Supreme Council of the Cooperation Council for the Arab States of the Gulf. (27-29 November 1984). The Closing Statement of the Fifth Session of the Su-

vidual state determines who becomes a GCC citizen with corresponding rights in all others.

The factors above have a heightened influence on demand for citizenship in the GCC member states, especially for individuals who have been resident there for long durations. Although most nationality laws in these states have been promulgated for more than two decades,[5] it is notable that most states have tried to issue internal regulations and expand the discretionary powers of the national authorities in this regard without amending the nationality law itself. Thus the nationality laws vary among the Gulf States, in contrast to the similarities among their constitutions, so that they are not as alike as one might expect. Some similarities are present in respect of women's and children's rights, but there are many differences in other provisions such as that of determining the status of native nationals and persons with multiple nationalities.

More contrasts can be found among the laws on nationality of the Gulf States concerning naturalisation, in terms either of the conditions needed to obtain nationality or reasons to withdraw it from naturalised persons. For instance, the period needed for a foreigner to be legally resident in the state before filing a nationality application varies among Gulf States. Thus, the UAE has three categories based on the foreigner's origin, requiring 3 years residence for Arabs of Omani, Qatari or Bahraini origin, 7 years for other Arabs and 30 years for non-Arabs.[6] Other Gulf States stipulate a fixed period without categorisation: of 10 years in Saudi Arabia,[7] 15 years

---

preme Council (in Arabic). Retrieved 22 May 2008, from <http://www.gcc-sg.org/indexf3c2.html?action=Sec-Show&ID=107>

5 With the exception of Qatar, with its new Nationality Law published in 2005.

6 Articles 5 and 6. UAE. Federal Law (17/1972). Concerning Nationality and Passports, Issued on 18/11/1972. Amended by Federal Law no. 10/1975 dated 15/11/1975.

7 Art. 9. Saudi Arabian Nationality Regulations – 1374 H. and its amendments.

in Kuwait,[8] and 25 years in Qatar,[9] with the exception of Oman, which reduces the period of 20 years to 10 years if the person marries an Omani.[10]

The conditions under which nationality can be withdrawn from naturalised persons also vary, although all states agree on the withdrawal of nationality if this was acquired by means of fraudulent conduct or by providing false information and in cases where the naturalised person has been convicted of crimes against national security. However, some states have extended this to include any 'shameful' crime or one against honour or the Secretariat.[11] Some take account of continuous residence outside the country without justification; 4 years under UAE Law[12] and 1 year for Qatar.[13] Some even consider dismissal from public office or the Secretariat for reasons of honour.[14] The Qatari system allows the Minister of the Interior to withdraw nationality for reasons of public interest, which also reflects the broad and unrestrained criteria applied with arbitrary power under each system.

Hence, each system is distinct and has different approaches over the granting and the exercise of nationality rights and over means to promote or reduce other rights and freedoms. An example in Oman is the loss of nationality based upon a person's religious beliefs,[15] which does not apply under more religiously based systems such as that of Saudi Arabia. Another area of interest is the distinction between native and naturalised citizens in terms of the rights

8 Art. 4 Kuwaiti Nationality Law no. 15/1959.

9 Art. 2 Qatari Nationality Law no. 38/2005.

10 Art. 2 the Law on the Organisation of the Omani Nationality (R.D. 3/83).

11 Art. 16 UAE Nationality Law, Art. 21 Saudi Nationality Law, Art. 13 Kuwaiti Nationality Law, and Art. 12 Qatari Nationality Law.

12 Art. 16 UAE Nationality Law.

13 Art. 12 Qatari Nationality Law.

14 Art. 12 Qatari Nationality Law.

15 Art. 13.2 Nationality Law.

and freedoms granted. Oman,[16] for instance grants its naturalised citizens full civil rights, while the UAE has a different attitude, granting election and nomination rights for any ministerial or parliamentary positions only to those of Omani, Bahraini or Qatari origins if they have held UAE nationality for no less than 7 years. Kuwait has extended such rights to all naturalised persons but with no less than 10 years residency. Finally, Qatar is more restrictive, in that it stipulates the granting of the right to work in public posts to natives, with no election or nomination rights for naturalised citizens.[17]

This chapter provides a comprehensive account of nationality law in Oman, based on the Nationality Statute and its amendments, highlighting the main issues and articles related to the right using comparisons with other Gulf States as a prism to illustrate and offer an incisive analysis. It ends with a list of recommendations concerning the Statute and the way it is dealt with to align with international standards in this matter.

4.2 Nationality under the Basic Statute

According to the Royal Decree 91/99, which established the Administrative Court, it is one of the main mandates of the court to review all administrative orders by governmental institutions in case of disputes.[18] Moreover, in the absence of a Constitutional Court in

16 Art. 7 Nationality Law.

17 Art. 16 The Qatari Nationality Law allows naturalised persons to hold a public post after 5 years.

18 In Art. 2.a of the European Convention on Nationality 1997, nationality is defined as "the legal bond between a person and a State [which] does not indicate the person's ethnic origin". Retrieved 13 April 2008, from <http://conventions.coe.int/Treaty/en/Treaties/Html/166.htm> It is a guiding principle of International Law that it is for each state to determine under its own law who are its nationals. Nevertheless, with the expansion of human rights since the adoption of Universal Declaration of Human Rights 1948, the tendency has been towards acknowledgment of the right to a nationality as a human right and it has been accepted that, in matters of nationality, states shall also take individual interests into account.

Oman, the Administrative Court is responsible for ensuring that statutes and regulations have been implemented according to the law, making it the most important judicial guardian of public interests today.

However, Article 7 of the same decree exempts all sovereignty matters, royal decrees and royal orders from the Court's jurisdiction. Two years after establishing it, a Royal Order required the court to exempt, with the exception of employment disputes, all matters relating to the Ministry of the Interior, including nationality, from its jurisdiction, based on the Ministry's jurisdiction over them as falling within the scope of sovereignty.[19] Moreover, Article 7.3 of (R.D. 3/2009) explicitly excludes all nationality issues from the Court's jurisdiction.[20]

This exemption has an influence on the personal right of nationality, as the Ministry of the Interior is the body responsible for nationality decisions. The court's decision and the latest amendments to the Administrative Court's legislation have not catered for the mechanism of judicial review, thus leaving nationality matters unprotected. This gives the executive branch, specifically the Ministry of the Interior and the Nationality Committee, full authority to decide on them without any restriction or limitation. These are not obstacles to the resolution of nationality issues, as the main obstacle comes from the statute itself. Nationality is governed by the Law on the Organisation of the Omani Nationality (R.D. 3/83) (hereinafter referred as the Nationality Law) which was adopted fourteen years before the promulgation of the OBSS, but which is still the main statute today. While there have been some amendments, these have not changed its main principles and articles,

19 The Royal Order 467/2000 sent to the Administrative Court by the Minister of the Diwan Royal Court.

20 Recent amendments to the legislation regulating the Administrative Court came into force in January 2009.

some of which are still unfair and may violate the principles of the OBSS and of human rights.

The Basic Statute recognises nationality as a fundamental right, listing it as the first right under the 'Rights and Duties' section. Article 15 states that "*Nationality is regulated by the law and it is prohibited to denaturalize or revoke it except within the limits of the Law*". Other Gulf States have almost identical articles in their constitutions, with the exception of Qatar, which gives constitutional status to the Nationality Law provisions.[21] Saudi Arabia, on the other hand, while listing nationality as a right under its Basic Law, leaves all nationality matters to ordinary statutes without any precautionary provisions to prohibit denaturalisation or the revoking of nationality, as it is the case with most constitutions in the Gulf States.[22]

The importance of nationality under the Omani system arises from the fact that social, legal and economic benefits, and several rights and freedoms which are listed under the OBSS, are granted explicitly to 'citizens' rather than to all people.[23] While Article 35 of OBSS grants some rights to non-citizens, foreigners have to be legally resident in the country to enjoy such rights,[24] there being no constitutional rights for illegal aliens, thus making nationality the central plank of freedoms and rights under the Basic Statute, which government and public authorities are legally obliged to respect.

Indeed, the importance of nationality and citizenship as legal

21 Art. 41 Qatar Constitution.

22 Art. 35 Saudi Basic Law.

23 Such as the principle of equality before the law, non-discrimination, and the right to assembly (Articles 10, 17 and 32), and the Sultan's obligation to safeguard citizens' rights and freedoms (Articles 7, and 42).

24 Non-nationals comprise around 30% of the Omani population. According to the final results of the Oman's Census 2010, the total number of Oman population is 2,773,479 and the expatriate are 816,143. See the Census 2010 'Final Results' from Ministry of National Economy website: <http://www.mone.gov.com/documents/Census_2010.pdf>

concepts reflect the connection between the person and the state and the individual's consequential political dependence upon it. However, such an approach should not hinder the general principle of equality for non-citizens as granted by the International human rights law; which is founded on the premise that everyone, by virtue of their humanity, should enjoy all human rights without discrimination.[25] The exceptional discrimination allowed in the International human rights to distinct between citizens and non-citizens "should serve a legitimate State objective and are proportional to the achievement of that objective",[26] by taking into account the followings:

(a) The interest of the State in specific rights (e.g., political rights, right to education, social security, other economic rights);
(b) The different non-citizens and their relationship to that State (e.g., permanent residents, migrant workers, asylum-seekers, temporary residents, tourists, undocumented workers); and
(c) *Whether the State's interest or reason for distinguishing between citizens and non-citizens or among non-citizens (e.g., reciprocity, promoting development) is legitimate and proportionate.*[27]

The nationality law in all GCC countries is one of the most important and far-reaching areas of legislation, which determines the primary element of the state and the rights and freedoms that ac-

25 The 1948 Universal Declaration of Human Rights recognises this principle in its article 2 (1): "[e]veryone is entitled to all the rights and freedoms set forth in this Declaration, without distinction of any kind, such as race, colour, sex, language, religion, political or other opinion, national or social origin, property, birth or other status"

26 Office of the United Nations High Commissioner for Human Rights (2006) *The Rights for Non-Citizen*, HR/PUB/06/11, p. 7. downloadable from: <www.ohchr.org/Documents/Publications/noncitizensen.pdf>

27 *Ibid.* According to Weissbrodt D. (2008) in his book 'The Human Rights of Non-citizens': the human rights of non-citizens should be viewed "not as an amalgamation of the rights of various non-citizen subgroups (refugees, asylum seekers, migrant workers, etc.), but rather as a unified domain", p. 5.

crue to citizens.[28] Nationality also has important consequences for both the individual and the state: for the state to exercise its sovereignty over its people, where the state alone has the right to move international liability in cases of infringement of the person's rights in a foreign country; and for the person to enjoy all public and private rights granted by the state's laws, being obliged to abide by all the duties imposed by it. As the right to a nationality serves as the basis for the enjoyment of many other rights, it entails co-responsibilities and duties under social contract theory. Therefore, nationality is regarded as a membership token that confers entitlement to social goods provided by the state.

The right to a nationality is proclaimed as the main principle in Article 24 of the International Covenant on Civil and Political Rights and Article 15 of the Universal Declaration of Human Rights which states: "*Everyone has the right to a nationality. No one shall be arbitrarily deprived of his nationality, nor denied the right to change his nationality*".[29] Regional treaties, such as the 1969 American Convention on Human Rights,[30] the 2004 Arab Charter on Human Rights,[31] and the 1997 European Convention on Nationality, also ac-

---

28 Black's Law Dictionary defines a State as: "A people permanently occupying a fixed territory bound together by common-law habits and custom into one body politic exercising, through the medium of an organized government, independent sovereignty and control over all persons and things within its boundaries, capable of making war and peace and of entering into international relations with other communities of the globe". Black's Law Dictionary, Sixth Edition, p. 1407.

29 It is also contained in Articles 7 and 8 in the Convention on the Rights of the Child, Article 29 of the International Convention on the Protection of the Rights of All Migrant Workers and Members of their Families, Article 6 of the Convention against Torture and Other Cruel, Inhuman or Degrading Treatment or Punishment. See: Claiming Human Rights. (18 December 2008). *Definitions of the Right to a Nationality.* Retrieved 3 March 2009, from <http://www.claiminghumanrights.org/nationality_definition.html>

30 Art. 20.

31 Art. 29.

knowledge the right of every person to a nationality and seek to illuminate the rights and responsibilities of states in this regard. The international instruments leave it to each state to determine by domestic law who are its nationals, while requiring such determination to be consonant with the general principles of international law, especially relating to the possession, loss or denial of nationality.[32]

Most Gulf States have progressively regulated the process of obtaining citizenship and nationality during the last five decades, enhanced by the impact of economic development in the region, especially the experience of immigration and its legitimate expectations. As a result, most states have tended towards increasingly complicated naturalisation policies.[33] Thus, with economic development the requirements and processes involved in obtaining nationality have become more restrictive, directly or indirectly, such as in the cases of the naturalisation of immigrants or of marriage between a citizen and a non-citizen.

A number of issues related to nationality rights may directly violate other rights in most Gulf States, such as those of stateless persons, minorities, women and children. This will in turn also indir-

---

32 50th Anniversary of the 1954 Convention relating to the Status of Stateless Persons.

33 Sometimes, the naturalisation polices are derived from the State's political attitude, and it might regarded as the most influential role in deciding over the naturalisation process in Gulf States, such as naturalisation is carried out selectively based on tribal or sectarian origin and not based on the equal right of foreigners in getting the nationality. For instance, the contrasting policies in Bahrain regarding dual nationality; where its nationality law regarded as the most restrictive statute in this regards among other Gulf States, however, the Bahraini Government had granted its nationality to citizens of other countries based on the sectarian security policy or who share the same tribal origins as the ruling family and its allies. for more details see chapter 4.5, and the Report of Bahrain Center for Human Rights (2006) Political Naturalization in Bahrain: Various Violations of Citizens and Foreign Workers Rights, downloadable from <http://www.bahrainrights.org/en/ref06090302>

ectly violate rights such as the freedom of movement and residence or other economic, social and cultural rights based on nationality.

Judicial and Executive Frameworks in the Practice of Nationality Law

Executively, the Minister of the Interior plays the leading role in nationality issues. In addition to his department's responsibilities for nationality applications, all acquisition, renunciations and recovery applications must be addressed to him, with additional powers given to the Nationality Committee. However the Minister has other powers over the National Committee such as over its financial affairs, such as deciding on the fees for applications, certificates and licences.

Another major player with great influence and powers is the Nationality Committee established by Article 15 of the Nationality Law which authorises it to rule on all nationality disputes.[34] The Committee does more than resolve disputes, as it has a deliberative influence by recommending to the Sultan when to allow a person to hold multiple nationalities,[35] as well as a judicial power to rule upon nationality cases, including the imposition of imprisonment and fines.[36]

The law does not provide the defendant in nationality cases any opportunity for legal review or appeal as the Committee has the power to make final decisions. The individual citizen's rights to nationality can be seen to be at risk from the committee's membership, its political approach, its discretionary powers, the confidenti-

34 It has six members, four of whom occupy high governmental positions: The Interior Minister as chairperson, the Minister at the Royal Palace Office, the Inspector General of Police and Customs and an official of at least undersecretary rank from the *Diwan* of the Royal Court. The other two Committee members are judges, but while they are from the judicial branch, they have to be chosen by the chairperson, which reflects the political stance of the Committee and enhances the power of the Ministry of the Interior.

35 Art. 10.

36 Art. 16.

ality of its deliberations and the lack of an appeal procedure, all enhanced by the 'supremacy' of nationality affairs'.

4.3 Obtaining and Losing of Nationality

In 1972, the first Omani Nationality Law (1/72) was issued. The aim of the law was to maintain Omani nationality, for two reasons. First, the Omani people were at the time politically divided by historical events into two main camps: the Sultanate and its followers on one side and the Imamate with its citizens and rebels on the other. Secondly, Omanis abroad were scattered throughout the Gulf States. The emergence of newly independent states[37] where many Omanis had settled to work and live, combined with the return of Omanis from the former colonies of Zanzibar and East Africa, made it essential to determine and unite the Omani nation.[38] It was however, difficult to define the nation and its members without laws and regulations at a time when increasing numbers of people were entering the new state.

This first law was replaced after 11 years by Royal Decree no. 3/83. The law which accordingly came into force on 12th January 1983 is still the main legislation that regulates Omani nationality today. Amendments have been made to this later statute in line with the state's development.

4.3.1 Obtaining Nationality

According to the Law and its latest amendments,[39] a person may be an Omani citizen by law (native) or by application (naturalised). The legal opinion of the Ministry of Legal Affairs states that people possessing their nationality at birth are treated as natural-born cit-

37 The UAE, Qatar and Bahrain.

38 Especially after the Sultan's call to Omanis abroad to return and build their own country in one of his first speeches in 1970.

39 In 1986, 1993, 1994 and 1999.

izens or native Omanis,[40] to distinguish them from naturalised persons, who are subject to legal limitations, such as to their eligibility for public office, or must have possessed nationality for a minimum period to be eligible for some government services.[41]
Natural-born citizens or native Omanis (by Law) have rights of blood or of territory:

- Right of blood, *jus sanguinis,*[42] is conferred by descent and covers any child born inside or outside Oman of an Omani father, without any provisions concerning the father's status,[43] or of an Omani mother, with several provisions and conditions.[44]
- Right of territory, *jus soli,*[45] is literally conferred 'by soil' and is enjoyed by those born in Oman of unknown parents, or of a stateless father who was also born in Oman and still had stateless status.

40 MLA/MO/6/4/1625/99 dated 26/12/1999.

41 Despite the fact that there will appropriately always be certain privileges that attach to nationality or citizenship; as functions for the constitutionally protected area of social regard and mutual obligation; the rights and freedoms stipulated in the OBSS to Omani citizens should not go against of the whole concept of human rights. Such as the guarantee of educational adequacy for Omani nationals (Art. 13 OBSS) and to extend it to children who are formally non-Omanis. – The modern international community recognised the three principles of human rights, which are the universal inherent, the inalienability, and the rule of law. "People have basic rights by virtue of being human. They are not earned by paying taxes to a particular government and do not come with possession of a particular passport ... it is indeed non-citizens that are most often in need of human rights protection". See the paper 'Is a British Bill of Rights needed?' from UK Parliament website: <http://www.publications.parliament.uk/pa/jt200708/jtselect/jtrights/memo/britishbill/uc1802.htm> Taking into account that, a right is defined in many law dictionaries as an entitlement or power, which is far different than a privilege or a service which are granted by a legal authority such a statute made by a state legislature.

42 Art. 1.1 and 1.2 of Nationality Law.

43 Even if the child is born out of wedlock or is married to a non-Omani citizen.

44 As will be discussed later under 'Women and Children's rights'; section 4.4.

45 Art. 1.3 and 1.4.

On the other hand, naturalised Omanis are those who fall within one of the following categories:

- Aliens who have acquired Omani nationality: Article 2 of the Nationality Law lists five requirements for the applicant to adhere to before he or she can apply for nationality, referring to age, language, period of residence in Oman, health condition and work. Moreover, it stipulates application procedures including the taking of an oath.
- Exempted by a Royal Decree, without being committed to the conditions listed under Article 2, which is one of the Sultan's powers.[46]
- Non-Omani wife married to an Omani or who was married to a naturalised Omani before he obtained nationality.[47]
- Non-Omani child under 18 years of age at the time his father obtained Omani nationality.[48]

The distinction between native or natural-born and naturalised Omanis is eminent under the Basic Statute, as possessing a native status is one of the main requirements for appointment as Prime Minister, Deputy Prime Minister or to any ministerial position.[49] Additionally, it is one of the requirements for candidacy to the *Ash-Shura* Council or to be appointed as a member of the State Council.[50] Unfortunately, the distinction also goes beyond political rights to cover other privileges of nationality, so that naturalised Omanis are ineligible for certain privileges or services from the state unless they have held nationality for a minimum period. This is the case with the social accommodation provided by the government, where a naturalised citizen must have held nationality "for no less than 3

46 Art. 3.
47 Articles 4 and 5.
48 Art. 4.
49 Art. 49 OBSS.
50 Articles 13 and 22 of 'the State and Shura Councils Regulation' (R.D. 86/97).

years before he or she can apply" for such accommodation.[51] Similarly, is required in order to acquire government-owned land.[52]

It may be considered reasonable to have some distinctions for a high ranking military position or sensitive public office, such as is the case with naturalised US citizens who are not eligible to become President or Vice President of the United States under Section 1 of Article II of the Constitution. The state also has the right to determine certain requirements and conditions for election candidates, where natural born citizens are treated as more privileged than new citizens. However, it could be said to be unfair and excessive to deny a person's political right to hold elected office for ever. Such a person may be more loyal and affiliated to the country than a natural-born Omani who was born of an Omani father outside Oman and has lived most of his life outside the country.[53]

Moreover, the fact that the nationality status acquired will effect on other rights seems unfair; it violates both the right to equality which is granted by Article 17 of the Basic Statute and Article 7 of the Nationality Law, which grants the naturalised citizen all civil rights. It is unjust that a naturalised citizen who has obtained Omani nationality after fulfilling all requirements, such as living in the country for a minimum of 20 years, is not treated on equal footing as a natural-born citizen.

The privilege of birth does not necessarily make a person more loyal to the state than one who has had to undergo the renunciation of his previous national status in order to acquire Omani national-

51 Art. 1.a of the Social Accommodations Law (R.D. 35/77) amended by (R.D. 27/88); see also the Legal Opinion (MLA/MO/8/1/79/94) dated 25/1/1994.

52 Art 1.1.a of the Acquisition of Government Lands Regulation (RD 81/84); also Legal Opinion by the Ministry of Legal Affairs (MLA/MO/20/1/546/97), dated 17/5/1997.

53 Such as the case of a child of stateless parents or of an Omani mother and non-Omani father, or the case of a person from the second or third generation of migrants, who was born in the country and has lived there since then, but is unable to obtain nationality as a natural-born citizen.

ity for whatever reasons. Such distinctions not only violate the basic rights and freedoms of the person as protected by the Basic Statute and international instruments; they can be argued to create a second class nationality, where discriminations exist. Discrimination against naturalised persons is also present in the General Mobilisation Law.[54] Article 5 of the law requests all nationals from countries enlisted by the Defence Council to submit additional documents with other information to the nearest police station as soon as this list is published. The provision includes any naturalised Omani whose origin is from the enlisted countries.

This requirement causes an imbalance in the equality between naturalised Omani and native Omani and other foreigners from unlisted countries. Naturalised Omani will most likely be the subjects to any dispute or conflict between Oman and his or her country of origin. Moreover, imposing the requirement to report and to submit additional documentation and information beyond that submitted earlier to obtain the Oman nationality may indicate the unstable situation of a naturalised person and violates the principle of equality. Such suspicions may also result in violating the person's rights and freedoms and may lead to withdrawal the nationality on the accusation of treason if any connection with his country of origin has been proved.

Once a person has obtained Omani nationality, it ought to be their right to be treated equally, especially as naturalised citizens usually achieve their status by pursuing a long process with the final word of the state, which has the sole right to refuse a naturalisation request, even in cases exempted by the Nationality Law, without giving a reason.[55] Thus, no distinction on the rights and freedoms should be made once nationality is granted.[56]

54 R.D. 76/08 promulgated the authorising of the announcement of mobilisation upon outbreak of war or of its revocation by Royal Orders.

55 Art. 6 of Nationality Law.

56 Unless it was granted based on false information.

The 'equality' between citizens referred to in Article 17 of the Basic Statute is interpreted according to the legal opinion of the Ministry of Legal Affairs as a 'legal' rather than an 'arithmetic' equality.[57] This means that every citizen has the right to receive the same treatment if he or she meets the conditions established, thus being subject to equal treatment in the pertaining conditions.[58]

However, this interpretation deals more with the conditions applicants must fulfil rather than with the equality of rights of the person that are transferred. It is possible, for example, that the conditions stipulated by any law or regulation violate from the beginning the basic principle of the person's rights or even ignore his entitlement to such rights or freedoms as are mentioned by a higher legal document, such as the Basic Statute.

The Nationality Law allows the 'recovery' of nationality for those who have lost it under Article 12 at the initiative of the individual and Article 14 where it has been lost at the initiative of the state. This allows a person the right to retain his Omani nationality through an application to the Minister of the Interior. Although it is a positive right, it also lacks some fundamental features, because the number of cases covered by Article 12 are very limited and do not cover all cases of loss of nationality at the initiative of the individual, but only those of minor children who lost their nationality as subordinates and followers of their fathers, and cases of an Omani wife married to a non-Omani who has obtained her foreigner husband's nationality and has obtained permission from the Ministry of the Interior to relinquish her Omani nationality. Therefore, it does not cover her right if she did not have such permission, nor does it cover the male's right in either case.[59]

Article 14 is restricted to cases of loss of nationality at the initi-

57 MLA/MO/6/4/1625/99.

58 Both naturalised and native have different conditions to fulfil which has impact on other rights related to nationality.

59 i.e. whether or not he has obtained the relevant licence.

ative of the state, which all fall under the reasons listed in Article 13 for depriving a person of his or her nationality. It allows the recovery of nationality if the reason for the deprivation no longer applies, but it does not grant such a right in less extreme cases, such as those of dual or multiple nationalities. Neither statute, regulations nor case law make it clear whether the recovery of nationality means that the person enjoys the legal standing of his previous status, or whether he should be treated as a naturalised person.[60]

4.3.2 Loss of Nationality

While it is "*prohibited to denaturalize or revoke it except within the limits of the Law*",[61] Nationality Law has several provisions stipulating when a person may lose his nationality at the initiative of the individual or of the state, whether voluntarily or punitively.[62] While there is only one case where a person may lose his nationality voluntarily, which is by acquiring another nationality, he is bound to obtain a licence from the authorities to do so. A reason beyond the need for such approval is "*To ascertain the compliance of all duties and obligations towards the Sultanate*",[63] albeit a person would lose his nationality automatically in the case where he did not have this permission. However, the consequences are different in each case.[64]

60 One may assume from its natural interpretation that 'recovery' means the restoration of the former status. However, the Qatari Nationality Law takes a different attitude, treating anyone who has recovered his nationality as naturalised, with fewer privileges and rights than natives (Art. 15 of Qatar Nationality Law).

61 Art. 15 OBSS.

62 Voluntarily means the nationality holder applies for renunciation, and punitively means nationality is withdrawn by the government as a punishment.

63 Art. 8 Nationality Law.

64 Art. 9 Nationality Law. The Law has different terms for one who has lost it accordingly to the provisions stipulated by law (those who obtained the license), and they will lose their nationality by a Royal Decree, and those who have lost it without a permission, thus no Royal Decree is needed although loss of the nationality will take effect according to the law.

The law distinguishes between a person who complies with licence requirements before acquiring another nationality and one who does not. In the first case, he will lose Omani nationality voluntarily, which has legal consequences for the person himself but no impact on his dependants, whereas the minor children of a person who does not receive the necessary permission will be affected, in that they too will lose their Omani nationality accordingly.

Multiple nationalities are prohibited under the Nationality Law, being permitted only under licence from an authority which must be explicitly declared by a Royal Decree.[65] Therefore, one of the requirements of naturalisation is the renunciation of the nationality of origin.[66] The Law has left the right of multiple nationalities to the recommendations submitted by the Nationality Committee.[67] It seems a positive development to allow some cases of multiple nationalities, especially in cases like the example mentioned above.[68] However, perhaps because of the composition of its membership, the recommendations of the Nationality Committee usually seem to prioritise political issues rather than humanitarian or social needs. Nevertheless, no official statistics are available as to the number of multiple nationalities and no official statements or elaborations are made concerning the types of recommendation submitted to the Sultan.

It is worth noting that while the Basic Statute refers to denaturalisation and revocation as different ways in which nationality may be lost, each having its particular reasons and thus effects, the Omani Nationality Law does not use these terms, instead referring to 'loss' or 'deprivation'. The obvious explanation is that the Nationality Law predates the Basic Statute and is older than the nationality laws of most Gulf States; whereas denaturalisation has a

65 Art. 8 Nationality Law.

66 Art. 2.5.

67 Art. 10.

68 About minor children.

direct effect upon a person who has been naturalised. A revocation would apply to all nationals, natives or naturalised, and may affect the person's spouse and dependants too.[69]

Article 13 of the Omani Law lists five main *ex lege* reasons for loss of nationality at the initiative of the state, two being limited to naturalised citizens and the rest applying to all Omani citizens, native or naturalised. The Law does not guarantee protection for a person who becomes stateless upon losing his nationality, which creates another problem.[70]

Nonetheless, some of the reasons leading to the loss of nationality are recognised under most laws, internationally. Similar examples include:

- Acquisition of nationality by means of fraudulent conduct, false information or concealment of any relevant fact attributable to the applicant;[71] and
- acting in the service of an enemy state or against the interests of the State.[72]

Other provisions are more controversial and some may violate other basic rights. The most notable being Article 13.2, which directly violates the freedom to practice religious rites and the freedom of opinion and expression, which are listed under Articles 28 and 29 of the Basic Statute. This is because it allows a royal decree to strip off anyone the nationality if they have been proved that "*The person espouses the principles of un-religious faiths, or belongs to a group or party that espouses such beliefs or guidelines*". This provision is outdated and while such provision may have been widely accepted at the time it was enacted, it is today archaic as it creates various social, political and legal contradictions as well as being contrary to the modern attitude of the state and the Basic Statute. This is more

69 Art. 15 and Art. 16 UAE Nationality Law.

70 This will be discussed on section 4.5.

71 Art. 13.1 Nationality Law.

72 Art. 13.4 Nationality Law.

so considering that adherence to Islam is not a requirement for obtaining nationality.

There are no official statistics or statements indicating whether this provision has been used, and most of the Royal Decrees related to loss of nationality do not state the reasons for the loss. Additionally, no court cases are allowed on this matter, based on the fact that nationality affairs are beyond the courts' jurisdiction. This provision should be amended or deleted as it conflicts with a more authoritative legal document.

There are two other provisions which involve some degree of state intervention in matters of individual freedom. Article 13.3 allows the state to deprive a citizen of his nationality if he has not obeyed the government's request to cease working for a foreign state. This raises two doubts, the first being one of imprecision; the article does not specify the meaning of 'foreign state' or the type of work covered, that is, whether it includes employment by the public, private or military sectors, which gives the government wide discretion. Whereas Article 13.4 specifically prohibits working with an enemy state or against the interests of Oman, there is no such clause in Article 13.3 and it could be interpreted as covering any work for a foreign firm or organisation, inside or outside the country, even if there is a strong relationship between the two states.

The second uncertainty arising in Article 13.3 is that it conflicts with the guarantee of the right to work, which should be upheld; it is unfair to have this level of governmental control over individual interests. Despite the fact that there are cases where the interests of the state are eminent, such interests should not be incorporated under this article, where it seems to be no more than unfettered discretionary government power. The final questionable provision allows a naturalised person to be deprived of his nationality if it is proved that he has been involved in any crimes against national security or belongs to a group or organisation plotting or conducting attacks against the country's security. The degree of discrimination against naturalised citizens under this provision is when one assesses the interpretation given to national security.

4.4 Women's and Children's Rights under the Nationality Law

> *"States Parties shall grant women equal rights with men to acquire, change or retain their nationality. They shall ensure in particular that neither marriage to an alien nor change of nationality by the husband during marriage shall automatically change the nationality of the wife, render her stateless or force upon her the nationality of the husband ... States Parties shall grant women equal rights with men with respect to the nationality of their children."*[73]

The United Nations Development Programme (UNDP) has recognised Oman as one of the more progressive states in the Gulf region in the area of women's and children's rights.[74] Indeed, Oman stands out as a model for other countries in the Gulf, as its government has actively promoted female education, with impressive results, and women now have the right to vote and be elected. Oman has acceded to three of the seven major United Nations conventions on human rights relating to women and children's rights, namely: the International Convention on the Elimination of All Forms of Racial Discrimination (ICERD),[75] the Convention on the Rights of the Child,[76] and the Convention on the Elimination of All Forms of Dis-

73 Article 9, CEDAW.

74 UNDP (n.d.). Programme on Governance in the Arab Region: Oman. Retrieved 9 April 2009, from <http://gender.pogar.org/countries/theme.aspx?t=4&cid=13>

75 Oman adopted the convention on 1st of February 2003. See Arab Human Rights Index website: <http://www.arabhumanrights.org/en/countries/ratification.aspx?cid=13>

76 The accession was on 12 September 1996 and came in force 1st August 1997. From Arab Human Rights Index website.

crimination against Women (CEDAW).[77] It also acceded in 2004 to the two optional protocols of the Rights of the Child Convention concerning the involvement of children in armed conflicts, the sale of children, and their exploitation in prostitution and pornographic materials.

However, areas of discrimination persist, and nationality is one of the main areas where it can be seen most clearly. The connection between nationality and patriarchalism is manifest in most Arab nationality laws; therefore, many nationality issues are not merely based on gender discrimination and the violation of the equality of rights, but they also involve dependants' rights and interests. In Oman, as in many Arab states, the male line is considered as primary for purposes of nationality; thus a woman married to a foreigner cannot transmit her nationality to her children born in wedlock. Such provisions are largely influenced by old laws, and until the 20th Century, wives and children were not autonomous citizens almost anywhere in the world, but were subject to their husbands and fathers.

Such provisions in the nationality laws of many Arab countries have since been amended or replaced, even in some leading Arab and Islamic states, such as Egypt, where in 2004 a law was passed allowing Egyptian women marrying non-Egyptians to bestow Egyptian nationality on their children, while before 2004 Egyptian women were not allowed to pass on their nationality to their children. Advances were made by Algeria and Morocco in 2005 and 2006, when both passed laws to let women married to foreigners bestow their nationality on their husbands and children. Iran also made progress in September 2006 when its parliament passed a law allowing children with an Iranian mother and a foreign father to acquire Iranian nationality under certain conditions. However, most Gulf states are still exceptions to this general trend, particularly in

77 On 2nd July 2006.

the question of the acquisition of nationality by children, though Article 29 (2) of the 2004 Arab Charter on Human Rights, which came into force on 15 March 2008, requests all States parties to allow a child to acquire its mother's nationality.[78]

The right to a nationality is especially underlined in relation to children, by such important international treaties as the International Covenant on Civil and Political Rights[79] and the United Nations Convention on the Rights of the Child.[80] These documents take into account the fact that children are the most vulnerable human group with regard to various violations of their rights and freedoms; a group which has very limited opportunities to defend these rights by itself, with the need for protection and stability, and the right to education, health and public services.

It is a positive aspect of the Omani Nationality Law that it does not make any gender discrimination among children in obtaining or losing their nationality, since most discrimination cases are based on the gender rights of adults; nonetheless, children's rights are always connected to their parents' situation. Thus, the parent's nationality status as a citizen, a foreigner or a stateless person will affect the child's nationality, since a child is deprived of Omani nationality in different cases, most of them based on the father's status as non-Omani or stateless. Later, it continues with the influence of the father's actions so that children may obtain or lose Omani nationality when, for example, the father acquires another nationality, as a consequence of which his children will lose their Omani nationality and will have to acquire their father's new nationality. There are nevertheless some conditions which have to be met in the interests of such children; for example, that the law gov-

78 Oman signed the "Arab Charter of Human Rights/Amended" prepared by the Arab Summit in Tunisia in May 2004.

79 Art. 24.3.

80 Art. 7.

erning the new nationality allows the father to bestow it on his children.

Notwithstanding these safeguards, such a penalty violates a person's rights in different ways. First, it seems to constitute a collective punishment, which is prohibited under many international instruments including the Basic Statute itself,[81] that children can lose their nationality because of their father's actions even though they have a residual right to recover Omani nationality when they reach the age of majority, while this is not the case if the father has obtained a licence before acquiring another nationality.[82] It also violates the children's rights without consideration of the mother's rights towards her children. A child's rights, for instance, can be maintained by its mother, its family or the community as whole, and the father is not necessarily the best person to uphold them; although the laws of most Arab countries recognise the mother as a better guardian of the child's interests than the father when considering the nursing and raising of the child, they nevertheless ignore this principle in matters of nationality.

Let us take the example of a divorced father who chooses to adopt a new nationality; his children are under the guardianship of their mother according to the Custody of Children Chapter under the Personal Status Law (32/97),[83] but according to the Nationality Law they will lose their Omani nationality automatically when their father loses his.[84] They will then be treated as foreigners with a number of consequences, such as the need for a visa to stay in Oman, difficulty for the mother in exercising her guardianship of her own children in a desirable manner, and limited access to gov-

81 Art. 21.

82 Art. 9.

83 Art. 130.

84 If he had not acquired the license from the government.

ernment facilities and public services which are mostly free for citizens, especially health and education.[85]

The nationality law does not mention the status of a child of a non-Omani mother and unknown father, but according to the response of the Omani delegation to the Committee on the Rights of the Child, "*When the father of a child was unknown, it would be given Omani nationality, regardless of the nationality of the mother*".[86] Unfortunately, the law has left the case of a child of Omani mother married to a stateless person without any solution; instead of granting the child the right to obtain his mother's nationality, it leaves him without one, so instead of reducing statelessness it creates a new generation of stateless children. It violates the child's right to nationality according to Article 24 (3) of the International Covenant on Civil and Political Rights and Articles 7 and 8 of the Convention on the Rights of the Child.

The Omani government made a number of reservations upon its accession to CEDAW, the first concerning Article 9, paragraph 2, which provides that States Parties shall grant women equal rights with men with respect to the nationality of their children.[87] Art. 17 of the Omani Nationality Law explicitly determines that the words 'Omani' and 'foreigner' shall cover both genders unless stated otherwise, yet at least seven out of eighteen articles have elements of

---

85 It was one of the observations by the Committee on the Elimination of Racial Discrimination that 'non-national children experience disparities in the enjoyment of economic and social rights, particularly the rights to health and education'. See document (CERD/C/459/Add.1) regarding 'Questions Put by the Rapporteur in Connection with the Consideration of the Initial Report of Oman'.

86 According to the government delegation to the Committee on the Rights of the Child; see the report Oman (second periodic report), Meeting of the 43rd Session (Geneva, 11–29 September 2006). Retrieved 16 June 2008, from <http://olddoc.ishr.ch/hrm/tmb/treaty/crc/reports/crc_43/crc_43_oman.pdf>

87 UN, CEDAW. (2009). Declarations, Reservations and Objections to CEDAW: Oman. Retrieved 16 June 2008, from >http://www.un.org/womenwatch/daw/cedaw/reservations-country.htm>

direct or indirect gender discrimination in rights to nationality, and most cases related to women have automatic effects on their children too.[88]

4.4.1 Gender Discrimination

The Omani Law Articles containing gender discrimination can be categorised under two main headings, applying to mothers and to wives, and can be explored by considering three different situations.

The right to transmit the nationality to the children (as a mother)[89]

The law does not provide a fair passage of citizenship to children. Article 1.1 refers to *jus sanguinis*, that is the right by descent, but it mainly covers children born of an Omani father inside or outside the country. On the other hand, a mother can transmit her nationality only in two cases: if the filiation of legitimate children is not proven or the child's father is unknown, or if the child's father was an Omani who became a stateless person.[90] Such discrimination is obvious and unacceptable, because it gives the Omani male the right to transmit nationality to his children without provisions or conditions, whether they are born in or out of wedlock, while it makes such transmission by the female an exception subject to several conditions. It may also contradict other legislation such as the Law of Personal Status, whereby the father does not have financial

88 Articles 1, 2, 4, 5, 8, 9, 11 and 13 Nationality Law.

89 Although the provisions of the Saudi Nationality Law may be more advanced than other Gulf States by allowing the child of a citizen mother and non-citizen father to obtain Saudi nationality, the government does not in practice allow the female child to obtain nationality when she reaches the age of majority unless she marries a Saudi husband, but the male child can obtain it by application when he reaches the age of majority without provisions.

90 Art. 1.2 Nationality Law.

responsibility for a child born out of wedlock, as the *Shariʿa* does not sanction adultery.[91]

Article 1.3 awards nationality based on *jus soli,* which covers those who were born in Oman of unknown parentage and also gives the right by soil to foundling children over the woman's right to transmit her nationality to her children. Even in some critical cases, the Omani mother cannot bestow her nationality on her children if she is married to a stateless person unless he first was Omani then lost his nationality and became stateless.[92] Moreover, the law gives more rights regarding nationality to a stateless male than to an Omani female and a stateless female. Thus, under the right to nationality by soil, a child born in Oman of a stateless father has the right to Omani nationality in a case where the father was also born in Oman and is stateless.[93] This right is denied to the children of stateless females and indeed to Omani females.[94]

Taking all the aforementioned cases together, the effect of the law is to treat women as no more than a receptacle of pregnancy; and irrespective of conflicts with other legislation it also causes more dilemmas, such as creating unacceptable traditional and religious situations, where it gives those who were born out of wed-

---

91 It was one of the observations about Oman of the Committee on the Rights of the Child at its 28th session (Geneva, 24 September to 12 October 2001). CRC/C/78/Add.1; Retrieved 16 June 2008, from International Service for Human Rights website: <http://olddoc.ishr.ch/hrm/tmb/treaty/crc/reports/crc_23-41/CRC_28.htm#_ftn3>

92 Art. 1.2 Nationality Law.

93 With the conditions of regular residence and with a time of the children's birth, the father was and continues as a stateless person.

94 Other examples of the male-oriented approach to nationality can be found under different aspects of the nationality law, concerning the loss of nationality, where children may lose their nationality because of their father's behaviour, even if it conflicts with their interests. Moreover, in naturalisation cases, all children automatically follow their father's application status to obtain Omani nationality or lose it. (Articles 4,9 and 13.1.) For more details, refer to the 'Loss of Nationality', section 4.3.2.

lock a stronger right to nationality than those born of an Omani mother. It may also encourage the stateless person or foreigner not to disclose his situation as a father, thus giving his child the opportunity to obtain Omani nationality immediately under Article 1.2, which is against the prevailing religious and social attitudes to the family and marriage.

The right to transmit the nationality to the husband (as a wife)

It is an advantageous aspect of the law that it grants the right to transmit one's nationality to one's spouse; however, this right is compromised under the Nationality law and inconsistent with the equality of rights guaranteed by the International Covenant on Civil and Political Rights and other international instruments. It can be illustrated by the comparison of an Omani male married to a non-Omani female with an Omani female married to a non-Omani male. In the first case, the law gives the wife of an Omani the right to obtain nationality if they have been married for no less than five years and remain living together, without any further conditions,[95] the same provisions applying to native and naturalised Omani husbands.[96] However, in the second case, where the Omani female is the one transmitting the nationality to her non-Omani partner, the marriage must have lasted for at least ten years.[97] Moreover, the husband has to fulfil all the naturalisation requirements of age, language, health and so on listed under Article 2, whereas most of these conditions do not apply in the first case.

This comparison clearly reflects gender discrimination as there is no need to have different provisions for males and females in this respect. For instance, what gives the non-Omani wife married to an Omani male the right to obtain nationality earlier and in an easier

95 Art. 5 Nationality Law.

96 Art. 4.

97 Art. 2.2.

manner than a non-Omani husband married to an Omani female, beyond the male domination enshrined in the nationality law? It does not merely reflect unequal treatment; it also creates some difficulties for any non-Omani male married to an Omani wife, as he will be treated as a foreigner until he obtains nationality, so that his rights and freedoms will be ignored in some areas such as political and civil rights, or restricted in other areas, such as work and movement. Moreover, his right to establish a stable family will be highly affected too, given that the child is always connected to his father under the law.

The right to recover Omani nationality (as a wife)

Article 11 gives the right to recover nationality to an Omani female married to a non-Omani, who had renounced her nationality for that of her husband's. However, she cannot do so unless she has made Oman her permanent home or has returned to Oman and proved her desire to remain. Again, such conditions are not imposed upon the male seeking to recover his nationality,[98] which also reflects gender discrimination.

In Oman, such provisions and the operation of the Nationality Law violate Article 17 of the Basic Statute, which guarantees equality under the law; Articles 3 and 24 of the International Covenant on Civil and Political Rights, which ensure the equality of men and women in the enjoyment of all civil and political rights and guarantees every child's right to acquire a nationality; Article 9 of CEDAW, which guarantees women equal rights with men to acquire, change or retain their nationality and with respect to the nationality of their children; and Article 2 of the Convention on the Rights of the Child, which respects and ensures these rights irrespective of the child's or its parents' or legal guardians' nationality.

The Committee on the Elimination of Discrimination against

98 Art. 9.

Women has shown its concerns that women and men do not enjoy equal rights to nationality and that Omani women's legal inability to transfer their nationality to their children if and when the fathers are non-nationals or to their foreign spouses, whereas Omani men are able to do so for their children born of foreign mothers or to their foreign spouses, which constitutes a clear violation of women's equal rights under the Convention.[99]

Therefore, the State should correct the discriminatory status and operation of the law to further amend it to eliminate such discrepancies, which result mainly from gender discrimination and continue to affect new generations. Unfortunately, all Gulf States have followed the same path by enshrining similar discrimination in their statutes.

4.4.2 Adoption and Nationality

One major aspect of children's rights in the Islamic world concerns adoption. Most Islamic states adhere to the provisions of the Islamic *Shari'a* as the main source of legislation, especially over their personal status and family laws. Thus they do not approve or provide for adoption, including inter-country adoption, but only for fostering or what is called the *Kafala* system. This entails the provision of substitute care to children who cannot be cared for by their own parents without the legal effects of adoption upon the child-parent relationship. The Declaration on Social and Legal Principles relating to the Protection and Welfare of Children, with Special Reference to

99 The Committee calls upon Oman to withdraw its reservation to article 9 of the Convention and to amend its domestic laws to grant Omani women equal rights with men in regard to transmission of their nationality to their children who have foreign fathers and to their foreign husbands. See CEDAW/C document CEDAW/C/OMN/CO/1, Committee on the Elimination of Discrimination against Women Report 'Concluding observations of the Committee on the Elimination of Discrimination against Women: Oman' (21 October 2011). Downloadable from: <http://www2.ohchr.org/english/bodies/cedaw/docs/co/CEDAW-C-OMN-CO-1.pdf>

Foster Placement and Adoption Nationally and Internationally recognised the *Kafala* system as a valuable alternative institution.[100]

Oman made a general reservation to Article 21 of the Convention on the Rights of the Child 1989 on any obligations that are not consistent with Islamic law and with enforced Omani legislation, especially the provisions on adoption.[101] Similar reservations were made by several Islamic states, such as Kuwait, Qatar, UAE, Jordan, Egypt and Iran.[102] Another reservation made by Oman, Kuwait, and the UAE was to Article 7 of the Convention, which is related to the child's right to identity, nationality and protection from being stateless; their main reservations were based on national legislation which was to regulate these cases. The nationality law in most of

100 UN (3 December 1986). Declaration on Social and Legal Principles relating to the Protection and Welfare of Children, with Special Reference to Foster Placement and Adoption Nationally and Internationally - A/RES/41/85. Retrieved 4 August 2008, from <http://www.un.org/documents/ga/res/41/a41r085.htm>

101 The reservations on the Convention on the Rights of the Child have been repeated observations by the Committee on the Rights of the Child documents, such as CRC/C/OMN/CO/2 (29 September 2006) and CRC/C/OMN/Q/2 (21 June 2006) about 'Implementation of the Convention on the Rights of the Child' List of issues to be taken up in connection with the consideration of the second periodic report of OMAN CRC/C/149/Add.1 (21 June 2006), and CRC/C/Q/OMA/1 (2 February 2001) List of issues to be taken up in connection with the consideration of the initial report of Oman CRC/C/78/Add.1 (18 July 2000) downloadable from Arab Human Rights Index website: <http://www.arabhumanrights.org/en/countries/reports.aspx?cid=13&ct=3#199>
Recently, Oman has withdrawn all reservations it has made on the Convention on the Rights of the Child, but without withdrawing the reservation on Article 14 on the right of choice of religion. See Appendix 3 for more information.

102 Most Islamic States have made broad, general reservations that aim to modify or exclude the application of any provisions of the Convention that are at variance with Islamic values and laws. Oman, Kuwait, Jordan and Egypt were more specific on their reservations concerning adoption. See UNDP, Arab Human Rights Index website (n.d.). Reservations on Conventions: All Countries. Retrieved 2 June 2009, from <http://www.arabhumanrights.org/en/resources/reservations.aspx>

these states limits the acquisition of nationality by a child born of unknown parents. On the contrary, it will result in the revocation of the child's right to nationality and its subsequent rights and services in different situations, even if the guardians of the child are citizens under the *Kafala* system, which is recognised and permitted by the national legislation.

Social and traditional conventions are usually deemed to constitute further obstacles to protecting the child, taking into account that a woman who gives birth out of wedlock may face criminal charges, which will result in an increasing number of unwanted children or orphans, who may also face socially discriminative treatment. Unfortunately, GCC States lack any legislation to protect the child from such violations and to grant the mother guardianship and protection, although the Omani system tries to avoid such discrimination by giving the child a full traditional four-part name.

Under Article 19 of the Omani Civil Status Law (R.D. 66/99) and the Children in Need of Care Regulation,[103] responsibility for children of unknown parents lies with the Ministry of Social Development, which shall ensure the welfare of the child by finding an appropriate alternative family that wishes to assume guardianship. The child will be given a full traditional four-part name based on the agreement between this family and the Ministry. In addition, the regulation prevents any indication being given of the fact that a child is of unknown parentage on any forms such as birth certificates or registration documents, to enable the child to live in society without any discrimination, which is another positive step.

4.4.3 Nationality and Mixed Marriage

Mixed marriage between partners of different nationalities will usually affect their children's nationality, as mentioned earlier, and

103 Ministry of Social Affairs and Labour and Vocational Training, Ministerial Resolution 88/96, Regulation of the children in need of care.

may affect the spouse's nationality too, but such influences are obviously reduced if each spouse is eligible for the other's nationality. The fact that the right to marry and found a family is enshrined in human rights instruments such as the UDHR,[104] ICCPR,[105] and the ECHR[106] does not prevent a state from enacting laws that place restrictions on the form that a valid marriage must take or on the ability of couples to marry. However, there is cause for concern when the nationality law interferes with the right to marry by allowing or preventing such mixed marriages.

In 1986, the Omani Royal Decree no. 5/86 amended some provisions of the Law on the Organisation of the Omani Nationality (R.D. 3/83); the amendments were based on the new regulation for mixed marriage between Omani and non-Omani partners. The regulation's conditions were strict and limited, requiring advance permission for such a marriage, but the most notable feature of R.D. 5/86 is that it deprived the citizen's dependant, child or spouse of his or her nationality even if the father was Omani. Moreover, it gave the authorities extremely broad discretionary power to withdraw such rights if the persons concerned had married without permission.

The reasons for issuing R.D. no 5/86 were mainly due to the social and economic conditions of the time, such as the increasing number of migrant workers with a high rate of spinsterhood among Omani females and a large number of Omani males marrying abroad due to the low cost of mixed marriages. The government attempted to prevent such marriages, even to women from the neighbouring Gulf States. Although this regulation violated the freedom of the individual to choose a partner and to form a stable family, it prevailed for almost a decade, resulting in numerous cases of loss of

104 Art. 16.
105 Art. 23.
106 Art. 12.

nationality and stateless persons for failing to obtain permission to marry from the State.

Fortunately, the regulation ceased to apply after eight years, when Royal Decree no. 58/93 came into force and abolished the previous decree and all of its conditions. The new decree was more flexible, although it gave the Minister of the Interior more power by delegating to him the authority to issue the new regulation for mixed marriage, which came into force in 1993.

The new regulation,[107] which still applies, also requires advance permission to marry. It does not impose any penalty connected with nationality, by withdrawing it or depriving either party of it, which is a step in the right direction. The new regulation applies different conditions and allows leniency for marriage with a citizen of the Gulf States, although it still punishes those who do not abide by its requirements, by the deprivation of public services and a fine, in addition to denying the spouse entry to the country.[108] Almost all Gulf States impose similar conditions, requiring their citizens to apply for permission before contracting a mixed marriage. However, their strictness varies, although most of them apply few or no restrictions at all if the partner is a citizen of another Gulf State.

4.5 Statelessness and Multiple Nationalities

Nationality is an essential ingredient of human security. In addition to its role in providing each person with a sense of belonging and identity, it provides a link between the individual and international law. Each state tries to avoid the presence of stateless persons within its territory due to the legal and social problems resulting from

107 Ministry of Interior, Ministerial Resolution 92/93, Regulation of the Omani Marriage to Foreigners.

108 Art. 4 of the Ministerial Resolution. However, a later Resolution by the Minister of Interior (154/99) came to ignore the depriving the spouse from entering the country punishment if the spouse is from one of the Gulf States. See also the Legal Opinion (MLA/MO/6/4/1/955/2000) dated 24/06/2000.

their existence. On one hand, the stateless person cannot easily be expelled by the state and on the other, he has an anomalous position in the state, being denied the status of citizen, which may reduce or eradicate his freedoms and rights. Under the statelessness position, the right to a nationality has itself been voided, as international law defines a stateless person as one "*... who is not considered as a national by any state under the operation of its law*".[109] Thus, the stateless person "*has been compared to a vessel on the open sea, not sailing under any flag*".[110]

Although the main international instruments of human rights refer to the right to nationality,[111] there are two particular international legal instruments concerning statelessness, the 1954 Convention relating to the Status of Stateless Persons, and the 1961 Convention on the Reduction of Statelessness, neither of which has been signed or ratified by any of the six Gulf States.

Statelessness in these countries is the first nationality's dilemma, in addition to multiple nationalities; sometimes they are connected and interlaced with each other. The existence of statelessness varies from one Gulf State to another, being a large and critical problem in Kuwait, for example, where there are up to 120,000 stateless per-

109 Article 1, 1954 Convention relating to the Status of Stateless Persons.

110 Weis, P. (1962). *The United Nations Convention on the Reduction of Statelessness, 1961.* Retrieved from The International and Comparative Law Quarterly, Vol. 11, No. 4, Cambridge University Press on behalf of the British Institute of International and Comparative Law. p. 1073. Article Stable URL: <http://www.jstor.org/stable/755987>

111 Art. 15 of UDHR, and Art. 24.3 of ICCPR. Regional treaties, such as the 1969 American Convention on Human Rights (Art. 20) and the 1997 European Convention on Nationality, also seek to clarify the rights and responsibilities of States in this regard. Other International human rights conventions and treaties intended to prevent or reduce statelessness, including the Convention on the Rights of the Child, the Convention on the Elimination of All Forms of Discrimination against Women, and the Convention on the Nationality of Married Women.

sons,[112] whilst the case in Oman is less serious, although no official statistics are provided by any state. Such variation in numbers comes mainly from their diverse nationality laws.[113]

A case in point is that of determining the status of native nationals. Most Gulf States connect the national origins with a person's longstanding settlement on the land; mostly at the first quarter of 20th Century.[114] However, there is great difficulty in determining status by such criteria, as most Gulf States were not officially existent at that time and had no entry or exit controls or records at that period.

Another example is that of multiple nationalities, as it is prohibited legally to have more than one nationality a time under the legislation of all Gulf States, while the conditions and the consequences are different. For example, Bahrain stipulates the loss of nationality if a person has obtained another nationality, whether voluntarily or under constraint,[115] while Kuwait and the UAE distinguish between the two cases, so that the person will lose his nationality only if the new one was obtained voluntarily.[116] Oman, Qatar and Saudi Arabia, on the other hand, have different approaches to

---

112 Approximate number of those who were resident in Kuwait estimated by Human Rights Watch in 2000; an estimated 240,000 were living outside the country, many of whom wished to return to Kuwait but had not been permitted to do so by the government. See the report by Human Rights Watch. (October 2000). Kuwait: Promises Betrayed: Denial of Rights of Bidun, Women, and Freedom of Expression. Retrieved 30 January 2009, from UNHCR Refworld: <http://www.unhcr.org/refworld/docid/3ae6a87e0.html>

113 In contrast to the similarities among Gulf States constitutions.

114 A large percentage of stateless people in the Gulf States make allegations that they are the result of failure to recognise people who were present on the lands prior to 1914 in Saudi Arabia, 1920 in Kuwait, 1925 in the UAE and 1930 in Qatar.

115 Art. 3 Bahrain Nationality Law (17 February 1937).

116 Art. 11 Kuwaiti Nationality Law, and Art. 15 UAE Nationality Law.

multiple nationalities depending on whether or not it was permitted by the government.[117]

In addition to the statelessness issue, multiple nationalities also represent a second dilemma in the Gulf States, with the influence of the political perspective on these issues. Many Gulf States have tried to avoid the existence of dual or multiple nationalities among their citizens, at least in their legislation. However, the existence of this problem is a fact and is recognised widely among different states. For instance, in 2002, Bahrain allowed the holding of dual nationality by nationals of any Gulf States, although its nationality law seems to be the most restrictive legislation precisely on this issue. According to officials, this was justified by the integrity of such nationals. Another example is that of Qatar, whose authorities in 2004 and 2005 stripped 5,000 persons of Qatari nationality, most of them dual citizens of Saudi Arabia.[118]

Positively, the Omani Nationality Law has also tried to reduce the number of statelessness cases by adopting a number of measures, such as:

---

117 The GCC states signed a Counter-Terrorism Agreement in 2004 to counter the dissemination of terrorism; although the agreement prevents dual nationality, its direct effects are still not clear in this regard. See: Gulf Cooperation Council (2004). *Counter-terrorism Agreement.* from <http://www.gcc-sg.org/indexd2c3.html?action=Sec-Show&ID=351>

118 Although this is allowed under nationality law by a Royal Order based on Art. 18 Qatari Nationality Law. However, some reports consider the political background of both cases, citing the desire to change the Bahraini national demographic before parliamentary elections in 2002 based on sectarianism background in the first case, and suggesting that Qatar's decision was in retaliation for support given by the al-Murra tribe to the former Emir.
Aljazeera News (2002, June 16). Bahrain Debate on Dual Nationalities (in Arabic). Retrieved 18 January 2009, from <http://www.aljazeera.net/News/archive/archive?ArchiveId=33995>
BBC News (2006, February 9). Qatar Resolves Citizenship Issue. Retrieved 18 January 2009, <http://news.bbc.co.uk/1/hi/world/middle_east/4698152.stm>

- Article 1.4 which is the most notable one and is unique amongst Gulf States. It allows third-generation stateless persons to obtain Omani nationality and has had the direct effect of reducing the number of long-term stateless residents, albeit it is connected to the condition of being born in Oman of a stateless father who was also born in Oman and still has a stateless status.
- Allowing a foundling child or the child of Omani mother and unknown father or a child who was born in Oman of unknown parents to obtain nationality as a right of the territory.[119]
- Protecting an Omani wife of a non-Omani from being stateless by several precautionary conditions, such as allowing her to keep Omani nationality, or allowing her to change her nationality and obtain her husband's if possible, or finally by allowing her to apply for a "nationality recovery".[120]
- Protecting children from being stateless. Although they are connected to their father's nationality status (whether he loses or obtains it), the law protects them from losing their nationality if they were born to an Omani mother and a stateless father who once held Omani nationality.[121] It also protects them if their father's new country of nationality does not allow them to obtain its nationality. Finally, it allows them to apply for a "nationality recovery" when they reach the age of majority in cases where they have obtained their father's new nationality.[122]
- Allowing "nationality recovery"[123] for those who have been deprived of it, if the reason for deprivation no longer applies, according to Article 13.

On the other hand, the same legislation acknowledges the existence of statelessness and of stateless persons who once held Omani na-

119 Art 1.3 Nationality Law.
120 Art. 11.
121 Art. 1.2.
122 Art. 9.
123 Art. 14.

tionality,[124] which reflects the complex challenges facing the legislation. It has also created new classes of stateless persons without remedies. Moreover, some provisions could create multiple violations of a person's basic rights by depriving or withdrawal his nationality, as in the example of stripping the nationality from those who follow or belong to a group of 'unreligious faiths'.[125]

The cases dealing with stateless status under the Omani Nationality Law can be categorised into a number of main types:[126]

1. Old generations of stateless persons: This covers those who have not applied for nationality as required by the Nationality Laws of 1972 and 1983 or those who are not entitled to nationality. Today, neither the law nor the regulations provide any remedies to those falls into this category.
2. Those who become stateless as a result of contracting a mixed marriage without permission; which applied between 1986 and 1993. This covers those who were citizens and became stateless as a result of the withdrawal of nationality, or the citizen's spouse and children who were denied nationality as a consequence of the voluntary withdrawal of nationality. The amendments to the mixed marriage regulations solved this problem as mentioned earlier.[127]
3. Stateless children: These involve the first stateless generation, those born of a stateless father, the children of an Omani moth-

124 Art. 1.2.

125 Art. 13.2.

126 The Office of the United Nations High Commissioner for Refugees lists ten reasons why people become stateless, as follows: conflict of laws; transfer of territory; laws related to marriage; administrative practices; discrimination; laws related to registration of births; *jus sanguinis*; denationalization; renunciation of citizenship; and automatic loss of citizenship by operation of law. See Weissbrodt, David S. and Collins, Clay, (2006) *The Human Rights of Stateless Persons*, Human Rights Quarterly, Volume 28, Number 1, February 2006, pp. 245-276.

127 See section 4.4.3.

er and a stateless or non-Omani father, and in some cases those whose status changes with that of their father in loss of nationality cases, either where he obtains another nationality without permission, or where he is deprived of nationality if it was obtained by means of fraudulent conduct or false information.[128]

4. Those who are deprived of nationality under Article 13 of the Nationality Law or those became stateless by renouncing Omani nationality without acquisition of another nationality or without permission from the Omani government.[129]

Statelessness cases in Oman are usually entangled with the right to nationality, as the situation of 'nationality recovery' often coexists with being stateless. However, such cases do not account for most applications to the Ministry of the Interior. These cases are usually connected historically with the events when Sultan Qaboos came to the throne in 1970, when many Omanis were abroad due to the political and economic situation. There was no nationality law at that time and many holders of either Imamate or Sultani passports settled in the neighbouring states or in former Omani territories such as Eastern Africa and coastal areas of Pakistan, foregoing to apply for a nationality status as requested on time.[130]

---

128 Articles 8 and 13.1 Nationality Law.

129 Art. 8 and Art. 9.

130 In an interview, the Minister of the Interior stated that "*many applications for Omani Nationality come from those who lived in Eastern Africa based on their descent as Omanis; or their fathers were Omanis but do not hold Omani nationality yet*". However, their actual number is vague, but according to unofficial estimates it is around 500,000; see Albayan Newspaper (28 December 1998). *Interview with the Omani Minister of the Interior.* Retrieved 18 February 2009, from: <http://www.albayan.ae/servlet/Satellite?c=Article&cid=1221054186674&pagename=Albayan%2FArticle%2FFullDetail>
Nevertheless, these cannot be treated as stateless persons, as they currently hold another nationality, although they are trying to reclaim their original Omani nationality, which makes their cases different from the cases that form the main basis of this Chapter.

4.6 Conclusion

The Gulf States are still far from implementing international standards with regards of nationality, or from emulating the integrationist example of the European Union with regard to nationality, reflecting their very different political attributes and their governmental structure as absolute monarchies.[131] However, their historical and traditional backgrounds are more integrated due to their geographical homogeneity. It is common to have a tribe which exists in one state and may have the same roots and affiliations as the main tribe which resides in a different Gulf State.

Nationality law is one of the main pillars of the sovereignty of any state; undoubtedly, harmonisation of the nationality laws, or at least setting minimum standards, will help to integrate the people of the Gulf States as well as reducing the differences between them. It would be a step forward if the GCC were to adopt a nationality convention similar to the 1997 European Convention on Nationality, as this would provide principles for how to avoid conflicts between the member states by combining priority for legal rights and obligations in the country of habitual residence with the reasonable exercise of free choice for the individuals concerned.

It should be taken into account that the process of naturalisation of any Gulf State will have direct and automatic effects on other states. For example, a foreigner with a higher medical degree who has lived in Saudi Arabia for ten years could acquire Saudi nationality and then move to Qatar and enjoy equal rights there with native Qataris in GCC matters, while an otherwise similar foreign national born and raised in Qatar would be deprived of such rights for not less than twenty-five years.

There are several obstacles facing the Gulf authorities in the ad-

131 The problem with the system of monarchy is the absolute power of the ruler, who can change or override the law, since he is the primary legislator, and the personal aspect of the ruler is obvious under these systems.

option of a regional convention or to be in accordance with international standards, as it would have to amend all conditions and provisions under the nationality laws to maintain equal rights and opportunities for all, and must take individual interests into account, without discrimination on the basis of race, sex, national origin, religion or age. This would require the reconsideration and review of many of the standards currently being applied. For instance, most Gulf States continue to treat women's nationality rights differently from those of men, thus violating the fundamental right of equality which is guaranteed under their constitutions. Therefore, the adoption of a convention based on gender discrimination would be a step backward; However, if it were adopted with equality of rights granted without each state first being persuaded of the need for such principles, this would lead to failure of the convention. Consequently, there must be a national consensus before the establishment of any regional convention.

Other areas to be covered by the convention are multiple nationality and statelessness. From one perspective, it is important to forbid multiple nationality amongst Gulf States, since each state would have direct and similar rights to other states, thus it is desirable to allow it only for the fewest possible cases. From a contrary point of view, there should be a free and unrestrained exchange of nationality between Gulf States. Nonetheless, it is recommended to take children's rights and interests into account, by implementing social research and allowing multiple nationalities for the child, if needed, until they obtain age of majority.

The approach to statelessness is another obstacle which needs to be solved nationally prior to the adoption of a regional convention, as it takes diverse political forms in the various states, with differences of strictness or laxity that make the issue particularly complex. Ultimately, there is a need to reduce statelessness by allowing more flexible conditions, for instance by granting the third generation stateless an immediate and automatic right to nationality.

Regardless of the adoption of the convention, Oman and all other Gulf States should withdraw their reservations to CEDAW 1979 and the Convention on the Rights of the Child 1989, especially on granting women equal rights with men with respect to their nationality and that of their children. The prohibition of any collective punishment should extend to all dependants or a whole family based on the father's behaviour and making all the amendments required to any provisions which violate other rights and freedoms, such as Article 13.2 Omani Nationality Law, which directly violates the freedom to practice religious rites and the freedom of opinion and expression.

Moreover, in order to guarantee equal treatment to each applicant, Oman and other Gulf States should aim to limit the discretionary powers of the authorities by converting more modes of acquisition and loss into entitlements, and through enlisting clearly defined requirements. The importance of judicial review and the right of appeal in nationality matters cannot be ignored. It is essential to provide the applicant or defendant the right to judicial review by allowing aggrieved applicants to appeal to a higher administrative authority or any other judicial court, rather than solely relying on the executive committee's decision. The attribution of nationality to a person should be based on a genuine link with the state whose nationality is acquired, and any lack of a genuine link between the State and a national habitually residing abroad should thus be taken into account. Suppressing a person's civil and political rights for long periods or permanently is not fair, and naturalised persons should be granted equal rights and freedoms to those of native nationals, avoiding any distinction between them.

5 Democracy, Shura, and Public Participation

"We hold these truths to be self-evident, that all men are created equal, that they are endowed by their Creator with certain unalienable rights that among these are life, liberty and the pursuit of happiness. That to secure these rights, Governments are instituted among Men, deriving their just powers from the consent of the governed ... That whenever any form of Government becomes destructive of these ends, it is the right of the people to alter or to abolish it, and to institute new Government, laying its foundation on such principles and organizing its powers in such form, as to them shall seem most likely to effect their safety and happiness".[1]

Democracy and human rights are perceived as universal values. Even if they are different from each other as political concepts, the two concepts are interrelated with 'democracy' referring to the running of the government by its people, and 'human rights' referring to inherent universal rights or status that apply to all individuals.[2] With the recognition of democracy as the most accepted form of governance and the best political system in the world today.

In the Secretary-General's words: "*Democratic government helps to guarantee political rights, protect economic freedoms and foster an environment where peace and development can flourish...because in the absence of genuinely democratic institutions contending interests*

1 The Declaration of American Independence of the Thirteen Colonies as originally written by Thomas Jefferson. (1776, 4 July). *The Declaration of the American Independence.* Retrieved 2 December 2009, from Indiana University School of Law, Bloomington: <http://www.law.indiana.edu/uslawdocs/declaration.html>

2 Democracy aims to empower "the people" collectively and who rules, human rights aims to empower individuals and how of ruling. See Norman, J. (2005) Human Rights and Democracy: Conceptualization and Application in Palestine, downloadable from: <http://www.phrmg.org/human_rights_and_democracy.htm#_edn22>

are likely to seek to settle their differences through conflict rather than through accommodation".[3]

Nevertheless, democracy has succeeded to exist in many places but does not necessarily protect human rights, while some non-democratic states are able to protect many human rights.[4] However, democracy's protection and guarantee of civil and political liberties are the reason that differentiates this political system from others. There is a debate of the linkage between both concepts, on one hand, with the claim for the separationist theory between human rights and democracy as the linkage will be harmful for the further acceptance of human rights within the international society. A recent outcome of the separationist theory is the "democracy as neo-imperialism" notion that charges that "democracy is a 'Western-centric' approach to government that is not found indigenously in all societies and is not desirable for all peoples". One the other hand, the claim for the linkage between both of them is necessary;

---

3 Report of the Secretary-General (1998) 'The causes of conflict and the promotion of durable peace and sustainable development in Africa'. Para. 77, from: <http://www.un.org/ecosocdev/geninfo/afrec/sgreport/report.htm#susdev>

4 Randall Peerenboom listed several examples such as Indonesia after independence from the Dutch, which ended when Sukarno declared martial law and Thailand which has gone through cycles of democratic elections followed by military-led coups with some seventeen coups attempts. He illustrated the situation by saying: "many studies using a variety of methods and definitions find that democracy reduces human rights violations. However, the studies also show that the biggest determinants of good rights records are political stability, the absence of wars, and high levels of economic development. Moreover, the studies that show democracy improves rights tend to assume a linear relationship: marginal improvement in democratization leads to a similar improvement in protection of human rights. Yet many qualitative studies have found that democratization has not led to better protection of human rights in the countries studied". See Peerenboom, R. (2004) Democracy, the Rule of Law, and Human Rights in Asia: The Empirical Record, UCLA International Institute. from: <http://www.international.ucla.edu/article.asp?parentid=6546>

otherwise "human rights without democracy are standards or norms, but not rights as such".[5]

Democracy and human rights are not merely complementary, rather, they are interdependent. The element of interdependence of both concepts is widely visible. This interdependence is enshrined in Article 21 of the Universal Declaration of Human Rights (UDHR), and Article 25 of the International Convention on Civil and Political Rights (ICCPR), where the rights of the person to take part in his country's government, to vote and be elected are defined as universal human rights.

Shura on the other hand, came as Islamic concept which have, to some extent and based on its interpretation,[6] different approach to democracy and human rights derived from its Islamic divine law. Some political scientist, such as Samuel Huntington claims that Islam is antidemocratic.[7] While Daniel Price in his book 'Islamic Political Culture, Democracy, and Human Rights' concluded that Islam "neither undermines nor supports democracy and/or human rights".[8] Maqbul Malik sees that Islam is in favour of human rights through his analysis of Islamic teachings: "Muslim jurists have divided rights into two categories: God's rights and human rights. Divine rights in the jurists' view stand second to man's rights. The Muslim jurists regarded human rights as an integral part of faith".[9]

5 For more information see: Anthony J. Langlois (2003). *Human Rights without Democracy? A Critique of the Separationist Thesis*, The Johns Hopkins University Press, Human Rights Quarterly, Vol. 25, No. 4 (Nov. 2003), pp. 990-1019. From: <http://www.jstor.org/stable/20069702>

6 as will be discussed later (5.2)

7 in his book 'The Clash of Civilizations: 1996'

8 Shahrough Akhavi (2000) Scholar Commons about 'Islamic Political Culture, Democracy, and Human Rights', by Daniel E. Price, University of South Carolina, Columbia. available from: <http://scholarcommons.sc.edu/cgi/viewcontent.cgi?article=1004&context=poli_facpub>

9 Maqbul Ilahi Malik (1981) *The Concept of Human Rights in Islamic Jurisprudence*, Human Rights Quarterly, Vol. 3, No. 3, The Johns Hopkins University Press (Aug., 1981), p. 57. available from <http://www.jstor.org/stable/761895>

5.1 Introduction

The Economist Intelligence Unit's Index of Democracy for 2008 and 2010 list most Arab and Muslim States among the Authoritarian Regimes, a political definition that is clearly at odds with democracy.[10] The Freedom House measurement which has the task to rank countries by their willingness to protect political rights and civil liberties assesses the majority of these states as 'unfree', or subject to undemocratic restrictions upon the political and civil freedoms of their people. The criteria used to assess different governmental systems worldwide are largely derived from the UDHR.[11] Unfortunately, while democracy and its freedoms have been adopted by many African, Latin American, Asian and European countries over the past few decades, the Muslim world still takes a largely anti-democratic stance.

The interrelationship between human rights and democracy in the Muslim and Arab States will thus be analysed in this Chapter with an aim of revealing a number of questions in relation to protection and engagement with rights of political participation. Moreover, this chapter will discuss the role of Islam in democracy and the protection of human rights under the *Shura* principle, as an alternative method of public participation. This chapter initially introduces the conceptualisation of democracy and *Shura* in terms of social mechanisms, institutions, and citizens' rights, their compatibility and contrariety. As it develops, this chapter will concentrate on the current Omani system in the form of a case study. Thus, the elements of public participation, its obstacles, its development and

---

10 The Economist Intelligence Unit. *Index of Democracy 2008*. Retrieved 13 June 2009, from <http://graphics.eiu.com/PDF/Democracy%20Index%202008.pdf> There were no status changes on the Arab States with the latest Report 'Democracy index 2010' from <http://graphics.eiu.com/PDF/Democracy_Index_2010_web.pdf>

11 Freedom House (2011) *Map of Freedom in the World*. Retrieved 29 March 2011, from <http://www.freedomhouse.org/template.cfm?page=363&year=2011>

its current efficacy as a means of granting political rights to Gulf citizens will be discussed.

5.2 Shura and Democracy

The relationship between secularism and democracy is a key issue of controversy among Arab scholars.[12] This is mainly attributable to the central influence of Islamic faith among Muslims and a governmental system which rejects the idea of public involvement. While liberal democrats reject any attempt to combine religion and politics, traditional Islamic thinkers reject this connection on the basis of democracy being an imported western commodity.[13] Although Islam is, in principle, against the notion of authoritarian regimes, the shifting political landscapes of Islamic States have instilled a *de facto* acceptance of such regimes, particularly without the critical influence of religious and secular intellectuals to offer a means of disavowal. As a result, some Islamic political intellectuals decided to treat the "*just autocracy*" ruler as the best type of government![14]

---

12 There are a variety of intellectual perspectives that cite democracy as necessitating secularism, because without it a democratic system cannot exist. Some Arab and Muslim States still persist with the view that *Shura* is a system within the state either as a governmental or parliamentary system. The underlying reasons for this belief lead to the existence of *Shura* or democracy in monarchies, especially within the absolute monarchies of the Arab Gulf States.

13 Bahlul, R. (2001). *Does Democracy Require Secularism* (in Arabic). Retrieved 24 November 2007, from <www.glo110.blogfa.com/post-55.aspx>

14 The 'Just Autocracy' is a translation term of the Arabic text '*al'Mustabid Al'adil'*. The Arabic term '*Mustabid'* means a person (as a monarch) ruling with unlimited authority who is assertive and does not hesitate in decisionmaking and implementation; this concept spread among Arabic traditional literatures to denote the quality of the ruler, especially if he is a 'Just', irrespective of the manner how he seized the throne (by heredity, by election or selection, or by force). This term should be distinguished from the Arabic term *Toghe'ian,* which describes the person who is an unjust dictator or tyrant. 'Just Autocracy' argument spread in the 19th and 20th centuries by several Islamists reformers such as Jamal Aldeen Alafghani and Sheikh Muhammad Abdo through their journal *'Al Urwa Al Wuthqa'* and Abd al-Rahman al-Kawakibi in his book *Tabai al-Istibdad.*

Shura, however, is an inherent element in Islamic States, regardless of the governmental structure adopted. *Shura* is the main Islamic political and constitutional principle, usually invoked by Muslims as a method of public participation. However, there is no straightforward comparison to be made between democratic and *Shura* principles. To understand the obstacles of implementing democracy in the Muslim world, it is essential to grasp the *Shura* principle from its linguistic, religious, historical and political manifestations.

Neither the term 'democracy' nor the term '*Shura*' reflect the clarity and simplicity of the meaning for which they traditionally stand as they have been interpreted in a variety of ways. While "democracy" literally means "rule by the people" and "*Shura*" means "consultation", both have long been associated with controversial terminologies, different manifestations and historical developments. Differing schools of thought have offered diverse interpretations of democracy, including liberal democracy, democratic socialism, and other linked concepts such as pluralism and the voice of society. While *Shura,* as a term reflecting the principle of consultation, also lacks agreement in the methods by which it is implemented and in its public dimensions.

'*Shura*' is an Arabic word derived from '*shara'*, which means "*extracting honey from hives*". One of its secondary meanings is "*taking the consultation and deliberation from its source*".[15] According to this purely linguistic definition, '*Shura*' is distinct from democracy in ways which could make it more complex.[16] It is a procedure of making decisions by consultation and deliberation rather than a systematic rule or decision making process. Although it is a mutual consultation process, the result is usually a one way com-

15 Al-Qurtubi, A. (2003). *Tafsir al-Qurtubi (in Arabic)* (Vol. 4). Riyadh: Dar Alam Alkitab. p. 249.

16 Since Shura is interpreted differently and no agreement on a common definition has been reached.

mitment instead of having an agreement between two parties.[17] Also, the consultant as its 'source' is a particular kind of person who could better relate to the subject of the consultation. For instance, *Shura* in the home involved family members, while in tribal issues it involves the leaders of families, with the most prominent figures of the tribes and secular groups implementing *Shura* at the national level.

It is believed that *Shura* was the method used by pre-Islamic Arabian tribes to select their leaders and to make major decisions. With emphasis on its political aspects, Islamic *Shura* may be defined as: surveying the opinions of the people involved or those who are knowledgeable in a certain subject, in order to reach a decision that is best and as close as possible to the truth.[18] Under this definition it is clear that *Shura* is distinct from democracy, which is commonly defined as the 'rule of the people, by the people, for the people'.

In the Quran, *Shura* is mentioned twice and there is a chapter named *Shura*. However, the Quran does not specify who should be consulted, what they should be consulted about, and whether or not this consultation is mandatory. The elements dealing with the extent and applicability of *Shura* have been the main issue of contention among Quran interpreters for centuries.

Historically, these arguments begin with the debate over the succession to Prophet Muhammad,[19] following different succession routes for the first four Caliphs, known as *The Rightly-Guided Caliphs.* Since then, *Shura* as a consultation council, or *Majlis Ash-Shura,* has taken different forms throughout many Islamic States. These different interpretations of *Shura* have been constituted by

17 The ruler and the consultants.

18 This definition is a mixture between several definitions of Shura which the writer believes as the most suits the meaning of Shura.

19 Died in 632 CE.

the council members,[20] the nature of consultation[21] and the decision's character; for instance, how the decision is made, and most importantly, the obligatory attribute of the final decision. Such diverse interpretation is largely the result of a weakness in the *Shura* principle. The majority of later rulers and caliphs made it into power by inheritance or by might, and were rarely chosen by *Shura*. Consequentially, concepts related to autocratic governmental systems, such as "*just autocracy*", became a part of many Islamic political schools. On the other hand, it is believed that *Shura*'s 'widespread meaning' is of a positive nature, since Quran and *Sunnah* never offer a single approach to it. Thus, it can be developed and adapted over time, as it may adopt any method which serves its principles. Therefore, it could be flexible enough to develop and reach the best of each society, people, or time without being limited by its core concepts.

Under its political and legal aspect, *Shura* as an Islamic term is used by a group of people who form the *Shura* council, usually consisting of the most prominent figures from the scholars and tribes. Nevertheless, the council's tasks are divided into three different notions. Al-Mawardi[22] in his book *"The Ordinances of the Government"* concentrated on the *Shura* council's main task to choose the best ruler. Other scholars focused on its deliberative function in which the council can exchange views with the ruler, without any say in his election.[23] The third group is connected to the notion of its com-

20 The membership method, and their qualifications.

21 When, why, and what they are consulted about.

22 (974 to 1058): Abu al-Hassan al-Mawardi was a 10th century jurist who wrote on many subjects, including interpretations of the Qur'an, religion, government, public and constitutional law, language and ethics. His work has long been recognised as a classic in its field, much discussed by Arab authors and Orientalists, and quoted in courses on Islamic law and government.

23 As it is in war issues. See al-Zamkhashari, *Tafseer Alkashaf, Beirut* 1/ p. 216.

bined tasks, both as a deliberative council for the ruler and the legitimate method of choosing him.[24]

The 'mandatory nature' of its deliberations remains the main issue in relation to these tasks and the involvement of the *Shura* council. History shows that whenever the council had the power to appoint the ruler or caliph spontaneously its decisions became mandatory with the ruler respecting their power, while in a situation where the council was appointed by the ruler its influences were weak. Obviously, the weaknesses of the *Shura* council usually come from the ruler who insisted on the non-mandatory approach of the council and its members, the consultants, who are usually chosen by the ruler himself and thus have no power to object the ruler's decision. Despite some exceptions, there are examples of influential *Shura* councils, such as the one in Omani history.[25]

Under *Shura*'s linguistic meaning, '*Shura*' is a simple procedure which is used by any individual or group for collective deliberation on a common goal. Thus, there is nothing which makes it intrinsically Islamic. *Shura* was used prior to the emergence of Islam and is used today by non-Islamic groups; hence, it is not inherently at odds with democracy. The connection between *Shura* and democracy may be seen from the illustration of the democratic method, that is, the people ruling and making decisions, ideally, by a collective deliberation in which all parties are exchanging counsel, which is the basic meaning of *Shura*.

Shura became a specifically Islamic term and principle as manifested in the Quran, although neither its definition, nor its historical-religious source gives precise accounts of it. However, *Shura*'s popularity is on the increase and is used today with political connotations. It is believed that *Shura* should be developed and used to serve people in the same manner as democracy. Mostly, this can be

24 It was adopted under the Imamate System in Oman.
25 One such example is the *Ibadi* Imamate system as discussed in Chapter Two.

done by using its greatest characteristics, such as the legal obligation on the ruler either of the *Shura* Council's legislative or consultative decisions, its function to appoint the government with the power to choose and dismiss the ruler, and most importantly, the people's right to elect and be elected. In this regard, the difference between *Shura* and Democracy needs to be ascertained, because in spite of their differences they also adopt a similar approach towards public participation.[26]

According to S. Sulaiman the main characteristics, common to any democratic system, are freedom of speech, free elections, majority rule and minority rights, political parties, separation of powers, supremacy of the rule of law, and freedom of action for individuals and groups.[27] Considering the chief elements, it is apparent that none of the above is against *Shura* or Islam in principle. Both *Shura* and democracy have the same view on collective deliberation and majority judgement, thus tending to be more accurate and fair, along with the affirmation that the rule of individuals through an autocratic system is most likely to infringe upon the human dignity and freedom.

Just as there is nothing inherent in democracy which makes it intrinsically secular (or Western), equally, nothing can prevent *Shura* from taking a secular form or for religion to play no part in it at all. However, integrating Islamic *Shura* principles with democratic elements does not imply that they should be identical. Nonetheless, the terms do not necessarily state their differences. It is therefore possible to have an Islamic democracy or an Islamic *Shura* system at the same time. The main issue to explore is the role of Islam

---

26 Idris, J. (2004). *Shura and Democracy: A Conceptual Analysis.* Retrieved 15 December 2007, from Islamonline website: <http://www.islamonline.net/servlet/Satellite?pagename=IslamOnline-English-Ask_Scholar/FatwaE/FatwaE&cid=1119503544462>

27 Sulaiman, S. (1996). *Democracy and Shura.* Retrieved 11 December 2007, from Al-Hewar Center: <http://www.alhewar.com/SadekDemAndShura.htm>

in determining the limitations and boundaries on the implementation of democracy, whereby in which Islam will undoubtedly play a fundamental role in its interpretation.

There is one important element of *Shura* that reflects a main principle of Islamic states which is based on the Law of *Shariʿa.* This is the idea that Islamic *Shura* is unnecessary if it involves any unanimously agreed upon rule from the Islamic Divine law.[28] Thus, the *Shura* council cannot discuss any matter which is against Islamic precepts, such as the legality of alcoholic drinks for Muslims, because according to the Law of *Shariʿa*, the absolute truth regarding this matter is already known, and there are clear texts in the Quran and *Sunnah* already regulating it.

Some Islamic intellectuals have put forward other controversial arguments about the elements that constitute *Shura.* For instance, applying the *'rule of God's'* approach instead of '*the rule of people'* which endows God with the absolute power of legislation.[29] Moreover, *Shura* is not a political system as most of the principles and values emanate from the divine Islamic law, whereas, *Shura* is only one component of it.[30] Additionally, *Shura* concentrates on the best decisions' outcome instead of on the vote of the majority as adopted by democracy. These arguments are marginal since 'divine law' constitutes the basis of any system adopted in Islamic States.

---

28 Quran and Sunnah.

29 Art. (2) of the Islamic Iranian constitution. The ruler under the Islamic concept is not absolute and it is the rule of God not the rule of Man and the ruler is just a 'vice-regent'. Under this concept the ruler is supposed to protect Islam and he should consult others (*Shura*) on state matters. There were several arguments about the ruler's commitments with the consultation, but it believed the ruler has the right to accept or ignore the consultation results since he is responsible for all of his actions in front of God. Under such a definition of *Shura* we can find many Muslim constitutions emphasising on *Shura* as principle which serves the ruler and his conscience to accept or ignore the consultation.

30 Idris, J. (2004). *Shura and Democracy: A Conceptual Analysis.*

They adopt the main core of Islamic *Shura*, and this is usually favoured by intellectuals who oppose democracy.

H. Goddard has tried to cover the different nature of Islamic responses to democracy, finding that those who stand firm on the perceived incompatibility of democracy and Islam usually base their arguments on an assumed relationship between democracy and secularism. The existence of a democratic system of government is thus regarded as impossible without retaining secularism as an integral part of the political system with which Islamic States operate. This reflects the interrelationship between democracy as a system and secularism as an ideology.[31]

A *Shura* without any form of Islamic restriction would be as un-Islamic as a liberal unconstrained democracy. On the other hand, there is no necessary connection between secularism and democracy. Thus, the whole issue centres on how to adopt democracy as a political system. The debate revolving around secularism, liberalism and democracy and their application in an Islamic orientated culture will not be resolved by the mere adoption of *Shura* instead of democracy.[32] Moreover, it is essential to know that the variation of *Shura*'s theories without adhering to its main concept in practice is part of *Shura*'s weakness, in contrast to democracy where both theory and practice diverged and gradually developed into a commonly accepted political system.

5.3 Basic Statute and *Shura* in Oman

Over the last three decades, Oman has emerged as a centre of political and economic stability in the Arab world, a stability which is an essential ingredient for any country to develop and flourish. Whereas democracy and public freedoms are at the core of stability

31 Goddard, H. (2002, January). *Islam and Democracy*. The Political Quarterly, Volume 73, Issue 1, pp. 3-9.

32 Idris, J. (2004). *Shura and Democracy: A Conceptual Analysis.*

in other parts of the world, the case in Oman is different. It is not a democratic state[33] and it did not adopt the modern concepts of human rights and public freedoms into its legal-political system until 1996 when the Basic Statute of the State was promulgated.

Several studies have tried to examine the reasons behind such stability in a state which is traditionally Sultanate (monarchic) and situated in a part of the world usually defined as 'unstable'. Among other factors, most agree that the current Sultan's wise leadership is playing the most influential role in Oman's stability today.[34] However, the task of creating long-term stability extends beyond individual rulers and institutions; public participation in ruling and taking account of the government is also crucial. In addition, there are natural external pressures directing towards opening the political system in Gulf States, in that they are absolute monarchies in a world apparently flourishing with democracies.

5.3.1 *Shura* as Part of the Omani System

Shura, as the principle used by Islamic states allowing the public to take part in selecting or actively participate in their government, involves the interaction of several individuals, parties and organisations. From this perspective, it could be considered similar to democracy. *Shura* is an intrinsic part of the Omani political system, and Oman has its own *Shura* perspective although it shares common traits in its social and traditional aspects with other Gulf States. *Shura* is part of the traditional tribal system which still exists today. Under the traditional tribal system each tribe has its own consultative council called *Majlis or Sablah,* where all discussions and consultations related to the tribe would take place. These councils also serve as social gatherings and a means of exchanging of information and news.

---

33 Art. 5 OBSS. *'The system of government is Sultani, hereditary'.*

34 Manea, E. (2005). *Regional Politics in the Gulf: Saudi Arabia, Oman and Yemen.*

Distinguishably, *Shura*, in its legal-political aspects, was an essential pillar of the Imamate system which governed Oman for over twelve centuries by a theocratic stratum of the *Ibadi* sect, where most of the state's political and legal issues were governed by the *Shura* council, in particular electing and dismissing the ruler.

From his early days of rule, Sultan Qaboos has remained committed to Oman's heritage and traditions. He has developed his own unique vision of the practice of *Shura* as part of his rule. Hence, he makes annual tours of the country, including the remote regions, where he meets his people face to face to listen to their requests and views, as well as discussing his policies. As a result, he has enhanced communication between the government and the people, and with most of the government's senior officers attending the tours, it positively impacts on the potential of solving issues directly. The people have direct access to him and his government and they have called his meetings with his subjects the 'Open Parliament', although it is not an official title.[35]

As Oman modernised, it had to establish foundations for a reliable system, where all religious, heritage related, political and social values could be congregated. The modernisation process in Oman, tried to implement a system which is accepted by its people, allows popular participation without adopting the western democratic style, and without changing the monarchy's governmental system. All of these requirements can be fulfilled through the adoption of the various theories of '*Shura*', which have existed in Oman even before the promulgation the Basic Statute in 1996.

Oman's affiliation with the Islamic route has been asserted by Articles1 and 2 of the Basic Statute. Due to this assertion, Oman is

35 The term used heavily by government institutions and media; for example see Oman Newspaper (18 November 2010) *Meeting with Ash-Shura Council Chairman (in Arabic)*. Retrieved 8 February 2011 from: <http://main.omandaily.com/node/35840>

no different from its neighbouring states. Therefore, *Shura*, as one of the most important political and constitutional principles in Islam, has been embraced as a political principle guiding the state's policy in addition to being a pillar of the Sultanate's governance, along with justice and equality.[36]

5.3.2 The Term '*Shura*' Under the Basic Statute

> *"It is not our intention to import foreign brands of democracy into this country; the democratic process that you are witnessing is, and must always be an Omani one, which accords with our people's culture, religion and traditions and particular needs".*[37]
> Sultan Qaboos: 1995

Under several Arab and Muslim constitutions, *Shura* is not merely part of the Islamic tradition; it is also a method of state governance as is the case in Oman and Saudi Arabia.[38] Moreover, the word '*Shura*' is often used to name the parliaments in Muslim-majority countries who call it '*Majlis Ash-Shura*' or the '*Shura* Council' that can include different legislative bodies. The term '*Shura* Council' is also the name to be used either if the house is elected as it is in Oman or appointed as is the case in Saudi Arabia and Bahrain or mixed as in Egypt and Qatar.

Equally, several Gulf States' constitutions have used the term 'Democracy' to describe their governmental system in spite of the fact that all of them are traditional monarchies.[39] In Oman nothing related to democracy or '*sovereignty being in the hands of the people,*

36 Articles 9 and 10 OBSS.
37 The Middle East (1 November 1995). *Facing the challenges: interview with Sultan Qaboos bin Said of Oman.* Retrieved 4 September 2007, from The Free Library: <http://www.thefreelibrary.com/Facing%20the%20challenges.-a0 18763792>
38 Art. 5 OBSS and Art. 8 Saudi Basic Law.
39 Kuwait (Art. 6), Bahrain (Art. 1), and Qatar (Art. 1).

the source of all powers'[40] has been mentioned under its Basic Statute, meaning that Oman continues to be a monarchy where absolute powers are vested in the hands of the Sultan. However, the Basic Statute did incorporate the *Shura* principle as part of the state's political principles.[41]

The term *Shura* as used here does not just offer a parallel to Democracy; it is more akin to a substitute. This is seen in Article 9 where "*The rule in the Sultanate shall be based on justice, Shura, and equality*" and it limits the citizens' right to participate in public affairs "*... in accordance with this Basic Statute and the conditions and provisions stipulated by the law*". All the conditions and provisions affirm the consultative aspect of *Shura* without affirming the citizen's right to choose or dismiss their government. However, the related chapter in the Basic Statute concerning a parliament (Oman Council) allows an ordinary statute to change the power of parliament from time to time. The attempts by Oman to safeguard the use of the Islamic term '*Shura*' as a governmental system or as the name of parliament, rather than adopting the western term 'democracy' can be illustrated by different interpretations and reasons:[42]

- Avoid using foreign terminologies: It is a well-known trait of the Sultan that he eschews the use of un-Arabic terms; a prime example being the generalised use of the 'Basic Statute' term instead of 'constitution' where each term has a different linguistic source in Arabic.[43]
- Adherence to tradition by "*Consolidating the pillars of genuine Shura emanating from the country's heritage, values and its Is-*

40 Kuwait, Bahrain and Qatar.

41 Art. 10 OBSS.

42 Those reasons may be applicable as well for other Islamic states which use *Shura* under their constitutions.

43 See section 2.2.2.

lamic Shari'a".[44] It is part of the State's policy to implement the *'genuine Shura'*. Comprehending the meaning of *Shura* under the Basic Statute is essential. However, understanding what it really means is subjective. Does it mean that the consultative and non-mandatory aspect of *Shura* deriving from its linguistic meaning, or is it referring to the *Shura* under Imamate System in Oman as part of 'the country's heritage'? Since the Council of Oman's formation lacks the power of the old Imamate *Shura*, the phrase *'genuine Shura'* means the Basic Statute is currently adopting the first interpretation.

- Islamic legitimacy: The Basic Statute asserts the Islamic attribution in Oman.[45] This is shown by the reaffirmation that *Shura* in Oman emanates from "its Islamic *Shari'a*".
- Diminishing the need for external intervention by utilising the consultative aspect of *Shura*; ostensibly serving the government to some extent, by using the election aspect ensuring public participation without the need for a powerful, centralised parliament. As a result, any international intervention or allegations leading to calls for democracy in Oman will be diminished.
- The flexibility of the term *Shura* from its consultative role to its representative parliamentary aspect may be regarded as a step towards a fully democratic state or a constitutional monarchy, without the need for major constitutional amendments. *Shura* has played and will play an important role in Oman's potential developments.
- From a political aspect, it is clear that the consultative aspect of *Shura* will serve to maintain Oman as an absolute monarchy,[46] at least under the current Sultan. The reasons for choosing this

44 Art. 10.

45 Art. 1 and Art. 2.

46 Art. 5.

> type of governmental system at a time when democracy is the most desirable method vary. One possible explanation may be that the current Sultan, needed time to monitor the development process in Oman. A development process of the magnitude as the one that is taking place in Oman is much more efficient when overseen by one person. Otherwise, by giving his powers to others, the Sultan could delay this process and limit the potential results.

Regardless of the status of the neighbouring Gulf monarchies, which could influence the Omani system directly or indirectly, Oman has chosen its own distinctive way of governing. In fact, Gulf States are not ready yet to adopt democracy or even the notion of a constitutional monarchy, largely because of the dominant tribal mentality with the weak political and civil associations, enhanced by the influences of the monarchies in these states. The tribal mentality as embodied by the *sheikh* still plays an important role in the ruler-people interrelationship, to the extent that the sheikh's words are to be heard and respected over public opinion since he is the one entrusted with the responsibility for his people. The influence of the monarchy is obvious with power largely shared among members of the Royal Family.

Oman is different to some extent since the Sultan holds most of the power meaning that the Royal Family, as a whole, is less influential than in other Gulf States. Moreover, as it will be expanded upon later, during the early stages of his rule the Sultan tried to develop a tangible increase in public participation. This hints at the fact that he is willing, at least to some extent, to relinquish some of his power to other authorities. This was mentioned in his first speeches to the Omani people on the assumption of power. In his speech on 27th July 1970 he stated that:

> "*... the government and the people are like one body*",

Saying one year later:

> *"We shall work seriously to establish a fair democratic rule in our country within the framework of our Arab Omani reality, putting before our eyes the doctrine of Islam which always lights our way.*[47]

The concept of *Shura* can be extended beyond its consultative meaning. The use of the designated Arabic term '*Shura* Council' instead of 'parliament' does not necessarily reflect the advisory elements of parliament. For instance, Pakistan has a 'legislative parliament' and calls it precisely that. Several Arab States have given the term *Majlis Ash-Shura* to their parliaments, either the appointed council as is the case with Saudi Arabia and Bahrain, or a partially appointed council as in Qatar and Egypt. Omani politics followed a different route, commencing the transformation of the old council *Al-Majlis Al-Istishari* in 1991, by giving the *Ash-Shura* Council its elected character. This may reflect the traditional *Shura* in Oman where the majority of members are elected, or chosen by their own people, to represent their tribes. In addition to its specialised council attribute, *Shura* is also the means of succession under the Basic Statute, where the Royal Family Council determines the successor to the throne.[48] Hence, the presence of *Shura* in Oman does not negate democracy or its consultative nature as the term is flexible and can be extended to incorporate most democratic developments.

5.3.3 The Development of 'Public Participation'

Oman has a long historical relation to the Imamate, but never experienced modern public participation until Sultan Qaboos ruled the country.[49] During this period there were significant developments in terms of public participation. Since each step is mainly

47 *Royal Speech: Words and speeches of His Majesty Sultan Qaboos bin Said 1970-1995 (in Arabic).* (1996). Muscat: Diwan of Royal Court. pp. 29-30.

48 Art. 6.

49 1970–now

based on public consciousness, each step that follows will lead toward more development and participation. The rule of Sultan Qaboos can be illustrated by four phases which show the development of public participation.

- In the First Phase (1970–80), the Sultan's emphasis was mainly on building the infrastructure of the country. However, the Sultan established numbers of councils, such as Municipal councils, a Chamber of Commerce and Industry, and the Council of Agriculture, Fisheries, and Industries, which allowed some public participation, albeit very limited.[50]
- The Second Phase (1981–91), marked the establishment of the State Consultative Council (*Al-Majlis Al-Istishari*), an advisory body set up to discuss government politics with the private and public sector. It consisted of 55 appointed members who represent the seven geographic regions of Oman, 18 government members (sub-secretary level), 12 private sector members (commerce and industry), and 25 from the general public. While its functions and powers were very limited it was a tangible starting point for more participation.
- The Third Phase (1991–97), brought about the replacement of the '*Al-Majlis al-Istishari*' by '*Majlis Ash-Shura*', which is more representative and more powerful. During this phase there were two parliament terms: The first one (1991–1994) had 59 seats, 3 candidates nominated for each *wiliyat* (Province) and the Sultan selected one. There was no voting, no ballots and no female candidates. Ballots were introduced for the second term (1994–97), which had 80 seats, with each province occupying at least one seat. Provinces with populations over 30,000 had 2 seats and the voters elected 2 candidates per seat, with the ultimate decision being the Sultan's. Voters were very limited in number,

50 Al-Hashmi, S. (2000) p. 52.

and for the first time female candidates were allowed in the capital district, winning 2 seats.[51]

- The Fourth Phase (1997–Now): 1996 was a turning point in the Omani system, because the Basic Statute of the State had established the second house, the State Council (*Majlis Ad-Daula*) which started functioning in 1997, at the end of the second term (1994–97) of *Majlis Ash-Shura*. All members of the State Council are appointed by the Sultan and this has allowed more opportunity for the public to choose their candidates for the Elected House (*Majlis Ash-Shura*).[52]

One fact about these developments is that they came as internal motivations declared by the Sultan himself as a subjective conviction. This is distinct from other parts of the Arab world where most of such developments in the last decade sprang from American and western pressures to co-opt Arab States as weapons in the 'war on terror',[53] or currently by the internal revolutions of Arab Spring.[54]

5.3.4 Basic Statute and Bicameral Council

Although over the last few decades the Sultan has created consultative bodies, Oman has no legislature yet, the legislative power being solely vested in the Sultan's hands. At the present time, the Basic Statute has developed the parliamentary system in Oman by

51 Majlis Ash-Shura (2001). *Majlis Ash-Shura Formation 1997-2000 (in Arabic).* Muscat. pp. 12-25.

52 Majlis Ash-Shura (2004). *Majlis Ash-Shura Formation 2000-2003 (in Arabic).* Muscat. pp. 11-29.

53 President Bush stressed the importance of democracy as a weapon in the war on terror in his annual State of the Union address in February 2005. "Hopeful reform," he announced, "is already taking hold in an arc from Morocco to Jordan to Bahrain." See Crystal, J. (2005, July). *Political Reform and the Prospects for Democratic Transition in the Gulf.* Retrieved from <http://www.fride.org/download/WP11_ReforPoli_ENG_jul05.pdf> see p. 1

54 See section 1.1.

adopting the bicameral council, a purely consultative body. It is called "*The Council of Oman*" (*Majlis* Oman) and is made up of members of the State Council (*Majlis Ad-Daula*) and the Consultative Council (*Majlis Ash-Shura*), as stipulated in Article 58 of the Basic Statute. The Council meets at the request of the Sultan to study and discuss matters raised by him, making all of its decisions on the basis of a majority vote.

The Basic Statute does not specify the roles of both houses, as it was left for ordinary statute to determine each council's jurisdictions, sessions and procedures. Royal Decrees 86, 87, and 88 of 1997 are the main statutes regulating both councils, although nine amendments have been declared for both councils so far. Neither the Basic Statute nor the Royal Decrees specify clear distinctions between both houses beyond their membership and their main objectives to assist the government in formulating the general policies of the state and via different methods. But it could be deduced from both the Royal Decrees and government practice that the Elected House is more concerned with the local society, social-economic development and constituency matters, with representatives for all regions, while the Upper House focuses more on the State's top-level policy formulation.[55]

The membership of the State Council differs from the elected *Ash-Shura* Council's membership in that its members are appointed by the Sultan and must be natural-born of at least 40 years of age. Members must also possess suitable experience stemming from a government, academic, military or business career and notables. The number of State Council members must not exceed the number of *Ash-Shura* Council members. Their membership is for a four-year term and may be renewed. The Council will offer seasoned advice to the Sultan and work closely in co-ordination with *Majlis Ash-*

55 Economist Intelligence Unit (2001). *Country Report 2001: Oman.* London: EIU. p. 7.

Shura, "... thus strengthening Omans' consultative process and widening participation in the public life of Oman".[56]

Oman is the first among the Gulf States to adopt a bicameral parliament although it is a deliberative one. This step has been described in similar terms as the relation of the House of Lords to the House of Commons in the U.K system. In fact, it also followed the traditional Omani way of building the *'Ahl al-Hall wa al-Aqd'* council 'the Council to Dissolve (Impeach) and Convene (Instate)'. This Council used to have the authority, through its members who would largely be people of religion, scholars, wise and learned men and respected members of the public, to appoint into power (*'aqd'*) or remove from office (*'hal')* sheikhs and rulers.

A. Rabi suggests several reasons for establishing the second house ('the State Council') in Oman with appointed members:[57]

- It is parallel to the direction and path of the Sultan's thinking, thus it would not develop any radical policies.
- It balances and restrains the elected assembly ('the Shura council') which could challenge the government's policies.
- It rewards membership to elite, tribal leaders and established families.

In addition, it is clear that appointed members will be less sympathetic towards constituents, which could help to set the State's priorities and overall formulation more efficiently. The bicameral Upper House of parliament as selected on a specialised basis was one of the recommendations made in the U.S report "*In Support of Arab Democracy; Why and How*". However, the aim of such a recommendation is actually '*To ensure that extremists do not come to dom-*

56 Ministry of Information (2000). *Oman 2000.* Muscat. p. 36.

57 Rabi, U. (2002, October). *Majlis al-Shura and Majlis al-Dawla: Weaving Old Practices and New Realities in the Process of State Formation in Oman*. Middle Eastern Studies, p. 46.

inate democratic systems'.[58] Nevertheless, it seems that Oman has its own inducements which were planned years before publishing a report in response to the various terrorist attacks by radical Islamic movements during the last few years. Therefore, the adoption of a second assembly in Oman could be more complex, although it will lead to a much needed expansion of public participation.

5.3.5 Democratic Elections and the *Shura* Practice

Additionally, several changes are occurring in unison; the global information revolution is making the world smaller and the demographics of Oman are changing. Taking a country from its old traditional system where most of the people were uneducated, to adopting a western system without an affiliation to the country's traditions and history will be hazardous and fraught with risk. Therefore, the Sultan believes that Oman has to initiate its own plan for the development of democratic institutions. The Sultan states that progress towards democracy and public participation in Oman: "... *will expand with time, but slowly, so there are no earth-quakes* (sic). *But we are still largely a tribal society, and it's still the government's due to defend the country*".[59] It seems to be within his vision to push his country (albeit cautiously), which was subjected to diversity rebellions and illiteracy, towards a semi-democratic status.

For the first 25 years of his reign, the Sultan tried to build several councils with different degrees of public participation. This could be regarded as steps towards an increased participation, although most of these stages are based mainly on absolute nomination methods or with government involvement.[60] The expansion of pub-

58 *In Support of Arab Democracy: Why and How Report of an Independent Task Force No. 54* (2005). Retrieved September 14, 2007, from Council on Foreign Relations: <http://i.cfr.org/content/publications/attachments/Arab_Democracy_TF.pdf>, see p. 45.

59 Miller, J. (1997) p. 16.

60 As mentioned earlier at 'The developments of public participation', section 5.3.3.

lic participation increased in the *Shura* Council after the Basic Statute was promulgated, thus establishing the second house of parliament 'the State Council' with nominated members in 1996. The *Shura* Council became increasingly electoral with each term; it continues to its previous developments, the new ones after promulgating the Basic Statute can be elaborated by each electoral term. This is explained in the following four paragraphs.

- From the third term of *Majlis Ash-Shura* (1998–2000) there were some major developments, such as an increase in the number of members to 82, voters represented around 10% of population and female candidates were allowed to vote throughout the whole country. The highest vote won, although the Sultan still wielded the power to decide the final results, so 11 candidates with the highest vote in their state were replaced with the second candidate from the same state.
- In the fourth term (2001–2003) there were also some new developments, such as having 83 seats with direct elections (it was previously a hybrid system called nominations and choice); any citizen over 21 had the right to register in his state as elector; the public participation was limited to 25% of the population eligible for voting and female participation was more pronounced. The highest vote was declared the winner directly without the Sultan's intervention.[61]
- The fifth term (2004–2007) built upon the previous developments by increasing public participation to comprise all the national population eligible for voting, and extending the council's terms to four years instead of three. There were 15 women from 506 candidates and the council had 83 members including two women.
- In the sixth term (2008–2011) for the first time the candidates were allowed, to some extent, to advertise and campaign. There

61 Majlis Ash-Shura (2004). pp. 13-30.

> were 631 candidates competing for 84 seats representing 61 provinces. 388,683 Omani citizens had registered to vote and out of that number it is said that 63% showed up to vote, making it the highest voters' turnout in Oman's short electoral history.

Irrespective of the civil, legal and educational developments that have occurred in the last decade,[62] the last elections saw slower and weaker steps towards democracy than elections at earlier stages. This raises the question of future developments towards achieving full democracy. The specific developments the Sultan intends to put into place remain unclear, as does the time scale for the implementation of a powerful *Shura* and an expansion of public participation, which could wield full legislative power instead of playing a solely advisory role.

Indeed, the election process in Oman is adopting many "... *useful contemporary methods and tolls*"[63] such as secret ballot. However, the most integral elements of democratic elections are still not in place, such as the role of political parties and, most importantly, the legislative aspect and the accountability of the government which are hoped to be adopted in the near future.[64] Nevertheless, the *Shura* Council could be regarded as the most important political institution, embodying political rights and freedoms, within the Omani system today. Therefore, 'Democracy' does not seem the best way of describing the Omani political practice as it lacks many key features of western democracy. A more accurate term would be 'the consultation *Shura*' or more precisely 'mere public participation', since most of the legislative powers are not conferred in the Elected House or in the other nominated house.

62 Following the adoption of the country's first constitution.

63 Art. 10 OBSS.

64 See Chapter Seven about the recent developments.

5.4 The Council of Oman and Human Rights

Oman is a novice in terms of the concept of modern democracy, thus it is essential for the concept to become a central element of its institutions, in order to consolidate and instil a democratic culture within the Omani society. There are various institutions that can play important roles in establishing a democratic behaviour and culture as a way of life, such as the family, tribe or sect, social, educational institutions, civil societies, and the media. However, the most important institution is the Elected House (*Majlis Ash-Shura*), whose role is manifested in educating citizens through its own practices given that its members are the representatives of the people.

Its dialogues, methods, and behaviours through discussions and voting are part of its education and commitment to democratic norms and traditions. Its role as a national representative body based upon the people's interests and monitoring the government's performance, will consolidate the democratic concept and ensure its practice among the people. In reality, the *Ash-Shura* Council is a representative and advisory institution that can review legislation without any power to amend the country's laws. This remains the sole right of the Sultan. However, its position, elections, and decision making process all follow the democratic route, thus it could serve to educate the community on the basics of democracy.

Majlis A'Daula 'the State Council' on the other hand, is the body responsible for affirming the principles stipulated under the Basic Statute, of which human rights and civil liberties are a part.[65] However, its role and efforts in this area, apart from the affiliation of the 'National Human Rights Commission' to it, remains vague and it appears not to be taking effective steps to protect human rights in

65 According to the amended Art. 17 of '*the State and Shura Councils Regulation*' (R.D. 74/2003) and Art. 97 of *Ash-Shura* Council's Internal Regulation (R.D. 88/97).

Oman.[66] Despite the Council of Oman's consultative aspect, so far no issues relating directly to human rights have been discussed by either house; their annual reports concentrate mainly on economical, educational and social development issues.

One of the main objectives in establishing the Council of Oman is '*to expand the area of popular participation*';[67] yet unexpectedly, this objective has been implemented surreptitiously. The law has allowed members of both Councils to express their opinions freely, although their deliberations are withheld from the public. The confidentiality of the meetings of both houses is regarded as an obstacle for non-members. It reflects the ambiguities and uncertainties of its work as well the limiting of freedom of information. [68] Thus, media coverage of internal discussions of the Upper House is not allowed, and it is very limited in the *Ash-Shura* Council; this coverage is reserved for the meetings with Ministers of service departments. These restrictions extend into the media coverage regulations prescribed by law which use a loosely phrased clause that coverage should be "*... in accordance with the followed customs of the Omani society*". However, this gives the executive branch the power to interpret such clauses in accordance with its own interests, thus allowing the broadcast of parts or all of the meetings.[69]

The following sections will highlight the different perspectives of the Council of Oman and its role in protecting human rights. Most discussions will focus on the Elected House (*Majlis Ash-Shura*) based on the idea that '*If the members of the Parliament's rights are violated by any way, the parliament itself is weak to protect other*

66 The Commission is affiliated with the State Council 'Majlis Ad-Daula', but it exercises its functions independently. See section 3.6.2.

67 Preamble of the Council of Oman Affairs (R.D. 86/97).

68 Regulations forbid any public attendance to the meetings in either house. Art. 56 of the State Council's Internal Regulation (R.D. 87/97) and Art. 80 of *Ash-Shura* Council's Internal Regulation (R.D. 88/97).

69 Art. 81 of *Ash-Shura* Council's Internal Regulation (R.D. 88/97).

civil rights'. The power and existence of political parties and the role of women in Omani political life will be discussed at a later point.

5.4.1 The Power of the Elected House (*Majlis Ash-Shura*)

The Elected House is supposed to be the guardian of the public's interests. The *Majlis Ash-Shura* in Oman is the elected council which consists of 84 members chosen by direct and free elections. In addition to its advisory tasks, the power of the house is also weakened by 'the chairman' who is the speaker of the house, as he is appointed by the Sultan,[70] although his two deputies are elected by the members on the first meeting. Many politicians foresee that one of the next developments of the house is to introduce "the elected chairman".[71]

Elected House Membership and Privileges

There are different criteria for the candidates to become a member of the Elected House. According to Article 22.a of '*The State and Shura Councils Regulation*',[72] the candidate must be at least 30 years and should have native Omani nationality in accordance with the law.[73] Further qualifications and disqualifications include that the candidate should:

- Represent the electoral state that he or she belongs to.
- Not have been convicted of any serious crime or immoral offences, unless he or she has been rehabilitated.

Section 2 of R.D. 2/2007 has added five more criteria to the above requirements:[74]

- Be registered on the electoral register;
- Not be member of any military or security forces inside Oman;

70 He is the only appointed person in the House.

71 Probably the next election in late 2011 or in 2015.

72 The Council of Oman Affairs (R.D. 86/97).

73 As discussed earlier under Chapter Four dealing with Nationality Right.

74 Amendment to 'the State and Shura Councils Regulation' (R.D. 2/2007).

- Not be subject to a bankruptcy restriction order, unless he or she has been rehabilitated;
- Should not be interdicted by a court judgement; and
- Not be diagnosed with severe mental deficiency.

There are other "loose qualifications" such as *having a good reputation* and being *reasonably well-educated* which allows room for unfettered discretion in the government's intervention to define such qualifications, even if they have never been used.[75]

According to Olson, D (1980) "*Members of the national parliament tend to have more education than does the general population whom they represent*"[76] However, the case seems different in Gulf Countries which tribal society controls. For example, many members of parliament in Oman from the year 1991 to the year 2000 were the tribal leaders in their states and were not usually well-educated, having used their tribal powers to win the election. This led the Sultan to add a new provision for the Elected House's membership after the 1997 election, limiting the number of parliamentary terms that can be served to two.[77] While this provision could be depicted as an injustice, it was necessary to add new, young, educated members.[78] This provision has not remained current for long, however, and was changed after 6 years by the Royal Decree 74/03 to allow the renewal of the membership for more than two terms.[79]

The representatives of the people must enjoy certain guarantees to underline the importance of their standing, but, more importantly, to give them the peace of mind they need to implement their

75 Economist Intelligence Unit. (2000). *Country Profile 2000: Oman*. London: EIU. p. 7.

76 Olson, D. (1980). *The Legislative Process: a Comparative Approach*. New York: Harper and Row. p. 99.

77 Art. 2 'the State and *Shura* Councils Regulation', (R.D. 86/97).

78 For instance, In 2000 election, there were 61 new members as 73%, and 50 new members as 60.25% of the Elected House seats in 2003 elections.

79 Art. 2 of amendments of 'the State and *Shura* Councils Regulation' by R.D. 74/2003.

mandate. Therefore, parliamentary privileges and immunities are part of the parliament's custom, since the primary function of parliament is to debate and pass resolutions freely on subjects of its own choosing. Thus, it is important to exercise their functions freely and to protect parliament against "*... disruption and interference both by outsiders and from within its rank*".[80]

'Inviolability' or immunity, which is generally interpreted as the freedom from arrest,[81] is another Omani privilege, although the scope of its applicability, which derives from the purpose of the immunity, seems limited exclusively to criminal actions. These cover detention and/or imprisonment, investigation and opening of procedures, prohibition of searches on the members' premises and the prohibition of court (or tribunal) summons' against parliament members. However, there are some exceptions to immunity according to Article 6 of the *Ash-Shura* Council's Internal Regulation (R.D 88/97), which include:

- That immunity does not apply in the case of apprehension at the time of the act being committed. (*flagrante delicto*)
- With the authorisation of the Council if it is in session.
- With the authorisation of the Council's chairman between the sessions.

Among the financial and statutory privileges which most members of parliament usually obtain, the most important is that of '*freedom of speech and debate*' as Article 3 of *Ash-Shura* Council's Internal Regulation states.[82]

However, many restrictions on this freedom have been stipulated in the council's meetings with ministers of service departments.[83] These include the subject, methods and the time of the

80 Alder, J. (2007) p. 220.

81 ECPRD (2001). *Rules on Parliamentary Immunity in the European Parliament.* p. 5.

82 R.D. 88/97.

83 Articles 81 and 92 of R.D. 88/97.

member's speech, all of which resulted in giving the government member (the minister) the right to ignore the requests of the council's members.[84] Moreover, the jurisdictions and limitations of the Council remain the weakest link in protecting human rights.

5.4.2 The Limitations of the Council of Oman

> *"A number of regimes in the Gulf, if not all, are interested in reviving, activating and deepening the representational institutions for purposes other than institutionalisation. These purposes may entail pragmatic and political aspects aimed at sharing the blame, though not the authority, for decision-making and policy setting".*[85]
> Al Mukhaini: 2002

In addition to its consultation boundaries, there are several other limitations to the Council of Oman which includes the two houses *Ash-Shura* Council and the State Council. These limitations and restrictions are part of the institution's weakness and reduce its influence in efficiently protecting or even in demanding human rights. The Sultan is still the most influential factor; the legislative power is in his hands and, most importantly, he has absolute power to amend the Basic Statute. All Royal Decrees and statutes are declared by him without any power to object by the councils, although most social-economic statutes and regulations are reviewed by both houses.

Members' privileges and the Council's regulations are an example of the Sultan's intervention and power, in that he can determine such privileges by a Royal Decree, and undoubtedly he can limit or change them without any subject limitations.[86]

84 Art. 82.b.

85 Al-Mukhaini, A. (2002). *State Institutionalisation in the Oil Producing Monarchies: A Discussion on the Role of the State in Oman and Kuwait.* Muscat: Unpubl.

86 According to Youngs: "*The constitutional rules are more important than other legal rules ... and a particular government will not be able to change the rules about how it could lose power*". Youngs, R. (1998) *English, French and German Comparative Law.* London: Cavendish Publishing.

Other limitations can be classified in three main categories, the executive branch, between the houses, and the jurisdictional limitations.

The Cabinet plays the central role in relation to the state's policies, as it extends its reach beyond its own executive jurisdictions to cover legislation more than other Councils. Although the Sultan meets the Cabinet occasionally, and the Deputy Prime Minister of the Council of Ministers usually presides over Cabinet meetings, the Sultan's position as prime minister and head of the Cabinet is illustrative of the extremist power of the executive branch. The Basic Statute provides for a Prime Minister under Article 48 although the Sultan has not nominated one. Neither house has power to accept or veto the Prime Minister or any governmental minister's appointment.

The relationship between the executive and the Council of Oman takes a harmonious form due to the weakness of the Council to oppose the government. The government possesses both executive and legislative powers, the latter being exercised by the government more than by the Council. Both houses have to submit their initial bills, requests and recommendations to the Cabinet, with the majority of financial affairs dealt with by Cabinet members rather than members of the Council.

Another clear intervention by the government is visible in the role of the Ministry of Interior over the election. Instead of an independent committee or department, the Ministry has the responsibility of organising and supervising the election process and commissions, as well as the election's disputes.[87] With the absence of electoral law, the Ministry is also responsible for the electoral regulations and it introduces new developments for each term.[88]

The relationship between both houses regarding new bills and

87 Resolved by the Central Election Commission in the Ministry of Interior, headed by its Under Secretary and consisting of several members. Articles 15-19 of *Majlis Ash-Shura Elections 2003-2007 Regulation's Board.*

88 Art. 21 of R.D. 86/97.

statutory proposals was previously more integrated than it currently is. Most socio-economic bills were initially introduced to the Elected House for its recommendations, followed by the Upper House, with both opinions then being submitted to the Cabinet, which in turn would refer them to the Sultan for ratification.[89]

Unfortunately, this arrangement was dissolved through amendments to the *'The State and Shura Councils Regulation'* in 2000 and 2003. These amendments have weakened both houses positions in relation to the Cabinet, when what was actually required was the strengthening of their positions. Most statutes today are submitted from either house to the Cabinet without the compulsory reviewing from the other house. Unfortunately, these amendments have severed the relations between the two houses, instead of ensuring a stronger co-operation.[90]

For instance, amendments introduced by R.D. 104/2000 for Article 18.d have not merely severed (to a great extent) the relationship between both houses; they have also given the Cabinet the right to recommend statutes directly to the Sultan without being reviewed by either house. The 2003 amendments[91] have extended the council's legislative power to review all bills; nevertheless it restricted all recommendations by "*submitting them to the Cabinet*". Both amendments still ignored the relationship between the two houses.[92]

The majority of regulations by the Council of Oman contribute

---

89 Art. 18.d and Art. 29.a R.D. 86/97, and Art. 54 of R.D. 88/97.

90 The amendments have allowed, to some extent, both houses to give joint recommendations to the Cabinet.

91 R.D. 74/2003.

92 According to a report published on 27th May 2008 by the '*Azzamn*' newspaper in Oman showed that there were around 10 Statutes on the last few months have been promulgated by the Sultan after they have been reviewed by the Cabinet only without being reviewed by *Ash-Shura* Council. Azzamn Newspaper (2008, 27 May). *Government and the Shura Council: "Partnership to Where?" (in Arabic).* Retrieved 11 November 2008, from <http://www.azzamn.org/news_details.php?id=11502&dt=2008/05/27&st=Archive>

to its limitations and weaknesses, as it purports to be a parliament which can hold the government accountable.[93] However, the most important element of the regulations relates to jurisdictions. For instance, *Ash-Shura* Council is allowed to question government ministers, although it does not have any power to remove them from office.[94] Therefore, it is ultimately more about creating a forum for public discussion, primarily restricted to socio-economic matters that can only address their respective ministers.

The 2003 amendments to *'The State and Shura Councils Regulation'* had extended the *Ash-Shura* Council's authority to review all bills and statutes. However, it also limited the bills by a provision that "*The council cannot review bills which are submitted directly to the Sultan according to the national interest*".[95] The term *'national interest'* relates to the Cabinet's role,[96] and reflects the fluidity of the Council's boundaries and Jurisdictions, according to the Cabinet's determination.

In addition to other limitations, stipulated mainly in '*The State and Shura Councils Regulation*' and other related statutes, there are three clear categories in which both houses of the council have little or no jurisdiction. These are Internal Security and Defence, External Foreign policy and affairs, and the State's Monetary System. These areas are placed outside of the Council of Oman's jurisdiction for four reasons:

- The seriousness and sensitivity of the related departments on the State's overall public policy and the outlook of the Sultan's ruling. Since Oman is a traditional monarchy, the policies on these categories are highly personal and remain the exclusive domain of the Sultan and very small ruling elite. For instance, foreign policy decisions reflect the Sultan's "*middle-of-the-road*

93 Discussed earlier under section 5.4.

94 As is the case in Kuwait, for example.

95 Amendments to Art. 18.d and 29.a of the R.D. 86/97 by a R.D. 74/2003.

96 *Ibid.*

position on regional conflicts", although he has been consistently pro-Western.[97]

- The existence of specialised councils consisting of ministers responsible for each category. For instance, all questions relating to national security will be considered by '*The National Security Council*',[98] defence issues will be considered by '*The Defence Council*',[99] and all matters related to its economic system and the preparation of the annual General State Budget, as well as drawing up the state's fiscal policy will be considered by '*The Financial Affairs and Energy Resources Council*'. These councils are comprised of members chosen on the basis of rank or position.[100]
- The ministries or the councils related to these categories are headed by the Sultan himself; he has nominated responsible ministers for the Defence, Foreign Affairs, and Finance ministries. These councils also hold their sessions at the Sultan's direction and under his chairmanship.
- The law has stipulated explicitly that the Council of Oman shall pledge allegiance to the Sultan.[101] Consequently, the jurisdictions of the Council of Oman should not cover the Sultan's authority.

5.5 Omani Basic Statute and Political Parties

Freedom of association has been recognised as an international right in Article 20 of the *Universal Declaration of Human Rights* of 1948 and in Article 11 of the European Convention on Human Rights (ECHR), where both have declared that "*Everyone has the right to freedom of peaceful assembly and to freedom of association*",

97 Riphenburg, C. (1998). *Oman: Political Development in a Changing World.* Westport: Praeger.

98 R.D. 63/2003.

99 R.D. 105/96.

100 Refer to section 3.3 for more details.

101 Art. 3 (R.D. 86/97).

including political parties.[102] Political parties appear as one of the most prominent institutions of modern political pluralism. However, the subject of political parties in Gulf States is one of the most controversial issues, raised spontaneously with every election term,[103] although political parties are not permitted in all Gulf States' systems. Calls for permitting political parties are usually based upon the dictum *'no democracy without politics, and no politics without parties'*. Unambiguously, such calls reflect the pluralism within these societies even though the prevention of political parties appears to suggest otherwise.

All of the Arab Gulf States are on the *Authoritarian Regimes* list, positioning them as the most undemocratic among nation states according to the "*Economist Intelligence Unit's measure of democracy: Democracy Index 2010*".[104] Thus, what is the need for instituting political parties in these states? What does their current political situation reflect? Is it an appropriate cornerstone suggesting more political freedoms? In order to answer these questions it is essential to find out how this basic right is prevented and the reasons behind such prevention.

In Oman, as well as in other Gulf States, the prevention of political parties is not expressed under its Basic Statute or constitution. The Omani Basic Statute gives the citizens the right to assembly and the freedom to form societies,[105] although these rights and freedoms are provided within the '*limits of the law*' and '*the legitim-*

102 Although this part is connected to the freedom of association (Chapter Six), it has been brought here to draw the connection with Shura as one of the political rights in Oman.

103 The discussion of political parties issue raises with every election by those who want to adopt the western democracy or to avoid the tribal and sectarian influences over the elections. It is one of the hot topics during election periods due to the political atmosphere attached with the election environment.

104 Economist Intelligence Unit (2011). *Democracy Index 2010.* Retrieved 22 March 2011, from <http://graphics.eiu.com/PDF/Democracy_Index_2010_web.pdf>

105 Articles 32 and 33.

ate objectives', as interpreted by the government itself. It is illegal to force anyone to join any society under Article 33.[106] The types of societies which are explicitly prohibited under the Basic Statute include those whose activities are '*hostile to the order of society, secret, or of a military nature*'.[107]

Between the allowances and the prohibitions of the Basic Statute text, the government has largely restricted freedoms of association, which include the formation of political parties, according to the interpretation of 'the legitimate objectives' and the 'limits of the law', Furthermore, the government must approve the establishment of all associations.

There is no Electoral Statute under the Omani system as yet. The Royal Decree no. 86/97 on *'the Council of Oman Affairs'* and the Royal Decree no. 88/97 *'Ash-Shura Council's Internal Regulation'* are the key legal documents relating to the candidacy and elections.[108] Therefore, most restrictions upon political parties are not extracted from these decrees or regulations. The restrictions come solely from the Law of Civil Association issued by Royal Decree no. 14/2000, which states that all associations must register with the Ministry of Social Development. This body is responsible for approving association by-laws and includes any type of not-for-profit associations and societies such as professional, charitable, cultural and other Non-Governmental Organisations and associations.

Since declaring the law in 2000, no application to institute political parties has been raised to the Ministry, whose disapproval is predictably based on Article 5 of the Law. This article clearly pro-

---

106 This is identical to Art 20. s2 of the UDHR "*No one may be compelled to belong to an association*".

107 Most of other Gulf States constitutions have almost the same approach (Kuwaiti Constitution Articles 43 and 44, UAE Constitution Art. 33, Bahraini Constitution Art. 27, and Qatari Constitution Art. 45).

108 Along with the Electoral Regulations for most election terms issued by the Ministry of Interior.

hibits any political work by an association as well as preventing the institution of political parties. Article 11 gives the Ministry the power to refuse association requests based on '*the community need*', '*state security*' and '*other evaluated reasons of the ministry*'. This allows the Ministry alone to decide the proper interpretations for these conditions. Moreover, the Ministry is solely responsible for the evaluation of these conditions, with no recourse to an independent body or the authority of Parliament.

Another level of prevention arises from the Council of Ministers where the law gives it the power to allow or prevent any association which does not fit an extremely limited set of acceptable criteria, including women, children, the elderly and people with disabilities.[109] Moreover, neither the courts nor parliament has the power to override or even review the Council of Ministers' decision, reflecting to some extent the legislative power of the executive branch over the parliament.[110]

Political parties, as a concept, can provide communities with a clear view of various ideologies, which is not the case in Oman. The incompatibility between ideological streams is not present in the press nor in the political forums and the Omani Council, or even within any student society, all of which facilitate the idea of political harmony. Thus, anyone that stands as a constituency candidate for *Majlis Ash-Shura* will do so in a personal capacity based upon his own campaigning as an independent individual.

Although there is some door-to-door campaigning, the majority of campaigns are executed through the tradition of the *Sablah* or *Majlis*, where men get together and discuss issues of the day. During election campaigns these gatherings are held in the Majlis, or in large open-air tents, which serve as campaign headquarters where

109 Art. 4 of the Law of Civil Associations (R.D. 14/2000).

110 More analytical study of the Law of Civil Associations will be discussed under next Chapter 'The Freedom of Association'.

the candidate tries to convince those attending to support him before holding a banquet.

The weakness of political maturity and the problematic nature of cultural diversity are the main obstacles to instituting political parties in Oman. Otherwise, establishment political parties without any cautionary steps could be disastrous, and those steps should include clear ideologies which should represent the country's culture and the people's interests. If political parties were allowed to work freely today, two main factions could emanate: The tribal affiliation, and the religious affiliation.

Traditionally, the political systems of the Arabian Peninsula States have been largely dictated by their tribal structure and religious sects of Islam. This is so even in States which allow political parties to be part of their democratic system. Yemen is an example where the most influential party leaders are also tribal leaders and the tribe still plays a key role within their society. As the last elections showed, the tribal vote is also the main influential factor in Oman. Therefore the most effective way to gain votes is to draw on the support and power of the candidate's tribe in his state or constituency, rather than by recourse to his merit and qualifications.

Iraq is another example where the religion, precisely the sectarian, is the basis of many influential political parties today. Bahrain and Kuwait in which political parties are prohibited and where several political groups act as *de facto* parties are other examples where religious sects form the ideology of the main political groups.

These examples clearly illustrate the reasons for banning political parties in Gulf States. In both cases, the institution of political parties in Oman today would be a setback for its democratic development and political pluralism. It would deepen the divisive internal disputes which remained masked for decades. In contrast, ethnic minorities would suffer from further marginalisation and vulnerability.

It should be borne in mind that all of the Gulf States are *'oil monarchies'* where the "*tacit social contract in which the regime provides social and economic welfare in return for political loyalty*" is based upon a policy of 'no taxation and no representation',[111] thus making the prohibition of political parties a foregone conclusion. This is largely due to the oppositional nature of political parties, an anathema to the absolute monarchies of Gulf States. Allowing political parties to work freely will lead to a necessary opposition to the government which is usually headed by the monarch himself.[112]

Other reasons for the prohibition of political parties are various and can be categorised under three main lists; the traditional, historical, and ideological. Traditionally speaking, the prohibition in Oman could be explained by the need to avoid traditional tribal or sectarian parties having an impact on the nation's policies, hence allowing other minorities to participate.

Historically, the models of political parties present in other Arab States do not offer encouraging examples, leading as they have to a one-party government in practice,[113] or tyrannical governance,[114] and internal wars.[115] Moreover, the lack of a solid historical-political base in the Arab Gulf States, which would otherwise aid comprehension of the diversity of political parties, is another dilemma. People in these states have rarely experienced any other affiliations than their tribe, sect or religion. The principle of the devolution of

---

111 Rathmell, A., & Schulze, K. (2000). Political Reform in the Gulf: The Case of Qatar. *Middle East Studies*, 36,4, p. 47.

112 Indeed, Gulf States' governments have succeeded in gaining the loyalty of formerly leftist members and leaders, as is the case in Oman. This has been achieved by way of the Sultan's pardon or by awarding them high government posts as a way of winning their loyalty in an effort to instil a model of a harmonious state; such as the cases of Imamate supporters, the Dhofar revolution (the liberation of Oman) leaders, and coup plotters in 1994 and 2005.

113 such as Syria.

114 Former Egypt and Tunisia regimes.

115 Algeria, Palestine and Lebanon.

power based on the multiplicity of ideologies of each party is missing, the discrepancy between Islamic and liberal groups in Oman is, for instance, almost not sure. The principle of keeping religion out of the political arena is an unacceptable phenomenon for those lacking knowledge about the party's conception, and this combination with an inhibitive cultural environment will create serious obstacles.

Under Islamic jurisprudence many intellectuals believe that Islam is not against the formation of political parties.[116] However, some people try to ignore such a conception based on the linguistic or religious reflection of the term 'party' which they avoid using. This is because it reflects the disunity and divisions between people, a fact which is avoided by the believers of the unity of the Islamic society. A diversity based on tribal or religious grounds is more acceptable as a *de facto* feature of these societies. Oman may also have another reason for prohibiting political parties, stemming from its own ideology of '*genuine Shura*'.[117] Thus, if a political party's conception is an essential aspect of the democracy it is not within the *Shura.*

Indeed, political parties play an important role in society and there would be numerous benefits were the state to allow the existence of such parties. In addition to the key rights entailed in their existence,[118] there are palpable benefits attached to the distribution of services to the party's members. Political parties are essential to the protection of freedom of speech and expression. They play an active role in the country's political life and "*make an irreplaceable contribution to political debate*",[119] as well as providing the structure

116 Such as Ammara, M. in his book *Islam and Human Rights,* and Aljabri, M. in his book *Democracy and Human Rights.*

117 See section 5.2.

118 Political parties can be seen as embodying the principles of freedom of speech and human rights.

119 See Case of United Communist Party of Turkey and others v. Turkey, 133/

required to train the national cadres needed to work in the different governmental fields; particularly the political ones. This provides a peaceful means to the devolution of power. As a result pluralism emerges from within the community's homogeneity and integration.

However, there are three structural features that are key in successfully establishing a political party: the existence of a clear political vision able to implement the party line; the existence of a genuine public awareness of and belief in the respective parties and, most importantly, an overarching respect for the constitution in its essential role as the forum for all parties and individuals.[120] When ascertaining the prevalence of these features within the Gulf States, it becomes clear that there is a prevailing reluctance towards a cultural and legal shift accepting this. The concept of civil society has not been sufficiently developed in the Gulf States in order for it to mediate between the ruler and the people, an essential principle for political parties. As it is inevitable that these states will move from absolute to constitutional monarchies, a level of political freedom will be required, and these should not be far from political parties' movements.

Although political parties are prohibited, there are currently some semi-political parties at the other end of the spectrum of the Gulf States, in Kuwait and Bahrain. Both of these states have experienced modern democracy and public participation decades before the other Gulf States; even if they are still struggling to legally permit the existence of political parties.[121] This is despite of the fact that political societies were legalised in Bahrain and informal polit-

---

1996/752/951 (European Court of Human Rights, Strasbourg, 30 January 1998). Retrieved on 13 July 2008. From: <http://www.icnl.org/knowledge/pubs/CommunistPartyTurkey.pdf>

120 Aljabri, M. (2002) *Democracy and Human Rights.* Beirut.

121 Kuwait and Bahrain have experienced the calls for democracy and instituting political parties in 1921 and 1938.

ical groups are tolerated by the Kuwaiti government. Some claims in both States, especially from educated elites, concentrate on the need to institute and sustain stable democratic politics through the establishment of national political parties. However, these claims do not necessarily represent the views of people as a whole, as many of these views have little to do with the reality of social, economic and political structures of the countries.

Nevertheless, the cornerstone is to have an effective parliament before allowing political parties to be established, to ensure that the party is guided by national principles. Only when the political standards and practices of parliament have been properly established can the system cater for political parties and their related consequences. Historically,[122] the formation of most of the political parties has occurred from the internal level of the parliament.

This said, the question arises as to whether these States should necessarily adopt the concept of political parties or if a 'non-partisan democracy' would be more beneficial. The allowance and acceptance of political parties is not enshrined in the legal method itself, the central concern of the Gulf States being the formation of political parties at a distance from their national and political bases. There is currently no purpose for the existence of political parties in Oman since national politics remains external to both parliamentary houses (the upper level of policy making still solely the Sultan's responsibility). The next step towards increasing public participation, and in which the presence of *Shura* in Oman has, to some extent, begun to be effective in focusing on service at the local level as it can be more effective.

Today, it is appropriate to demand an increase in political participation and a democratic government with more parliamentary legislative power instead of asking for the possibility to institute political parties that neither the people nor the whole society are

122 Pre-twentieth century.

ready for yet. Bearing in mind that most of the successful political experiences, such as the European, Asian and American States, did not attain political stability and maturity instantly but rather this developed over many decades, often centuries to reach their current political status. Therefore, the same principle should be adopted by the Gulf States where the democratic development should take their own traditional and regional aspects into account.

In the meantime, an increased focus on the civil and professional societies currently permitted by the Omani legal system, could be a step toward developing a political basis in future developments. It is necessary for those societies to play important roles in relation to parliament's decisions as they are the only legal organisations the country recognises and which could provide more political awareness.

5.5.1 The Role of the Omani Civil Societies and Trade Unions in the Election Process

In a state that prohibits political parties, civil societies and trade unions play the most influential role in elections, since both of them are permitted by the Omani legal system. Trade Unions are guided by the Omani Labour Law (R.D. 35/2003), its amendments, and Ministerial Resolutions by allowing their existence and regulating their roles.[123]

Local societies on the other hand, are governed by the Law of Civil Associations issued in 2000. There are 93 registered societies and organisations which cover women, charities, the disabled and the activities of various professionals.[124] Both trade unions and civil societies are far from having a direct influence over the Omani political life, due to the regulations and laws prohibiting any polit-

123 Labour Law (R.D. 35/2003) as amended by R.D. 112/2006. Refer to section 6.3.1 for more details.

124 As of November 2008.

ical activity.[125] Their ability to influence people's behaviour through education can be seen as an initial step towards the acceptance of political parties in the future.

Trade unions are still too weak to play a tangible role in elections and for two main reasons: the majority of trade unions have only recently been established, as the amendments of Labour Law only came into force in July 2006, and that law does not cover the military and public sectors where most educated Omanis are employed, thus prohibiting them from gaining the benefits unions could offer. According to the Ministry of National Economy's statistics, around 6% of the Omani population are covered by the social insurance for workers in the private sector or those who are self-employed; the numbers of trade unions are still low and their roles within the community as a whole remains unclear.[126]

Secondly, trade unions are far removed from the interests of the candidates of the *Ash-Shura* Council, since the Council's role does not include any issues directly related to trade unions. However, local societies and organisations have not experienced this difficulty, a fact which should result in their gaining more influence within the electoral system.

Although most societies have an immediate connection with communities, the previous elections in October 2007 highlighted their relative inability to influence and educate people about the elections. Female societies were the most pro-active in supporting and gathering support for female candidates, but have still not succeeded in their mission.

The lack of political experience and knowledge is one of the issues which need to be concentrated on in Oman, as the weakness of civil societies within the political life has resulted in them from

125 See next Chapter for more details.

126 Ministry of National Economy (2008, April). *Manpower in Private Sector.* Retrieved 12 December 2008, from <http://www.moneoman.gov.om/book/mb/Apr2008/T14.pdf> There are around 30 trade unions as on March 2008.

having a significant influence. However, the Kuwaiti example, where political parties are also prohibited, provides a context in which civil societies have reached a level of maturity that they can play a key electoral role. Thus, for example many members of the Kuwaiti National Assembly originate from a civil society background, as a result of the society's successful membership. There are various benefits which accrue to a civil societies' membership, such as an increased knowledge of the community's needs, more mature approach towards the political process, and the potential to gain influence with regards to the directions taken and strategies planned. Therefore, the civil society is treated as a 'small parliament' where the potential National Assembly's candidate starts his journey. This is, unfortunately, not currently a feature of Omani politics.

5.5.2 The Political Role of Women

> *"Arab women's entry into the political arena is not without its difficulties. With the lowest regional average of women Members of parliament in the world, the Arab world ranks at 3.5% only, according to the statistics from the Inter-parliamentary Union".*[127]
> A. Karam: 1999

The political situation for women in Gulf States is worse than in other Arab countries, because of many interlinked factors related to religious thought, conservative society and traditional tribal views, together with the overall attitude of political leaders in Gulf Countries. Oman is one of the most progressive countries in the Gulf region as far as women's rights are concerned. Today, it has three women with Ministerial positions, two of whom are part of the cabinet. Oman was also the first Gulf country which allowed women to vote and to be a candidate in the elected house. Such developments

127 Karam, A. (1999, October). *Strengthening the Role of Women Parliamentarians in the Arab Region.* Retrieved 9 April 2008, from UNDP: <http://www.pogar.org/publications/gender/karam1/karama.pdf>, p. 3

were necessary as 49% of the population are female, although this necessity was not recognised until 1994, when, for the first time, female candidates were allowed in the capital district, winning two seats. Since then, this principle has been applied to include all regions of Oman. Moreover, the Sultan has stressed that out of the 72 members of the State Council at least 14 should be women.[128]

Oman's experience in this matter set a precedent for other Gulf States to follow. Today, the *Shura* Council in Bahrain includes eleven women nominated by its absolute monarch (The Emir) with women allowed to vote and stand as candidates for the House of Representatives, and a female candidate won one seat at the last elections. In Qatar, the first woman was elected to public office, as a member of the 29-member municipal council, in April 2003. Kuwait, which had the first elected Parliament in the region, created in 1963 after a long struggle for the vote, finally became the fourth Gulf Cooperation Council (GCC) member country to grant women the right to vote and stand for public office in 2006. In the same year, one woman was elected to the Federal National Council in Abu Dhabi and women gained political rights for the first time in the United Arab Emirates (UAE). The only exception is Saudi Arabia, where women's suffrage remains a very sensitive issue.[129]

In the last Omani elections in 2007, it is believed that more women than men voted in the election. However, despite the higher

---

128 As on March 2010.

129 Accordingly, the regional average of women in parliament in the Arab world has risen from 7% in January 2006 to 9% in January 2007. These developments, and within such a short time frame, are a result of new election regulations in the GCC States. However, the regional level of women's political participation remains the lowest in the world, and far from the world average of 17%. See Inter-Parliamentary Union: Second Regional Conference of Women Parliamentarians and Women in Decision Making Positions of the GCC States. (2007). *Women Making a Difference in Parliament.* UAE, 30-31 October 2007. Retrieved 12 May 2008: <http://www.ipu.org/splz-e/abudhabi07/information.pdf>

participation, and the fact there were 21 female among 631 candidates competing in the election, not a single woman managed to get elected. In fact, the two female *Shura* members of the previous council both lost their bids for re-election.

There are two facts resulting from this last election: Firstly, female participation as a candidate is still weak even though women form half of the Omani population. Oman introduced female candidacy more than 10 years before the rest of the Gulf States, though they did not reach the 3.5% of overall candidates. As a result, achieving gender balance in political life will be far from easy to implement. Secondly, although the number of female voters is high compared to male voters, no female has won an electoral seat yet. This reflects the current obstacles faced by women demanding their rights. This could be attributable either to the mistrust of female voters, who form the majority of the population, or by the male influence as a whole on the female electorate decision.

Indeed, it is a long and difficult struggle for the attainment of women's rights in the Gulf States. This is largely due to the traditional mentality which posits 'male supremacy' and the religious or social restrictions ensuing from such a concept. The female candidates' difficulty in identifying with male voters will continue, along with the argument that women are less competent than men, lack political maturity, and would neglect their families if put into office.

Introducing electoral seat quotas for women had been considered an important political strategy, and the Omani Minister of the Interior hopes to examine such a strategy in relation to future developments,[130] particularly as the only two female seats for three parliamentary terms have been lost during the last election. Nevertheless, this issue should be included in electoral rules and strat-

130 *Media Conference about Ash-Shura Council Elections 2007.* (2007, 2 January). Retrieved 12 May 2008, from Arab Woman and Political Participation website: <http://www.awapp.org/wmview.php?ArtID=1588>

egies, as this will create the necessary context for traditional constraints to be overridden and for public awareness to be enhanced. Taking into account the most recent political experiences for women in Oman and other Gulf States, there are other recommendations to be made. These would include the strengthening of women's knowledge of political processes and their role in parliament, enhancing public awareness about advocated women's rights through media influences and religious support, and giving women more power and decision-making roles both in the government and in public life.

5.6 Conclusion

John Adler in his book, the '*General Principles of Constitutional and Administrative Law*' states that:

> *... the electoral system can only be assessed in relation to its aims; these could be to secure democratic local representation, to produce effective government or to produce an 'accountable' government.*[131]

An assessment of the electoral system in Oman can be made by connecting it with the principle of 'separation of powers'. However, in Oman the electoral system's aims were outlined in its early days through the *Shura* Consultation, and it was focused on the citizens' right to take part in public affairs rather than the creation of a democratic government under the people's sovereignty.[132]

The situation of separation of powers in Oman can be described as more harmonised, in the sense of absence of conflicts between the branches, such harmony stemming from the Sultan's and government's powers together with the limitations of parliament. Nevertheless, what should be noticed here is that Oman's Basic Statute was clear in specifying the powers which were in the hands of the

131 pp. 245, 246.
132 Art. 9 OBSS.

Sultan. Moreover, there are different councils and institutions in Oman which have taken some of the powers of the parliament.

Oman is the first Gulf Country to have a bicameral Parliament; all Upper House members are appointed by the Sultan and most of them have a variety of experience from different careers. The establishment of the Upper House was intended to offer seasoned advice to the Sultan while working closely in co-ordination with the Elected House.

In Oman, since parliamentary practice is in a fledgling stage, the people are still unfamiliar with parliament. It seems that many people, especially most well-educated people, do not see the Elected House as an effective body, which is mainly due to its functional limitations. However, some people, especially the elderly, believe and trust in the Sultan's rule. Thus, they do not demand more democracy or more parliamentary power, because they appreciate the governmental progress brought about by the current rule.[133]

There are certain other obstacles to the Elected House becoming more powerful, such as the newness of its parliamentary experience, its tendency towards tribalism, public lack of awareness of the parliamentary system, and the limitations of its functions resulting from its domination by the government.

The Omani system can be described as a developing system, in that with every election term new developments are introduced to the lower house system, with such developments contributing towards more public participation. However, what is actually needed today is an increased development of its powers and functions, such as the binding nature of its decisions, and more legislative power to influence and observe the executive branch. Currently, Oman is still

133 Of course, the media also plays an effective role in raising people's knowledge and points to the main problems existing between the Council and the government. The laws have allowed the media to criticise the government. However, the media in Oman it is not effective as it is slow to criticise the government, thereby not being the source of public awareness it is meant to be.

a way from having the parliamentary powers of a western democracy.

Though political rights are rarely mentioned directly under the Basic Statute, other human rights or civil liberties, which constitute one third of the articles of the Basic Statute, are far from being protected; neither house has discussed them in relation to specific cases or issues. For free elections to exist, substantial respect for these freedoms should be ensured, as these are also very limited and cannot be discussed by the advisory body which lacks its own rights.

6 Freedom of Association

Freedom of association is a right, and not something that must first be granted by the government to citizens.[1]

6.1 Introduction

The principle of political pluralism is one of the most important foundations of the democratic system; it allows the transfer of power based on the right of people to oppose peacefully, which is inherent in the right to associate and assemble and in their freedom of expression.

International human rights law recognises the right to freedom of peaceful assembly and the right to freedom of association with others in two stages; firstly as one right under Article 20 of The Universal Declaration of Human Rights, which was followed by a similar adoption in the European Convention on Human Rights under Article 11, of the Convention on the Elimination of Racial Discrimination of 1966,[2] and Article 24(6) of the Arab Charter on Human Rights. A later step came from Articles 21 and 22 of the International Covenant on Civil and Political Rights which admitted the right of assembly as a standalone right and separate from the right of association. This was also followed by several regional conventions, such as the American Convention on Human Rights,[3] and the African Charter on Human and Peoples' Rights.[4]

With the exception of Saudi Arabia, all other Gulf States guarantee the freedom of assembly and association under their constitutions. Kuwait, Bahrain, Qatar, and Oman have separated these rights and freedoms as standalone rights by recognising the assembly as a

1 Under Art. 22 of ICCPR, as well as other major international conventions.
2 Art. 5 (d) (ix).
3 Articles 15 and 16.
4 Articles 10 and 11.

right, and the association as a freedom, while the United Arab Emirates has combined both of them as freedoms under one article.[5]

The right to associate with others and form or join associations, trade unions and political parties is correlated with freedom of expression and opinion. The right to associate is also connected to freedom of peaceful assembly, freedom of movement, and other rights and freedoms that foster democracy and pluralism. In fact, the European Commission has defined freedom of association as "*A general capacity for the citizens to join without interference by the state, in associations in order to attain various ends*".[6]

However, this freedom may require more assurances other than 'run and join an association' as '*Governments could restrict the ability of groups to operate freely. They might interfere with the internal decisions and organisation of the association with devastating consequences*'.[7] Moreover, although the right to associate is protected by several international human rights instruments as an individual right,[8] it might also be regarded as a collective right when applied to unions, associations, corporations, and other entities, '*... assuming that the association itself had certain rights*'.[9]

---

5 Although there are no clear reasons for such a distinction.

6 X v. Sweden (preliminary objections), 6094/73, § 52, DR 9 (1978) (European Commission of Human Rights 6 July 1977).

7 Marshy, M. (April 2005). *Freedom of Association with regard to Political Parties and Civil Society in the Middle East, North Africa, and the Gulf: A literature review.* Retrieved 13 September 2010, from International Development Research Centre (IDRC): <http://www.idrc.ca/uploads/user-S/12018943281Pub_Mona_Marshy_doc.pdf>, p. 6.

8 'Everyone has the right to freedom of peaceful assembly and association' UDHR 48 (Art. 20), 'Everyone shall have the right to freedom of association with others.' ICCPR (Art. 22.1)

9 Such as treating the associations as groups with a separate identity, thus having the right to protect their interests and identities; see Human Rights First (February 2007). *The Neglected Right: Freedom of Association in International Human Rights Law.* Retrieved 8 May 2010, from <http://www.humanrightsfirst.org/pubs/descriptions/neglrt.htm>

Although, the Freedom of association is guaranteed by many national constitutions worldwide,[10] governments in the Middle East have the ultimate power to restrict and hinder this right in their own country. Their constitutional provisions usually provide the right of association by highlighting the guidelines for the right in general and leave the details to be implemented by relevant laws and regulations.

It is important for a community to consider the adoption of fair and clear laws to regulate this freedom and to protect and support the formation of associations for several reasons. Since freedom of expression and freedom of assembly promote pluralism and tolerance within a society, this in turn reinforces social stability and the rule of law. However, the power to enact laws usually resides with the legislative branch, and this is the preserve of an elite few in most Middle Eastern countries.

This chapter seeks to explore the freedom of association in Gulf States' systems in general and in Oman in particular; and the extent to which these civil societies and labour unions have fulfilled their potential to support the right of association. It analyses the obstacles limiting associations' abilities to increase influence and improve society.

The term 'association' in these systems refers to three different types of associations based on legal statutes and current practices. These are: Civil associations including non-governmental organisations (hereinafter referred to as NGOs), trade unions and political parties. Political parties will not be covered as no Gulf State permits

10 Constitutionally, the right of the people to assemble peaceably is explicitly guaranteed in the First Amendment of the Constitution of the United States of America without including the protection of the freedom of association. Although it is not expressly protected in the constitution, the Supreme Court ruled it to be a fundamental right protected by its Fourteenth Amendment. On the other hand, the Canadian Charter of Rights and Freedoms which is constituted as Part I of the Constitution of Canada of 1982, has acknowledged each one as a fundamental freedom articulated under Article 2.

political parties,[11] therefore this chapter will further examine the freedom to associate with regards to civil associations (NGOs) and Unions.[12]

6.2 Freedom of Association in the Gulf States

The concept of association was manifested in most Gulf States with the existence of different types of civil and voluntary activities than those that also arose as the countries opened up and modernised subsequent to the discovery of oil and increased engagement with the rest of the world. Most associations were based on tribal and religious affiliation even if other civil orientations existed. Historically, the mosque played the most influential role in associations, as it was the focal point for any civil activities including charitable, religious missions, and voluntary activities. In Oman, endowment institutions, traditional irrigation management systems (*falaj systems*),[13] and the cooperatives of professions and traders in each village had various levels of influence in the construction of civil society. Other civil activities include cultural, social, and sport clubs.

The discovery of oil in the region in the 20th Century profoundly transformed the political, economic, and social structure of both society and the state. This transformation resulted in the emergence of new forms of civil works and activities in states. As a result, most Gulf States have introduced legislation to control changes to civil

11 Please refer to earlier discussion in Political parties, section 5.5.

12 For convenience, this Chapter will refer to organisations in general, interchangeably as any non-governmental entity, whether the organisation is an "association", a traditional non-governmental organisation ("NGO"), a labour "union", club, or any such group.

13 The system of *falaj* consists of tapping the water table of the mountains and moving the water via man-made subterranean channels and siphons across the wadi beds to the plains where it is used for irrigation and other domestic purposes. See *The Traditional Aflaj Irrigation System.* (2005). Retrieved 13 September 2010, from Nizwa.NET: <http://www.nizwa.net/agr/falaj/chapter1.html>

societies, which had been predominately controlled by the rules of customs and traditions.

One may assume that non-democratic Gulf States are indifferent to civil societies or the establishment of NGOs, but some studies have shown otherwise. The Executive Office of the Council of Ministers of Labour and Social Affairs in Gulf Cooperation Council (GCC) estimates that there are approximately ten thousand associations with different objectives in the Gulf States, with an estimated one million members.[14] This statistic includes unlicensed organisations and their members, which shows that the majority of organisations work without official permission, as the number of officially recognised organisations do not reach a quarter of the above estimate.[15]

6.2.1 Gulf States Constitutions

With the exception of Saudi Arabia, all Gulf State constitutions guarantee freedom of association.[16] Each state presents this freedom differently in the respective constitutional text. Some constitutions sum up the right by guaranteeing it within the limits of the law,[17] without any further elaboration and lacking any reference to the illegality of forcing anyone to join an assembly.[18] However, this is

14 Mahmoud, H. (2009, July). *The reality of civil work and its constraints in the Gulf States*; paper presented at GCC Volunteering Forum, Abu Dhabi, (2009). Retrieved 17 September 2010, from Emaratalyoum website: <http://www.emaratalyoum.com/local-section/2009-06-28-1.151713>

15 For instance, the number of registered associations in Oman does not exceed 93 as of November 2008, and the establishment of civil associations is not permitted in Saudi Arabia. The two countries together are the largest in Gulf States with respect to the land size and population.

16 Hence, whenever Gulf States is used in this Chapter it does not include Saudi Arabia unless otherwise stated.

17 Art. 34 Constitution of the UAE and Art. 45 of the Qatar constitution.

18 As mentioned earlier, the UAE constitution has combined the freedom of assembly and freedom of association under one Article 34.

not the case in the three other Gulf States' constitutions, namely, Oman, Bahrain and Kuwait.

The Bahraini and Kuwaiti constitutions have explicitly mentioned associations and unions as part of the guaranteed freedom since they are formed on a national basis and by peaceful means.[19] However, none of the Gulf States' constitutions mention political parties as part of the freedom of association or as a right by itself.

Oman, on the other hand, is much more specific about this guarantee. The conditions in Article 33 of the Omani Basic Statute have expanded upon Article 32, which has simply noted the right was controlled by the limits of the law. Article 33 of the Basic Statute is unique and different among other Basic Statute articles in that it presents the conditions of this right. Other provisions under Gulf States constitutions relate to civil liberties typically use short phrasing with general rules, leaving the details and restrictions to be addressed through normal legislation other than the constitution and adapted from time to time to make it more flexible.

One might argue that the detailed provisions in Article 33 mentioned above are actually restrictions based on the political perspective enshrined under this right. It is possible, for example, to provide such details in a normal statute instead of listing them in the constitution. This shows the regime's caution with respect to granting this freedom to citizens and the possible threats inherent in the right of association importance of the Basic Statute.

When comparing Oman's Article 33 to Article 27 of the Constitution of Bahrain and Article 43 of the Constitution of Kuwait, the Basic Statute has not explicitly listed unions and as such the right to unionise is not part of Oman's freedom of association provisions. Moreover, Article 33 is focused on other conditions that are not contained in other constitutions, namely that '*this freedom is not in conflict with the provisions and objectives of the Basic Statute*' and '*it*

19 Art. 27 Bahrain Constitution and Art. 43 Kuwait Constitution.

is prohibited to form societies the activities of which are: adverse to the order of society, secret, and of a military nature'.[20]

While it might be acceptable to mention those conditions in any ordinary law, raising these issues in constitutional text gives them an importance and seriousness that is significant. There might be several political-historical reasons for including them under the Basic Statute. During the current rule of Sultan Qaboos and before the promulgation of the Basic Statute, several groups were formed in Oman. Many of these groups were motivated by ideologies antagonistic to the monarchy, and most of these groups fall within the listed prohibited conditions, such as secrecy or an activity of a military nature. Some were even in conflict with the provisions and objectives of the Basic Statute, including that '*The system of government is Sultani (royal), hereditary in the male descendants of Sayyid Turki bin Said bin Sultan*'.[21] Other reasons might stem from the historical and religious background of the country, particularly the background of the *Ibadi* sect and its doctrine of the Imamate governing system, which is based on choosing a ruler by election and does not acknowledge the hereditary system. One of the Imamate system stages is based on a state of concealment and secrecy (*Kitman*) when it is not possible for *Ibadis* to rule the country.[22]

6.2.2 The Statutes Regulate the Freedom in Gulf States

In the Gulf States, as well as in many other authoritarian regimes, enacting statutes and regulations to control this right is the most ef-

20 Art. 32 OBSS.

21 Art. 5 OBSS.

22 *Ibadis* accept that there are times when conditions make it impossible to rebel against illegal Islamic rulers. Accordingly they defined four stages in which their true Muslim community could exist: the state of manifestation (*Zuhur*), the state of defence (*Difa'*), the state of self-sacrifice (*Shirah*), the state of concealment and secrecy (*Kitman*). See al-Nami, A. (2007). *Studies in Ibadhism.* Retrieved 11 October 2010, from Open Mind: <http://www.lulu.com/items/volume_62/1035000/1035883/1/print/STUDIES_IN_IBADHISM.pdf>

fective tool for governments to have the ultimate power to decide upon the formation of the associations, their membership, to impose taxes on them, to allow access to funds, to oblige them to report on activities or to obtain government approval for their activities and participants. Undoubtedly, through enactment of laws, governments can easily curb organisations that oppose them or at least organisations that the government perceives as a potential threat; especially if the legislator is not elected or is immune from accountability.

Almost all of the Gulf States follow the Egyptian model of imposing legislative restrictions on civil societies, which are the legal face of the hegemony exercised by the States.[23] Bahrain was the first Gulf State to legally regulate the freedom of association; even before obtaining independence and before its first constitution, the 'Licensing Act of Associations and Clubs in Bahrain', was announced on 24th February 1959.[24] After gaining independence and

23 Egypt's Law of Associations and Private Institutions was introduced in the second half of the 20th Century. It began in Egypt with the July Revolution of 1952 and the abolition of political parties and many associations and trade unions. It was followed by the sixth conference of Arab Social Affairs experts held in Cairo in 1960, which concluded that the need for Ministries of Social Affairs to impose full control over volunteer work in each Arab country; this was adopted accordingly in Egypt by the Law of Associations and Private Institutions (32/1964), and many Arab and Gulf States subsequently. See Farahat, M. (2006, February). *State, civil society and the law: 'Notes on some aspects of the legislative discrimination against women in the Arab World' (in Arabic).* Retrieved 3 October 2010, from Studies Centre; Working paper submitted for conference of civil society and the empowerment of Arab women – Bahrain: <http://www.amanjordan.org/aman_studies/wmview.php?ArtID=1082>
For the resolution see The Recommendations of the Sixth Conference of the Arab Experts on Social Affairs, (s1729/d p. 34/c 3) on 07/09/1960. (1960). Retrieved 12 May 2010, from Moqatel Encyclopaedia: http://www.moqatel.com/openshare/Wthaek/title/GamatDowal/AGamatDowal1730_87-1.htm_cvt.htm> #1730

24 The Act is downloadable in Arabic from Bahrain's Ministry of Legal Affairs website. Retrieved 14 May 2010: <http://www.legalaffairs.gov.bh/viewpdf.aspx?ID=K0559>

announcing its constitution, Bahrain enacted the 'Law of Associations, Social and Cultural Clubs, Special Committees Working in the Field of Youth and Sports, and Private Institutions' No. 21 of 1989. This law is still the main regulatory statute today.[25]

In Kuwait, the Law of Association No. 24 of 1962[26] is still the main law regulating NGO activities, although it was amended several times.[27] Some of these amendments were more restrictive than liberal, for example, the Law of 1965 raised the age of the founding members of an association from 18 to 21 years.[28] Qatar's Law number 12 of 2004, the Law of 'Associations and Private Institutions' changed Law 8 of 1998. The law of 12/2004 has already been put into the amendment process by Qatar *Shura* Council and the amendments are going to be approved by 2011.[29] In the United Arab Emirates (UAE), the current law issued in 2008, 'Law 2 of 2008 Concerning Associations and Public Welfare Associations' has made some positive changes on the old statute 'Law 6 of 1974'.

Despite the fact that Saudi Arabia has never guaranteed freedom

---

25 It was amended by Law 44 of 2002 and Law 42 of 2009, and other implementing Ministerial Resolutions which have the force of the law, as Article 91 of the Law of Association states that a violation of any of their provisions is punishable by a penalty not exceeding 50 Dinars. See: The International Federation for Human Rights (FIDH) report. (2009, March). *Freedom of Association in the Arabian Gulf: The Case of Bahrain, Kuwait and Yemen.* Retrieved 1 May 2010, from <http://www.fidh.org/IMG/pdf/etude.pdf>, p. 11

26 Enacted the same year as the constitution was promulgated.

27 Law no. 28 of 1965; Law no. 75 of 1988; Law no. 12 of 1993; Law no. 14 of 1994.

28 According to the Ministry, Law no. 75 does not exist although it is published in the Official Gazette no. 1804 of year 35 and does not seem to have been abrogated. The same restriction prevents unregistered NGOs from exercising any activities, which was not the case with the original law. For more details see: (FIDH) report '*Freedom of Association in the Arabian Gulf: the Case of Bahrain, Kuwait and Yemen*'.

29 Alraya Newspaper (13 April 2010). *Shura Council Recommends Amending the Law on Private Associations and Institutions.* Retrieved 22 July 2010, from Arab Legal Information Network: <http://www.eastlaws.com/news/news.aspx?id=3054>

of association, charitable and professional societies existed without any legal regulation until 1961. The establishment of the Ministry of Work and Social Affairs, followed by the adoption of several regulations, allowed limited charitable, scientific and professional associations. The NGOs that currently exist in Saudi Arabia were established either by separate royal decrees or because they fall under one of the regulations that have been declared for some types of associations. Most associations are subject to absolute governmental control and must comply with different regulations of licensing authorities.[30] Today, the Saudi system is still missing a single legal framework to govern the work of associations and NGOs. However, in 2006, Saudi Arabia announced that it would adopt a new law which will regulate all types of civil societies and NGOs. A draft by the Saudi *Shura* Council has been before the Council of Ministers for approval since 30 December 2007.[31]

Oman, on the other hand, has had 'The Law Concerning Clubs and Associations in Oman' since 1 January 1972. At that time, Oman was new to contemporary developments, and the law came into being to regulate NGOs and clubs, including sport clubs. Interestingly, it also regulated charitable organisations, including animal rights organisations,[32] an area the country was not familiar with at that time. This law might be regarded as the basis of the current Omani Law of Civil Association issued by Royal Decree no. 14/2000, (hereinafter referred to as LoCA) which replicates many provisions of the old law.

Today, the right of associations in Oman is governed by 2 different governmental bodies by different legislations. The Ministry of

30 Al-Shayeb, J. (2006). *Prospects and Constraints on Civil Society in Saudi Arabia.* Beirut: a paper submitted to the Conference in Support of Civil Society in the Arab Region from 3 to 5 July 2006.

31 Sometimes the draft bill from *Ash-Shura* Council will be used for the comparison with other Gulf statutes in this Chapter.

32 Art. 5.2.

Social Development is responsible about the Law of Civil Association, and the Ministry of Manpower controlling the Labour Law and Labour Union Regulation.

The Omani Law of Civil Association came to regulate the right to associate as mentioned under Article 33 of the Basic Statute, and it has been amended four times within seven years by Royal Decrees nos. 30/2001, 55/2001, 41/2002 and 23/2007.[33] Also, there are two main regulations governing the civil association in Oman; the 'Regulation of Foreign Communities Clubs'[34] and the 'Regulation of Conditions, Rules and Procedures for Granting Licenses to Raise Money from the Public'.[35] On the other hand, Oman's Labour Law R.D. 35/2003 with its amendments and Ministerial Resolutions are regulating the Labour Unions.[36]

6.3 The Law of Association in Oman and the Freedom

Most political theorists consider freedom of association to be essential to the development of civil society and democracy. However, based on the statutes that regulate the associations, the Gulf State regimes view free organisations and societies with suspicion and as threats to the regime or the system. Their laws do not reflect a true understanding of the importance of NGOs as partners with governments in society's development. These restrictions tend to control civil society instead of organising it.

The civil societies in the Gulf States region today are weak, and they work under increasingly heavy pressure from the government. Some of the NGOs, specifically the human rights organisations and

33 Some amendments added more restrictions. Such as Article 5.f. which restricts providing any support outside Oman to only through *Omani Charitable Organisation* and Art. 6 which increases the minimum number of founding members required from 20 to 40.

34 Ministerial Resolution 32/2003.

35 Ministerial Resolution 157/2005.

36 See section 6.3.1 for more information.

oppositions groups, encounter more obstacles and hindrances than other organisations, because of their role in discussing issues that some governments prohibit. These obstacles come in the form of legislation or administrative decrees to hamper or prevent the operation and activities of these groups.

The concept of freedom of association should not be limited to the right to form or join an association freely; this freedom should also cover the operational functions of associations, where most of the governmental interference takes place. Article 8 of the International Covenant on Economic, Social and Cultural Rights (ICESCR) requires state parties to ensure '*the right of the trade union to function freely*'. Although this refers specifically and only to trade unions, it shows an understanding that the right to 'form and join' an organisation may not be sufficient to enable an individual to fully realise a right to freely associate.[37]

In this regard, the following discussion will highlight the freedom of association in Oman from different perspectives through analysis of specific core provisions relating to the formation, function and dissolution of associations. It will examine the right to establish an association, to join an organisation, and to affiliate with international organisations. Moreover, it will check the status of NGO presence of independent judicial review and freedom to operate without unreasonable governmental interference. Labour unions, also called 'trade unions', which are often treated differently from other associations under Omani Law will also be considered. Finally, it will check the current sanctions and penalties listed by the law.

6.3.1 The Role of Labour Unions as Associations in Oman

The right to form a labour union ('union') is not mentioned under the Omani Basic Statute. This omission is contrasted in the Bahrain and Kuwait constitutions, which provide for the right to form a uni-

37 Human Rights First (2007). *The Neglected Right.*

on. Oman denied the right to establish labour unions until 2006, when new amendments allowed the formation of unions and protection of their activities. Today, unions are regulated through Oman's Labour Law R.D. 35/2003, its amendments (R.D. 74/2006 and R.D. 112/2006) and Ministerial Resolutions (294/2006), (311/2006), (17/2007) and (59/2010).

Customary international law recognises the right to organise unions as fundamental human right. For example, conventions promulgated by the International Labour Organisation (ILO) recognise the freedom to organise unions as universally applicable regardless of state ratification.[38] Oman joined the ILO in 1994, but has ratified only half of their core labour standards to date. Oman has not ratified, among other conventions, Convention 87: Freedom of Association and Protection of the Right to Organise, and Convention 98: Right to Organise and Collective Bargaining.[39]

After promulgating the Basic Statute in 1996, it was necessary to change several statutes which were not in line with it; such as the old Labour Law (R.D. 34/1973) which was changed by the current Labour Law (R.D. 35/2003) to regulate labour in the private sector. When it was published in 2003, the old restrictions on forming unions were also present in the new law. These restrictions were removed in 2006 when Oman attempted to conclude the US-Oman Free Trade Agreement (OFTA) to fulfil goals of diversification of income and attracting international investors. This agreement was criticised by many U.S. democrats and lobbies because of the Omani

38 The principles established in ILO conventions and interpreted in a long line of ILO cases are valuable and can help the right of freedom of association found in "traditional" human rights law.

39 The Government indicated that ratification of C.87 and C.98 are under consideration. See ILO. (2009). *Country Baselines under the 1998 ILO Declaration Annual Review (2000-2008): Oman*. Retrieved 6 July 2010, from <http://www.ilo.org/wcmsp5/groups/public/---ed_norm/---declaration/documents/publication/wcms_decl_facb_omn.pdf>

Labour Law restrictions on the right to assemble.[40] The objections and criticisms pushed Oman to issue a new Royal Decree which amended the law by allowing the existence of unions and collective bargaining (R.D. 74/2006). This was followed by another amendment (R.D. 112/2006), four months later, to allow the unions to establish several labour associations.

Based on the Labour Law amendment (R.D. 74/2006), the Minister of Manpower is responsible for issuing and enforcing regulations.[41] The latest Ministerial Resolution in this area is M.R. 59/2010 dealing with the 'Regulation, Formation, Work and Registration of Labour Unions, Labour Associations and the General Confederation of the Sultanate of Oman's Workers'; hereinafter called 'the regulation' or 'M.R. 59/2010'. It replaced the old regulation (M.R. 24/2007) and introduced new or more restrictive provisions and reduced the scope of freedom granted by the 2007 regulation.

The right to establish unions in Oman has created an opportunity for freedom, due to the new amendments, changing the old system of 'representation committees', where the government had absolute power. The regulation also eliminates the requirements that unions must notify the government at least one month in advance of any meeting and that union leaders must speak and write Arabic.[42]

6.3.2 The Right to Establish an Association

In parallel to the Basic Statute provision, the Omani Law of Civil Associations 14/2000 might be regarded as the most restrictive law in the Gulf States; even more than the pending new Saudi system;

40 Reuters (16 January 2005). *UAE, Oman must make new move for FTA, says US.* Retrieved 2 August 2010, from Citizens Trade: <http://www.citizenstrade.org/ctc/wp-content/uploads/2011/05/reuters_uaeomanlabor_01162005.pdf>

41 Art. 110 (Omani Labour Law).

42 International Trade Union Confederation (ITUC) (2009). *Internationally-Recognised Core Labour Standards in the Sultanate of Oman: Report for the WTO General Council Review of Trade Policies of the Sultanate of Oman.* Retrieved 4 May 2010, from <http://www.ituc-csi.org/IMG/pdf/TPR_Oman.Final.pdf>

which has already been heavily criticised by different researchers and institutions.[43] The strictness of the Omani system is clear from its initial articles, which includes the definition of association, the acceptable areas for NGOs, and the prohibited activities of registered NGOs.[44]

The definition of association under Article 1 of the law is vague and ambiguous enough to allow the government broad discretion in their interpretation of the terms used, resulting in arbitrary denial of registration for organisations. It tries to determine the individual responsibility in advance for any violation that might happen, which reflects governmental concerns about organisations.

Taking the example of the persons allowed to form an association, the definition only recognises 'natural persons' (not juridical persons) whereas both are recognised by all other Gulf State statutes.[45] On the other hand, under the same definition, it requests any non-governmental (juridical persons) to register their sub-branch NGO activities, '*... even if physical sports are among their activities*'.[46] Overall, the registration should be done by individual members, not institutions.

---

43 Saudi National Society for Human Rights. (2009) *Second Report on the Status of Human Rights in the Kingdom of Saudi Arabia 2008.* Retrieved 17 May 2010, from <http://www.nshr.org.sa/FCKFiles/Second_Report_on_the_Status_of_Human_Rights.pdf> Also the report from Al-Arabiya News (2008, January 30). *Saudi Arabia: Criticism to the new draft regulation of "Civil Society Institutions".* 3 May 2010, from <http://www.alarabiya.net/articles/2008/01/ 29/44907.html>

44 Art.1, Art. 4, Art. 5r and Art. 5r1 (LoCA). Articles 2 and 3 are more about nominating the Ministry of Social Development as the administrative department responsible for implementing the law, and to exempt some NGOs from this law; where they are organised by separate laws; for instance, the sports clubs and endowments which are regulated by Law 41/2001 and Law 65/2000 respectively.

45 Art. 1 (Qatar Law 12/2004), Art.1 (Kuwait Law 24/1962), Art. 4 (Bahrain Law 21/1989), Art. 2 (UAE Law 2/2008), and Art. 2 (Saudi Arabia: bill under consideration).

46 "unless sports are the main activity of the association or the club", Art. 1.3 (LoCA).

However, the main restriction in Oman actually comes from the set of acceptable areas for NGOs. The very short list originally stipulated under Article 4 of LoCA which is frustrating for most NGOs, as the list only contains five areas: orphan care, maternal and child welfare, women's services, aged care, disabled and special groups care. This orientation is different than other Gulf States, as none of them has been as specific as Oman regarding acceptable areas.

The law allows other areas to be added to the list only by the suggestion of the Minister of Social Development and after the approval of the Council of Ministers. Within a few months after issuing the law, a Ministerial Resolution (149/2000) included professional organisations in the list. This was followed by amendment to the law by Royal Decrees 55/2001 and 41/2002, which applied this law to the associations formed by foreign communities in Oman,[47] and gave the Council of Ministers full authority to allow (or disallow) the formation of associations that do not comply with any provisions of the law (Article 5r).

The Omani system in seeking to avoid any interference of civil societies with traditional tribal or religious policies does not allow any religious activities under the association law, leaving such responsibility to the Ministry of Endowments and Religious Affairs. Despite religious activities being one of the popular NGO's activities in other Gulf States, the law prohibits any religious sub-activities of any registered organisation.[48]

Reasons for denial also includes multi-activity work as it is not allowed for any organisation to work on more than one area or activity, unless it has received an approval from the minister,[49] and it cannot work on any activity that is not listed in its own regulations.[50] The Ministry has the full authority to reject the organisation

47 Art. 5r1 (LoCA).
48 Art. 5 (LoCA).
49 Art 4.6 (LoCA).
50 Art. 5.a (LoCA).

or to accept its application based on several other vague and arbitrary reasons; effectively, these give the Ministry the full power to interpret or decide an organisation's fate by itself. Reasons might include: the community not needing services; the existence of another organisation in the area of activity that meets the needs of society or that the establishment of the organisation does not enhance the state's security. The law also gives the Ministry the full discretionary power to choose other reasons not listed under the law.[51]

Regarding labour unions, the Labour Law, its amendments and the Ministerial Resolutions are only applicable for workers employed in the private sector. Other categories of workers, such as government and security personnel and those in the armed forces, are covered by different national laws that do not allow them to join or form a union. Additionally, the regulation[52] came with a new provision to prohibit an employer from becoming a union member, which was not the case with M.R 24/2007. This is contrary to ILO Convention 87, which allows the existence of an organisation of employers as well.[53]

Thus, the right to form or join a union is still limited to one sector and this right does not apply to all categories of workers in the sector, such as those who are working in fisheries, agricultural and domestic workers, those who have informal employment, and employers. In International Labour Law, public employees have the right to organise and the only exception applies to the police and armed forces if it is contrary to national law.[54]

Forming political parties is clearly and absolutely prohibited un-

51 Art. 11.

52 M.R. 59/2010.

53 Articles 2-11 of the c.87 (ILO).

54 Art. 9 of convention 87. Although the extent to which civil servants are able to enjoy these rights has been a matter of debate in a number of countries. See Human Rights Education Associates website (2007). *Freedom of Assembly and Association*. Retrieved 13 April 2010, from <http://www.hrea.org/index.php?base_id=146>

der Article 5 of LoCA and Articles 16.2, 28.2 and 39.2 of the Labour Union Regulation.[55] The same articles also prohibit any 'political activity'. This term is undefined and broad, and such ambiguity may give the government a basis for broad interference with union activity, allowing it to be used to disallow the existence of any human or civil rights activities, or NGOs working to monitor elections, provide legal aid, or defend the rights of political prisoners.[56]

Registration

In 2004, the then Special Representative of the United Nations Secretary-General on Human Rights Defenders stated in her report to the UN General Assembly that *'Decisions to deny registration must be fully explained and cannot be politically motivated'*, which is definitely not the case in Oman or in other Gulf States.[57] The Special Representative also states in her report that NGO registration should not be compulsory and that '*NGOs should be allowed to exist and carry out collective activities without having to register if they so wish'*. She also recommended the adoption of a 'declaration' or 'notification' whereby an association is considered a legal entity as soon as it has sent notice of its existence to the relevant governmental department.[58]

Oman, as well all other Gulf States, has a system of prior authorisation before an organisation may carry out any activity.[59] It is

55 See more details about political parties in Chapter Five.

56 Some Arab states, such as Egypt, have limited the scope of meaning to 'advancing political party interests and participation in party's election campaigns using NGO personnel or funds'.

57 59th session of the UN General Assembly. (2004). *UN Special Representative of the Secretary General on Human Rights Defenders Report (A/59/401).* Section 3, par 82.d; p21. Retrieved 13 April 2010, from UN website: <http://daccess-dds-ny.un.org/doc/UNDOC/GEN/N04/533/18/PDF/N0453318.pdf?OpenElement>

58 *Ibid*, section 3, par 82.a; p. 21.

59 The Laws of Association. Art. 2 (Kuwait), Art. 6 (Qatar), Art. 7 (UAE), and Art. 8 (Bahrain).

reasonable to require registration for an NGO to attain legal status; however, imposing registration as a prerequisite for an association to start its activity is a violation of Articles 22 and 25 of ICCPR. Article 1.3 of Omani law requires the registration of every kind of association, as prescribed by the definitions previously discussed, before the association can work in Oman.

Based on M.R. 59/2010, a labour union must have at least 25 employees. A union must submit: an application letter with the suggested union's name, address and the union's activities; a list of the founding members; the minutes of the meeting held to establish the union; and the suggested bylaws.[60]

Recent regulation does not authorise the creation of more than one union per company,[61] and it imposes several conditions on the union's membership, similar to the LoCA, which did not exist before, such as stipulating that the member has not been *'convicted of a crime or a felony of honour of dignity unless their rights have been restored'* and has to obtain a *'no-objection certificate'*.[62] The new regulation limits a union's freedom by discouraging new members from joining or by reducing the current membership after the new regulation was introduced. The conditions are a step back for the right to organise, and unnecessarily burdens union activities. Moreover, the Ministry holds the final word by its power, not to expressly reject, but to request more information that is deemed important for registration within one month of receiving the application.[63] It is not clear what kind of information would be important or necessary since the requirements under the current practice are clear. Transparency is a key issue in protecting the right to form a union, and if the meaning of the term 'important' is vague, this might result in denying or delaying the formation of a union.

60 Art. 4 (M.R. 59/2010).
61 Art. 45 (M.R. 59/2010).
62 Art. 3 (M.R. 59/2010).
63 Art. 5 (M.R. 59/2010).

On the positive side, the regulation stipulates a time limit for the registration process, which did not exist in the LoCA. As explained below, no time limit exists for associations that are not unions. For unions, the Ministry of Manpower must issue a certificate of registration within 90 days after its announcement in the Official Gazette.[64] However, the Labour Law and the regulation do not clarify what happens if the processing takes longer than the time allowed. It is necessary to have the presumption that an application is approved after a delay of more than the allotted period in order to protect the right to form unions.

Bureaucracy controls the registration process for civil associations, resulting in one of the obstacles that prevent many applications; although registration is cheap, the registration process takes a long time, and there is no time limit for the Ministry of Social Development to respond to applicants.[65] According to the '2009 Country Reports on Human Rights Practices: Oman', the average time to receive approval and register an association in Oman is approximately two years, often longer, although the process can be as short as two months.[66]

Unquestionably, the approval time is based on the set of requirements and the level of ministerial interference involved in formalising the NGO structure and bylaws, which could involve the Council of Ministers. The Special Representative emphasised in her report that governments should allow for quick registration, and the law must set short maximum time limits for governments to re-

64 Art. 6.

65 Most Gulf States give a time limit for the administrative authority to respond, 30 days in Bahrain (Art. 7), Qatar (Art. 7) and Kuwait (Art. 8), and 60 days in UAE (Art. 7).

66 U.S. Department of State, Bureau of Democracy, Human Rights, and Labor (2010). *2009 Human Rights Report: Oman.* Retrieved from: <www.state.gov/g/drl/rls/hrrpt/2009/nea/ 136077.htm>

spond to registration applications. If a government fails to do so, the NGO should be allowed to operate legally.[67]

The LoCA also limits the minimum number of founding members needed to establish an association,[68] requiring them to submit bylaws of the association signed by at least 40 individuals.[69] In the case of foreign communities clubs, 100 founding members are required, and they are not allowed to operate in Oman unless 2000 citizens from the nationality in question exist in Oman.[70] Raising the minimum number is proven to deter individuals from forming associations and reduces the number of applications received by the Ministry.[71]

One of the advantages of Omani law is that allows non-citizens to join, to be a founding member of an association, and to be one of the elected board of directors. That is not the case under UAE, Kuwait and Qatar Laws, which request that all founding members be of the state's nationality before he or she can apply as a founding member of an association.[72] However, formal registration of nationality-based associations in Oman is limited to one association for each nationality.[73]

---

67 59th session of the UN General Assembly (2004). Section 3, par 82.c, p. 21.

68 Art. 6 (LoCA).

69 The number was doubled from 20 members by the amendment of the law by a Royal Decree no. 23/2007.

70 Articles 3 and 4 of the foreign communities Clubs Regulation.

71 All other Gulf States require fewer founding members than Oman; 10 founding members are required in Bahrain (Art. 4) and Kuwait (Art. 4), and 20 in UAE (Art. 3.1) and Qatar (Art. 2.1.a). According to the International Federation for Human Rights (FIDH) report '*Freedom of Association in the Arabian Gulf: the Case of Bahrain, Kuwait and Yemen*'. <http://www.fidh.org/spip.php?page=article_pdf&id_article=6475> <01-05-2010> It appears that the Kuwaiti Decision 836 of 2004 stipulates rules and conditions that are not in the Law. For example, associations should have 50 founding members; p. 33

72 Art. 3.4 (UAE), Art. 4 (Kuwait), and Art. 2.2.a (Qatar), although the Qatar law has given the exemption power from such conditions to the Council of Ministers (Art. 2.2.d).

73 Art. 3 of the Regulation of Foreign Communities Clubs (M.R. 32/2003).

LoCA requires unnecessary personal information about all founding members, such as their religion, age, career, and address.[74] Other conditions exist for individuals to join any association;[75] a member has to be at least 18 years old, and not 'convicted of a felony or misdemeanour involving moral turpitude or dishonesty unless has been rehabilitated'.[76] Additionally, it requires a 'no-objection certificate', issued by police and security departments, although this requirement is more of a certification of good conduct or lack of criminal record.[77] Interestingly, this certificate is not required for a more critical position, such as running for *Ash-Shura* Council (elected house of parliament).[78] Thus, the requirement for a certificate can be interpreted to prevent those who are against the government's policy from running an association or from being one of the founding members by using security department services.[79]

Legal Status

Legal status confers several rights, such as the ability to open a bank account, rent premises and other operational activities, all of which enable the NGO to function. The LoCA has given the Ministry the responsibility to announce and disclose the approved or-

---

74 Art. 7b, and Art. 9.1. In the case (N.A.A.C.P. vs. ALABAMA, 1958) where the National Association for the Advancement of Colored People (N.A.A.C.P.) was requested to provide a list of the names and addresses of all its members and agents in Alabama, as well as financial and legal records, the American Supreme Court held that in practice there was a grave danger that NAACP members would be subjected to harassment and that the organisation's effectiveness would be compromised. For more information see *Human Rights First*, (2007).

75 Art. 7.f.

76 Those conditions are different under the foreign communities club, as the minimum age is 25 years Art. 4.c of the regulation (M.R. 32/2003).

77 Art. 9.5.

78 Art. 22 of the State and Shura Councils Regulation (R.D. 86/97) about the candidate's requirements.

79 The same requirement exists under Art. 8 of Kuwaiti Association Law and the certificate should be from the Ministry of Interior.

ganisation in the official gazette free of charge if it was not rejected.[80] Thus, the juristic and legal personality of any organisation is attained only after this publication.

The legal personality of the labour union is granted after the registration, within the time period mentioned in Article 6 of the regulation.[81] The legal personality will allow the union to represent its members, and seeks to protect and advance their interests by negotiating with employers regarding pay and work conditions. Unions may also conduct activities related to health benefits and education facilities for their members, to present grievances and represent its members in the courts or before the government.[82] These rights were not present in the LoCA.

However, there is limitation on the right of an organisation to possess properties or other kind of possessions, as the law has limited these '*to the extent necessary to achieve the purpose for which it was created*'.[83] Once again, the Minister can give special permission based on the Ministry's determination of the '*necessity*'.[84] The same article also contradicts Article 40 which allows the organisation's board of directors to exploit the surplus revenues of a profitable business to ensure a stable income for the organisation.[85] Other limitations cover opening branches of the organisation or even moving the organisation from one location to another, as it needs to obtain permission from the Minister 30 days before opening a branch or moving the main branch from its location.[86] Since the organisation

80 Art. 10 (LoCA).

81 Art. 110 of the Labour Law (R.D. 35/2006) and Art. 6 of the regulation (M.R. 59/2010).

82 Art. 7 (M.R. 59/2010).

83 Similar article under Bahraini Law (Art. 7).

84 Art. 13 (LoCA).

85 Article 40 (LoCA) was amended by a Royal Decree no. 23/2007 which cancelled the governmental approval before spending on profitable business, despite the fact that such cancellation is required for Article 13 too.

86 Art. 14 (LoCA).

has already received legal status, it should not be necessary to impose these restrictions, and which only reflect the government's absolute control over the organisation's daily work.

6.3.3 The Right to Join (or Not to Join) an Organisation

The LoCA gives each association the right to establish its own rules and regulations in its bylaws with respect to membership requirements and duties, thus allowing the association the right to retain the control over its members.[87] However, the Minister still has control over this right too, as he has the right to nominate temporarily a manager or a board of directors, based on several cases listed under Article 34.

Theoretically, a temporary nomination is regarded as a remedy for those non-functioning associations or organisations in violation of state rules; this power permits the government to take full control of the association's activity. It could be used to manipulate their work and to change their activities or directions, especially if the nominated members are government employees.

Article 34 does not mention the illegality of forcing any one to join an association, but this is covered by the Basic Statute, which states that '*It is unlawful to force any one to join any society*'.[88]The labour union's regulation allows unions to join other local unions, to form Labour Associations among five or more unions, and to join the 'General Confederation' of the Sultanate of Oman's Workers, which is regarded as the main association for all Omani labour unions. However, the Labour Law has limited the formation of federation to a single federation of unions in Oman, which is contrary to ILO Convention 87.[89]

87 Art. 7.d.

88 Art. 33 OBSS.

89 Art. 109 (Labour Law). Also see International Trade Union Confederation (ITUC), 2009.

6.3.4 The Right to Affiliate with International Organisations

There is considerable control over the freedom of associations and their right to communicate with outside organisations, as it is not allowed for any association to affiliate or even to join or participate with any club or association outside Oman, unless approval has been granted by the Minister. The restrictions cover sending delegates from the Omani organisation abroad or hosting any delegations coming to Oman without the Ministry's approval.[90] Those restrictions have an impact on an NGO's work and activities as it limits its abilities to communicate and participate with similar international NGOs. This in turn reduces its abilities to get regional or international experience and to develop, learn, and innovate.

There is no clear provision under the law as to how non-Omani NGOs can work in Oman. Apparently, the only way is to submit an application to the Ministry similar to other NGOs, and the founding members are required to be from Oman.

Due to international agreements, labour unions are provided with more freedom to associate with international organisations. Article 5 of ILO Convention 87 explicitly guarantees the right to affiliate with international organisations. Article 109 of the Labour Law mentions that the General Confederation of the Sultanate of Oman's Workers represents all unions at local, regional and international meetings or conferences. However, neither the law nor the regulation address a union's right to affiliate with international organisations, leaving this area as a grey area for the government to exploit whenever it deems necessary or expedient.[91]

90 Art. 5.d (LoCA).

91 The regulation also refers to the Unions' Associations and the General Confederation rights to organise their relationships with regional and international organisations, where such right is not present at the labour union level. Articles 24.8 and 34.2 of the regulation (M.R. 59/2010).

6.3.5 Financial Matters

One important aspect of LoCA is the concentration on the financial issues of an association, starting from the opening of a bank account, to sources of funding, its expenditures, checking and auditing of accounts and statements, and submitting financial reports to the Ministry. Each organisation must open a bank account with an Omani bank and inform the Ministry about the account.[92] The law does not allow for tax exemption for any NGOs, although such exemption is typically important to support an association's activities. The only government support granted to some associations is the financial support based on the authority's discretionary criteria and the conditions mentioned in Article 45.

Under LoCA, an association may only invest surplus revenues in profitable businesses,[93] but the law has not determined what kind of business is allowed, leaving such decisions to be made by the organisation's board of directors. However, engaging in financial speculation is not allowed.[94] Prior permission is also required from the Ministry to collect any money from the public, or to hold public parties, or to host a charity event.[95]

The suspicion of external interference in internal affairs exists in all Gulf States. For instance, the Omani government restricts the flow of funds to any association, particularly funds from abroad, even from individuals, unless permission has been granted from the

92 Art. 39.

93 Art. 40.

94 Art. 41.

95 Art. 5c and Art. 44 (LoCA). Permission is also required to accept donations, contributions, and bequests, or any other income not specified under the law (Art. 37 – LoCA). Although, these are the main financial sources for most organisations internationally, an organisation in Oman should obey the 'Regulation of Conditions, Rules and Procedures for Granting Licenses to Raise Money from Public' (M.R. 157/2005), which also regulates any charitable events by private companies and people. In all cases, the Minister of Social Developments has the final word in this regard without any right to appeal.

Ministry;[96] otherwise the person will be subject to criminal penalties.[97] Similar restrictions have been implemented in all Gulf States.[98] More restrictive provisions for sending funds internationally comes from Article 5r which prevents any kind of support to international third parties, individuals or organisations, except through the Omani Charitable Organisation.[99] Although this article came as amendment to the original law, it contradicts Article 42 which allows an NGO to transfer money abroad with Ministerial permission.[100]

6.3.6 Independent Judicial Review

A critical factor in the freedom to associate is the ability to be subject to independent judicial review. Article 11 of LoCA has given the Ministry the full right to refuse registration of an association based on general and vague terms as discussed earlier.[101] Unfortu-

96 Art. 42 (LoCA).

97 Art. 54.7 (LoCA).

98 Art. 31 (Qatar), Art. 43 (UAE), Art. 20 (Bahrain).

99 Art. 5r is an amendment provision in R.D 55/2001. The Omani Charitable Organisation was established in 1996 according to the Royal Decree no. 6/96 as a semi-official charitable organisation. It is a civil charitable organisation subject to governmental financial supervision.

100 The Human Rights Committee, in its concluding observations for Egypt in 28/11/2002, stressed that foreign funding should be accessible and unrestricted, and such restrictions are inconsistent with the provisions of Article 22 of the ICCPR. The Special Representative also stressed the same, and further that governments must allow access to foreign funding as a part of international cooperation. A civil society is entitled to the same consideration as governments, and transparency is the only legitimate requirement for NGOs. See (59th session of the UN General Assembly. (2004) Section 3, par 82.d, p. 22. Human Rights Committee (2002). *Concluding observations of the Human Rights Committee: Egypt - CCPR/CO/76/EGY. (Concluding Observations/Comments).* Retrieved 20 May 2010, from UN ICCPR: <http://www.unhchr.ch/tbs/doc.nsf/385c2add1632f4a8c12565a9004dc311/89189f6057f03fdec1256c68002f1ec4?OpenDocument>

101 Refer to the right to establish an association or a union; section 6.3.2.

nately, the association's right to appeal that decision to an independent judicial body does not exist.

Moreover, the law does not require the Ministry to respond to the applicants in a specific time, which gives the Ministry the right to hold applications for years without a formal decision. This might be done by the government for specific semi-political and human rights organisations; especially for the cases where external pressures exist, such as international organisations and governments.

The law gives the applicant the right to be informed by registered mail about a rejection and the Ministry should provide the reasons for the rejection. The law allows the applicant to write a petition to the Minister against the decision within one month of receiving the rejection letter. The decision about the petition rests with the Minister and is regarded as the final disposition of the complaint.[102]

The Labour Law explicitly prevents any government interference; however, it is notable under the regulation, mainly in the latest version, that the government controls many aspects of the right to form unions without any judicial review. Such review would be useful in cases of application rejection, as the regulation allows any third party to submit an objection with regard to registering the union to the Ministry within 30 days of announcement. The Minister forms an independent committee for such objections, mainly comprised of government staff, instead of members of an independent tribunal. Similarly, the right to dissolve a union remains within the Minister's power.[103] The Administrative Court has not received any complaints from unions in this regard yet. Future complaints may serve to examine the judicial review on the right legally.

Courts are not involved in any part of this law or in reviewing the decisions made by the executive branch, or even in determining

102 Art. 11 (LoCA).

103 Art. 46 of the regulation (M.R. 59/2010).

if the rules have been applied to the law or not. The only part where courts are involved in the freedom of association is Chapter 8 of the LoCA, which looks at sanctions and penalties. Even the right to dissolve the association is given to the Minister instead of a court.[104] This allows the Ministry to dissolve or suspend an association, or merge several associations without the need for a session before the courts. It has this right based on loose conditions, such as '*if the association has committed a grave breach of the law or regulations issued*' or '*violated public order or morality*', and these are ambiguous enough to be interpreted arbitrarily by the government and used to suspend the association. In all events, the law prohibits members from continuing activities after the association's dissolution.[105]

All of the above hinders the people's right to associate without any judicial review, and gives the executive authority, mainly the respective Ministries, to hold over one of the judicial aspects of the law, and this contradicts the Basic Statute, which states that the judicial branch is independent.[106]

6.3.7 The Right to Operate Freely without Unreasonable Governmental Interference

Unreasonable governmental interference permeates almost every aspect of the Omani Law of Civil Association. Out of 60 articles, more than half provide grounds for governmental interference, especially by the Ministry. In effect, the Ministry must approve any exercise of the freedom of association.

Governmental interference in the freedom of association occurs on two levels. The higher level is controlled by the Cabinet or Council of Ministers, which controls the formation of associations. It has the power to include new areas where associations are per-

104 Art. 47 (LoCA).
105 Art. 48 (LoCA).
106 Art. 60 OBSS.

mitted to work,[107] and the power to establish associations that do not have the terms and conditions set forth in the law or to exempt those associations from some provisions contained therein Article 5r. Undoubtedly, the royal decrees also play an important role in this regard, as the way of amending the law.

In practice, the Cabinet limits freedom by prohibiting associations whose activities are deemed '*adverse to the order of society*' or in '*conflict with the provisions and objectives of this Basic Statute*' as stated, by not approving the existence of organisations regarded as a threat to the predominant social and political views or the interests of the country.[108] These provisions serve as a "catch-all" provision allowing arbitrary government action.

The lower level of the interference is exercised by the Ministry of Social Development as the administrative authority responsible for the civil associations, and it supervises and control many aspects of an associations' work, thus limiting the right to practice freely.[109]

In addition to the abovementioned ministerial tasks and powers, there are more powers given to the Ministry in general or to its employees, including the minister. These include:

- The power for a Ministry employee, who is granted law officer status,[110] to access any association premises and to check all reports, resolutions, statements, documents, and correspondences. In addition, it has the power to close the association's premises and its branches for a limited time by ministerial resolution.[111]
- The Ministry has to be informed 15 days before any ordinary general meeting, and it has the right to delegate a governmental

107 Art. 4 (LoCA).

108 U.S. Department of State, Bureau of Democracy, Human Rights, and Labor, 2010.

109 Art. 3 (LoCA).

110 Art. 17 (LoCA).

111 Art. 58 (LoCA).

employee to attend the meeting.[112] The Ministry also has to receive the minutes of any ordinary general meeting and board of directors meeting within 15 days.[113]

- A great interference comes from Article 33 which allows the Minister to evocate the meeting or its resolutions or part of the decisions based on reasons that can be determined by the Ministry itself. Moreover, the Minister can change the whole board of directors for two years or nominate a person as a manager to control the association.

The Minister also has other powerful tools to exert full control of any association or organisation. Article 46 gives the Minister the power to merge more than one association and the merged associations have no right to object or refuse. Moreover, Article 47 has given the Minister, and not a judicial court, the right to dissolve the association.

Labour unions are more flexible than NGO's in this regards. Article 110 of the Labour Law has explicitly given unions the right to work free of interference and undue influences. In practice, the labour union is requested to submit two copies of its bylaws to the Ministry of Manpower,[114] which can cause the postponement, even rejection, of the establishment of the union. For instance, if a union's '*bylaw is inconsistent with the provisions of the laws and regulations in Oman*'.[115] This recently developed provision contains a great danger to the right to organise, which could lead to paralysis of union activity through, for instance, using the Law of Civil of Associations which has a list of several prohibited activities.

A new provision also has been introduced in the regulation to allow the Minister to dissolve a union based on a final judicial ver-

112 Art. 23 and Art. 31 (LoCA).

113 Art. 28 and Art. 32 (LoCA).

114 Art. 13 (M.R. 59/2010).

115 Articles 8, 24, and 35 (M.R. 59/2010).

dict in cases of grave breaches of the regulation or public order or morals;[116] this might open the door for infringement of the free exercise of union rights by the government. Although the dissolution must be based on a judicial verdict, it is desirable to leave the final word in dissolution to the court and not the government.

6.3.8 Sanctions and Penalties

In addition to the powers and the ministerial control over associations, the LoCA has listed several sanctions under Chapter 8, which includes imprisonment and/or fines, and without prejudice to any other penalty provided for by the Omani Penal Law or any other law.

Some of the reasons listed provide for highly reactionary penalties and these infringe the right to associate. They include the criminalisation of those who run a non-registered association without approval, or those who initiate an activity contrary to the purpose for which it was created, allowing non-members to participate in the deliberations of an ordinary general meeting, or even accepting donations without ministerial approval.[117]

The UAE law (2/2008) and the Kuwait law (24/1962) might be regarded as the best in this regard, as they do not have any imprisonment sanctions compared to Oman and the other Gulf States.[118] An exception exists for unions in Oman. An interesting point about the regulation of unions is the lack of any kind of sanctions or fine provisions.[119]

116 Art. 46.4 (M.R. 59/2010).

117 Art. 54 (LoCA).

118 Art. 57 (UAE), Art. 31 (Kuwait), Articles 89-92 (Bahrain), and Art. 43 (Qatar).

119 Laws and regulations usually provide for penalties, especially for those that organise any right or freedom related to expression and information. The Press and Publications Law (R.D. 49/84), the Law of Radio and Television Facilities (R.D. 95/2004) and the Law of Civil Associations (R.D. 14/2000) all listed several sanctions and penalties that weakened those freedoms and rights tremendously.

It is possible that the authorities have deliberately decided not to list the sanctions and fines regarding unions to show tolerance regarding this freedom to enter in the free trade agreement and demonstrate compliance with international labour standards. In either case, it is a positive step which should be followed with regard to the LoCA as well. Another positive step under the labour unions is that, the Labour Law bans the government and employers from punishing or dismissing workers based on their union activities, and introduced penalties for those who prevent workers from forming or joining union activities which could encourage the union's work;[120] if other constraints do not exist.

6.4 Conclusion

Several external factors influence the freedom of association in most Gulf States, mainly in the political context, where the regimes are either undemocratic or totalitarian. Thus, granting this freedom could lead to demand for more political freedoms and, perhaps political parties, which are prohibited in all Gulf States.

Article 22.2 of the International Covenant on Civil and Political Rights (ICCPR) permits restrictions on freedom of association only in certain clear circumstances as prescribed by law and as necessary in a democratic society in the interest of national security or public safety, public order, the protection of public health or morals or of the rights and freedoms of others. However, the restrictions stipulated in most Gulf States do not favour the protection of individual interests. Thus, Gulf States try to limit the number of approved associations in order to have more control over their activities. These laws include too many restrictions and grant the government power that is too broad. Although some states have semi-liberal conditions with limited freedom, Oman is different. Its Law of Civil Associations is a collection of the most restrictive provisions from its old

120 Articles 110r and 112 of the Omani Labour Law.

law and from other Gulf States' laws combined with new provisions.[121]

The current official statistics for registered labour unions in Oman show a lingering reluctance regarding the formation of new unions.[122] General lack of appreciation of the importance of unions may be due to historical experience with many government restrictions on forming unions. This incompetence may also be based on the current experience with NGO practices under LoCA and the restrictions implied therein. Many workers are hopeful about the results of the current exercise of the right to form new unions, but government enforcement regarding the protection of this freedom will be necessary to encourage workers to form new unions.

Comparing the Law of Civil Associations (R.D. 14/2000) on one hand with the Omani Labour Law (R.D. 35/2003) and Labour Unions Regulation (M.R. 59/2010) on the other hand,[123] shows how the latter law and regulations are more in favour of protecting the freedom of association than the former; although those amendments do not originate from the government's full understanding of the importance of the freedom nor from the suggestion of the Oman Council.

The amendments were part of the qualifying criteria for concluding the OFTA,[124] which pushed Oman to change its law; the Royal Decree was published just three weeks before a close vote (221 to 205) by the US House of Representatives approving the

121 Comparing Oman with other Gulf States, the most restrictive provisions are in Oman. Among the founding members, Oman needs 40 members to agree on its motions, whereas other Gulf States need only 10-20 members. The penalties are similar to Bahrain's law.

122 The official registered unions in Oman are 78 until May 2009.

123 Which allowed the existence of the labour unions and collective bargaining in Oman.

124 US-Oman Free Trade Agreement.

OFTA,[125] which came into effect on the 1st of January 2009.[126] Undoubtedly, it brings legitimate change in the exercise of the freedom to assemble with regard to labour unions.

Changes from inside a country without any external pressures or international interference, is clearly preferable, but external pressures often help to advance freedoms and rights. International agreements, in this respect, have great potential for protecting human rights in the Gulf States, as is the case in Oman and Bahrain (FTA).[127] It is also interesting to see that the right to associate under the Omani legal system follow different avenues with regard to NGOs and labour unions. NGOs are regulated in detail through the Law of Civil Association while the details of regulating labour unions are stipulated under the Ministerial Resolution (M.R. 59/2010). These organisations are regulated from different perspectives; labour unions concentrate on the private sector's companies and all other associations are covered by the Law of Association.

Another important issue to discuss is how the LoCA is more restrictive than the regulations of labour unions in almost every respect, such as the right to establish an association or a union, governmental interference and judicial review. Moreover, laws and statutes issued by Royal Decree are not under the Administrative Court jurisdiction. It might be beneficial to have a similar regula-

---

125 Democratic congressmen, prompted by US unions, had expressed concern at existing Omani labour law. See Economist Intelligence Unit (2010). *Oman politics: Unionised.* Retrieved 22 May 2010, from Zawya: <http://www.zawya.com/printstory.cfm?storyid=EIU20100401230354125&l=164500100309>

126 The Report of the Labour Advisory Committee for Trade Negotiations and Trade Policy (LAC) has criticised the original Omani Labour Law and the Ministry of Manpower resolutions 135 and 136, which had only allowed the formation of workers' committees, and prevented strikes and collective bargaining. Similar criticisms came from different US and International organisations and trade unions. Issued on 15 November 2005 and downloadable from <http://nyfairtrade.org/pdf/omanLACreport_11152005.pdf>

127 The U.S.-Bahrain FTA entered into force on 11 January 2006.

tion for NGOs and associations instead of the current law which regulates the freedom but cannot protect it legally.

Article 33 of the Omani Basic Statute lists several provisions for the right to freedom of association, along with more terms and conditions. The Law of Civil Associations is the main law that supposedly ensures and protects freedom. However, it has not succeeded in ensuring the minimum standards. On the contrary, it hinders these rights. The conditions stipulated under Omani law cover almost every aspect of freedom and day-to-day activities, which do not support the right to live freely and actively.

This law has limited civil society and freedom of association mostly centralised for women's associations and the care of children and the disabled. Ironically, most of these allowed areas listed under Article 4 of the LoCA are departments and centres in the Ministry of Social Development,[128] which conflict with Article 11. This article gives the Ministry the right to reject any application based on a similar activity or that Omani society has no need for this service. In essence, the government has veto power over the mere existence of an association. A natural response to such a situation is for an association and its members to refrain from asserting any opinions or views even slightly contrary to official government policies.

Is forming societies on a '*national basis and for legitimate objectives and by peaceful means*', as stipulated by the Basic Statute, only covered by the list of accepted areas as mentioned in Article 4 of the law? Is, for example, a human rights organisation within these conditions? What is more important for society than an organisation that spreads the awareness about civil rights? The existence and enforcement of this law in the Gulf states and Oman will not

128 Under the Ministry's current structure, several centres and departments are responsible for child care, orphan care, disabled care and aged care, and women's development; see the Ministry's website <http://www.mosd.gov.om> However, all of them are listed under Article 4 of the law.

only restrict the effectiveness of community associations and organisations, but will also make the freedom of association concept far from being achievable in the foreseeable future.

The Ministry of Social Development has a great deal of power and discretion to grant or deny registration to an organisation and interfere in its operations and resolutions, as well as its financial support or dissolution. Hence, individuals are not allowed to pursue their objectives because of tremendous restrictions, limitations and bureaucracy. These restrictions do not help the government to effectively control and supervise associations; instead, they lead people to set up secret organisations to fulfil their needs and to work freely. Such underground organisations are prohibited by the Basic Statute and by law.[129] The government has put many restrictions on the freedom to associate, and any organisation seeking to operate in Oman will be treated effectively, more or less, as a department under the ministry rather than as an independent organisation. For more than 10 years since the law was declared in 2000, the number of official authorised organisations has not exceeded 93,[130] which includes foreign clubs and professional associations. This number is not expected to increase in the near future under present conditions.

The current law has many negative aspects that reflect the government's mistrust and fear of promoting civic activities, and this has a great impact on weakening civil society in Oman.[131] Thus, it is

---

129 Art. 33 OBSS.

130 Until November 2008 (there were 51 Women's associations, 19 Professional Associations, 11 Charitable societies, 4 societies for Disabled Persons, and 8 Clubs for Foreign Communities). See Ministry of Social Development website: <www.mosd.gov.om> Retrieved 29 November 2008.

131 Al-Hashmi, S. (2009) listed several obstacles for Omani civil society to develop and work effectively, citing this law as an obstacle. His list includes several factors; financial dependence on governmental grants; people's reluctance and lack of experience; technical weaknesses; absence of symbols and role models; and low media coverage for the NGOs' activities. However, most obstacles

necessary to re-examine these laws and regulations now. Amending the current Omani laws with regards to freedom of association, however, is impossible, as the changes needed would be too numerous.

Thus, it is recommended that a new statute be introduced in line with international standards and with the participation of the Omani NGOs and international human rights institutions. Although the formation of political parties is unlikely in the near future, it is recommended that the law have clarity for permitting human rights organisations with clear definitions for '*prohibited political activities*'. Sanctions and penalties should be deleted from the law and any conviction for any offense or a crime should be reviewed by an independent judicial court with respect to the penal law. Legal protection for the associations and their members has to be introduced, with a clear legal right for any association to take unreasonable administrative decisions to court. Finally, it is recommended that Oman joins the ICCPR and ICESCR,[132] and ratifies the ILO's other core labour conventions, most importantly No. 87 dealing with Freedom of Association and No. 98 dealing with the Right to Organise and Collective Bargaining and other international conventions.[133]

---

are the results of the law and the government's practices. In addition to the government's emphasis on its absolute role as the only service provider for community needs, NGOs are not fully independent. The government's rationale is based on the argument that the community has not reached the age of majority or that such claims must be accompanied by political demands, such as democracy, which are undesirable. See Al-Hashmi, S. (2009, October 31). *Civil Society Institutions in Oman: Reality and Challenges (in Arabic).* Retrieved June 1, 2010, from Nizwa Journal: <http://www.nizwa.com/articles.php?id=3285>

132 Refer to section 3.5 for more details.

133 That will help the ILO and other international organisations to monitor and report on the freedom in the country with respect to international standards. It is also important to expand the union rights by including other sectors that are not covered by the current laws and regulations, especially the public sector, where most Omani citizens are employed.

Conclusion

Overall, the state's rights should be limited to supervising the organisations' activities without impinging on the freedom of association, which includes people's right to form, join and operate freely and peacefully. The role of the government, in fact, should be to ensure freedoms instead of rationing the basic civil rights of its citizens.

7 General Conclusion

This study has examined the OBSS and the factors that may maintain and safeguard basic human rights and freedoms in the Omani Law. From the promulgation of the Basic Statute of the State in 1996 until 2011, Oman has made dramatic developments in the area of human rights, perhaps more than any other Gulf State.[1] These areas of development cover almost every aspect of the citizen's life. Legislation issued in the last 15 years evidences progressive developments in legal, political, civil, social, cultural, economic and environmental rights; such as the rights of empowering women, protecting children and disabled persons, allowing for the existence of trade unions, and more public participation.

This study has explored the core developments from various respects. Overall, the cornerstone of these developments is the Basic Statute, which constitutionally protects the rights and freedoms of Omani citizens, changed the governing system to a bicameral parliament, and established a new semi-independent judicial system where the rule of law is paramount and, for the first time in modern Oman, holds the state accountable.[2]

However, the factors that may maintain and safeguard basic human rights in Omani law vary, as has been seen. This study illus-

1 One obvious example is the women right to elect and be elected where Oman became the first Gulf State guarantees this right. Although Oman is still under the "Not Free" status under the Freedom House Analysis 'Freedom in the World 2011: Oman', downloadable from <http://www.freedomhouse.org/uploads/fiw11/Oman_FIW_2011.pdf>, compared to Kuwait which is the best among Gulf States with the "Partly Free" status, Oman has made intrinsic developments in the areas of human rights and the rule of law during the last 15 years more than other states in the region, and that is witnessed via its legislations, regulations, enrolment to several international human rights instruments and norms, and its withdrawn some of its reservations from these instruments (such as the CRC; see Appendix 3).

2 Refer to sections 3.3 and 3.4 for more details.

trates the importance of international human rights treaties, norms and reports in influencing the state's policy. This has helped people to become aware about several areas which were ignored or denied from the authority. The government's failure to ratify and sign some core international human rights, in particular the ICCPR, ICESCR and ILO conventions without expansive reservations.[3] These sorts of reservations also serve to hinder the promotion of the protections needed for rights and freedoms.

Rule of law has been implemented to some extent and the Administrative Court offers its efficiency in protecting and promoting human rights and freedoms. However, its scope is still too limited to cover the constitutional aspects which are needed to give the rights and freedoms the protective shield which can be offered through a constitutional court.

The separation of powers does not exist in Oman with the absolute power of the Sultan and the domination of the executive branch over other branches. The legislative and judicial powers of some executive institutions and committees have impacts too, which make some administrative organs both an adversary and an arbitrator at the same time. The weak power of the Parliament, or 'Oman Council', is the main reason for such imbalance which also results in the dominance of the executive branch over other branches.

So far, the Sultan in his exercise of his absolute and unconstrained power has shown an inclination towards the role of protecting rights and freedoms. However, this power can be very dangerous if it is exercised negatively especially human rights aspects in Oman are promoted mainly by the Sultan's tendency, where such rights and freedoms cannot be sufficiently upheld in the absence of human rights being procedurally guaranteed. This is the basis of the need to reflect on a constitutional monarchy as a solution for future protections and guarantees.

---

3 Refer to section 3.5 for more details.

Therefore, the current problem in Oman is not about the procedural safeguards in human rights' matters,[4] rather it is about legislation and existing laws and regulations, the rules of the legislative, and the separation of powers, where most human rights and freedoms' violations are taking place. The power of the executive branch in determining and controlling these rights is obvious without independent legislative power that represents the people.

Other Basic Statute limitations than those above-mentioned, can be categorised as follows:

Constitutional limits: Most important are the citizenship and constitution amendment limits. The Basic Statute explicitly guarantees some basic rights and freedoms for Omani citizens, but leaves non-nationals without constitutional rights or protections, such as the principle of equality before the law and non-discrimination.[5]

Moreover, it allows the Sultan to change or amend it without any limitations. It is vital when it comes to people's rights and freedoms and the law just gives him such power without the approval from other institutions and councils such as parliament, the judicial branch or even by the Council of Ministers. It is a sole right of the Sultan. Even the oath which the new Sultan has to take before he can proceed as a ruler will not necessarily prevent him from changing the Basic Statute.[6]

The adoption of some guarantees in this regard is necessary. Other Gulf States might be a model for the Omani system, such as the Kuwait, Bahrain and Qatar constitutions. They prevent any discussion for amendment provisions concerning rights and public freedom

4 Such as, the recognition of the individual before the law, the right of access to a court, the presumption of innocence, the right to an appeal to a higher tribunal, the public trial, the prohibition to be tried more than once for the same offence after final judgment, and trial without undue delay and within a reasonable time.

5 For more information refer to sections 3.2.2 'The Right to Nationality' and 'Equality before the Law and the Prohibition of Discrimination'.

6 Art. 7 of OBSS.

except in cases where the purpose is to grant more rights and guarantees in the interests of the citizens.[7] They also went further by asking for the approval of two-thirds of parliament for any changes or amendments.[8] This has been recommended as a necessary change to the Omani system if the Basic Statute is to be amended soon.[9]

Loose Phrases and the Absence of Restraints over the Legislator: Using a variety of terms and formats to refer to the limitation of the right or freedom by the law in the constitution is a phenomenon that is used by all of the Gulf States' constitutions and by Oman's Basic Statute. For example, using terms that the right or freedom is guaranteed 'by law' or 'in the limits of the law' or 'in accordance with the law' or by using the general statements of the 'legitimate targets' and the 'foundations of national public' or 'national security' which are very general and could have more than one explanation and might be misused.[10]

That leaves their definitions in the hands of those who are in power and to their sole discretion and what they see as legitimate and patriotic. Giving them the power to make laws to restrict rights and freedoms becomes a tool to demolish them. This of course is risky since the constitution provision is limited by the ordinary law and not vice versa.[11]

---

7 Art. 175 Kuwait Constitution, Art. 146 Qatar Constitution and Art. 31 Bahrain Constitution.

8 Art. 174 Kuwait Constitution, Art. 144 Qatar Constitution and Art. 120 Bahrain Constitution.

9 See section 2.4 'Basic Statute in Practice'.

10 See section 3.2 'Constitutional References to Basic Human Rights'.

11 Similarly, adopted by ordinary statutes, especially those regulating rights and freedoms, such as Article 1 of the Law of Civil Association about the definition of association, which is vague and ambiguous enough to allow the government broad discretion.

Ordinary Statutes regulating Constitutional Issues: A crucial limitation of the Basic Statute is that it left the areas which are interlinked with rights and freedoms to be regulated by ordinary statutes, such as regulating the Oman Council, Constitutional Court, and political parties. The Basic Statute refers to these institutions or rights in general but leaving their status to ordinary law to regulate them will weaken them without any constitutional protection.[12]

Relevant Statutes: There are several statutes still missing that need to be adopted, such as the Civil Law, Law of the Child, and the law regulating assemblies and demonstrations. These illustrate rights and freedoms that are not covered by current regulations. Another important statute which is still missing is declaring the terms of reference of the Authority on Conflicts of Jurisdictions and Rules Law to cover the constitutional disputes and to be responsible about all constitutional matters as a Constitutional body or court.[13]

Court Jurisdictions: Certain issues are excluded from the jurisdiction of the courts, such as issues related to the sovereignty of the State, Royal Decrees and Orders and issues related to nationality and tribal affairs. This is expected from any state in terms of deciding on its sovereignty. However, it is necessary not to mix it with the basic rights of a person, such as his right to nationality and his right to having a name.[14]

Security Issues: The exaggerated security fears that has led the government to adopt several security procedures and regulations are violating the citizen's individual basic rights. Taking the right to assemble as an example, this is guaranteed by Article 32 of the Basic Statute without any legislation to regulate it; but Article 137 of

12 See sections 2.3.4 'The Oman Council', 3.4.4 'The Constitutional Court', and 5.5 'Omani Basic Statute and Political Parties'.

13 See section 2.4.

14 See section 4.2 'Nationality under the Basic Statute'.

the Omani Penal Law (R.D. 7/74) allows the authority to break up any kind of special gathering in a public place if the number of the participants is ten people or more. This can lead to several punishments including imprisonment and a fine.

Another is where the Higher Education Council has prevented all public and private universities from conducting political science courses in Oman.[15] Also, the Ministry of Higher Education has requested all higher education institutions to receive an official permit for any public lecture conducted by visiting professors from outside Oman 5 months before it takes place.[16] Both contradict freedom of information and expression and the person's right for education.

All of these laws and regulations are based on security cautions, which result in violating other rights and freedoms. It is recommended that unnecessary procedures are removed and deleted as well as policies that are based on security concerns when they contradict a person's rights.

Emergencies and Martial Laws: The UN recognises that human rights can be limited or even pushed aside during times of national emergency, although "*the emergency must be actual, affect the whole population and the threat must be to the very existence of the nation. The declaration of emergency must also be a last resort and a temporary measure*".

The State of Emergency Law (R.D. 75/2008) lists several areas where rights and freedoms are limited, for instance the freedom of movement and assembly, which have been accepted according to the UN standard. However, the Anti-Terrorism Law (R.D. 8/2007) lists several precautions and punishments that are very extreme. Some

15 Altawasil Report, p. 9.

16 Office of the Director General of Private Universities and Colleges. (24 September 2009). Official Circular 60/2009. Muscat.

rights and freedoms can also be violated for long periods and can reach up to five years, such as the precautions listed under Art. 19.[17]

The recent development in the Middle East or what is called 'Arab Spring' is one of the significant factors that is also driving Oman to pursue more freedoms and liberties, and might open the door to more democracy in the future. In February 2011, Oman witnessed a rare outbreak of discontent when demonstrators assembled in *Sohar* State to demand more jobs and increased wages. Later, the demands increased to include investigations into corruption and government accountability, and finally for political reform and constitutional changes. Sultan Qaboos responded quickly by promising more jobs and benefits and also promulgated Royal Decree no. 39/2011 which granted legislative and audit powers to the Council of Oman.[18] It is one major step towards the constitutional monarchy; although such changes have not been announced yet, waiting for the technical committee of experts, which was formed by a Royal Order, to submit its report to the Sultan about the draft amendment of the Basic Statutes.

It is not expected that many significant changes will be made to the Basic Statute based on the Royal Decree. Certainly, changing the governmental system to a constitutional monarchy is unlikely under the current Sultan.

The current political and legal developments in Oman are numerous, and during the first 5 months of 2011, the Sultan has issued several Royal Decrees which will play an influential role in promoting and protecting human rights in Oman. The most notable are:

17 Anti-Terrorism Law (R.D. 8/2007).

18 Issued on 12 March 2011, and it was part of the demands requested by demonstrators. See Chapter Two, section 2.5.

- Royal Decree 25/2011 on the independence of the Public Prosecution which gave the Public Prosecution full independence from its links to the Inspector General of Police and Customs.
- Royal Decree 27/2011 on amending the name of the State Audit Institution and expanding its prerogatives which gave the State Audit the jurisdiction over administrative affairs, in addition to its financial responsibility.
- Royal Decree 31/2011 on restructuring the Council of Ministers, removed very influential figures from its membership, who have been members for decades; brought new blood to the Council, and for the first time nominated 5 members of *Ash-Shura* Council to be members of the Council of Ministers.
- Royal Decrees 33/2011 and 34/2011 on nominating 2 members of *Ash-Shura* Council to hold the positions of the Chairman of the State Audit and Administrative Institution and the Chairman of the Tender Board respectively.

The Basic Statute obstacles, as mentioned earlier, are the main part of the limitations which human rights should override for a better position in the future. The current Royal Decrees and Orders will help Oman create the foundation for greater Human Rights awareness which will need further studies in the near future.

> *Yesterday's man must be very unhappy as it never occurred to him that he holds sacred rights, and therefore, did nothing to protect them. Today's man, however, would be much more unfortunate when he realises that he has such rights, but is unable to protect them.*[19]

19 Adbul-Malek, O. cited from Al Roken, M. (1997). *Human Rights under the United Arab Emirates: Guarantees and Restrictions*. Arab Law Quarterly, 12 (1), p. 107.

Bibliography

Administrative Court (2003). Set of Legal Principles Established by the Court for years I and II (2001-2002). Muscat: The Technical Office.

Administrative Court (2008, June 11). Introduction to the Administrative Court in Oman Conference. Sur.

Akhavi, S. (2000). *Scholar Commons about 'Islamic Political Culture, Democracy, and Human Rights', by Daniel E. Price'* . Retrieved from University of South Carolina, Columbia: http://scholarcommons.sc.edu/cgi/viewcontent.cgi?article=1004&context=poli_facpub

Al Abri, I. (2010). *The judicial system in the Sultanate of Oman (in Arabic).* Retrieved January 13, 2011, from Ministry of Justice website: http://www.moj.gov.om/HostedPages?c=&PageId=3

Al Busaidi, T. (2008, October). Organising the Constitutional Review in the Sultanate of Oman (in Arabic). *Journal of Law,* 11 (2), pp. 293-361.

Al Hashmi, S. (2000). Shura in Oman (in Arabic). *Unpublished Article,* 50,51.

Al Hashmi, S. (2009, October 31). *Civil society institutions in Oman: Reality and Challenges (in Arabic).* Retrieved June 1, 2010, from Nizwa Journal: http://www.nizwa.com/articles.php?id=3285

Al Jabri, M. (2002). *Democracy and Human Rights.* Beirut.

Al Khateeb, N. (Al Khateeb, N.). *Principles of the Constitutional Law (in Arabic).* Amman, Jordan: Dar Al Thaqafa.

Al Kiumi, B. (2009, December 12). *The Petition for Contractual Constitution: Why do we sign?* Retrieved January 3, 2010, from Alharah AlOmania: http://alharah.net/alharah/t13995.html

Al Mukhaini, A. (2002). *State Institutionalisation in the Oil Producing Monarchies: A Discussion on the Role of the State in Oman and Kuwait.* Muscat: Unpublished.

Al Mukhaini, A. (2002). Stepping into Democracy: The Shura in Oman. *Qatar Conference on Democracy and Free Trade,* pp. 1-4. Doha, Qatar.

Al Nami, A. (2007). *Studies in Ibadhism.* Retrieved October 11, 2010, from Open Mind: http://www.lulu.com/items/volume_62/1035000/1035883/1/print/STUDIES_IN_IBADHISM.pdf

Al Qurtubi, A. (2003). *Tafsir al-Qurtubi (in Arabic)* (Vol. 4). Riyadh: Dar Alam Alkitab.

Al Roken, M. (1997). Human Rights under the Constitution of the United Arab Emirates: Guarantees and Restrictions. *Arab Law Quarterly*, Vol. 12 No. 1, pp. 91-107.

Al Shayeb, J. (2006). Prospects and Constraints on Civil Society in Saudi Arabia. Beirut: a paper submitted to the Conference in Support of civil society in the Arab Region from 3 to 5 July 2006.

Al Shukaili, S. (2006). *The Mediator in Explaining the Omani Basic Statute (in Arabic)*. Cairo: draft book.

Alarabiya News (2008, January 30). *Saudi Arabia: Criticism to the new draft regulation of "Civil Society Institutions"*. Retrieved May 3, 2010, from http://www.alarabiya.net/articles/2008/01/29/ 44907.html

Albayan Newspaper (1998, December 28). *Interview with the Omani Minister of the Interior*. Retrieved Feburary 18, 2009, from http://www.albayan.ae/servlet/Satellite?c=Article&cid=1221054186674&pagename=Albayan%2FArticle%2FFullDetail

Alder, J. (2007). *Constitutional and Administrative Law* (6th ed.). Basingstoke: Palgrave Macmillan.

Aljazeera News (2002, June 16). *Bahrain Debate on Dual Nationalities (in Arabic)*. Retrieved January 18, 2009, from http://www.aljazeera.net/News/archive/archive?Archiveld=33995

Alqabas Newspaper (2009, April 21). *Government Backtracked the Decrees on Assemblies and Dual Nationality (in Arabic)*. Retrieved August 3, 2009, from http://www.alqabas.com.kw/Article.aspx?id=492109

Alraya Newspaper (2010, April 13). *Shura Council Recommends Amending the Law on Private Associations and Institutions*. Retrieved July 22, 2010, from Arab Legal Information Network: http://www.eastlaws.com/news/news.aspx?id=3054

Alroya Newspaper. (2011, January 20). *the Administrative Court: 11 Years in Judicial Service Report (in Arabic)*. Retrieved January 2011, from http://www.alroya.info/ar/alroya-newspaper/internal/13165----11-------

AlSulaiman, A. (2011). *Terminological differences between Morocco and other Arab countries*. Retrieved June 23, 2011, from Arabic Translators International: http://www.atinternational.org/index.php?option=com_content&view=article&id=49:2011-04-23-20-03-08&catid=36:2011-04-23-19-59-36

Amnesty International (2009, June 1). *Amnesty International Report 2009 on Oman.* Retrieved January 2011, 2011, from http://www.buzzle.com/articles/amnesty-international-report-2009-on-oman.html

Azzam, F. (1995). *Guarantees of Civil and Political Rights in Arab Constitutions (in Arabic).* Cairo: Cairo Institute for Human Rights Studies.

Azzamn Newspaper (2008, May 27). *Government and the Shura Council: "Partnership to Where?" (in Arabic).* Retrieved November 11, 2008, from http://www.azzamn.org/news_details.php?id=11502&dt=2008/05/27&st=Archive

Bahlul, R. (2001). *Does Democracy Require Secularism(in Arabic).* Retrieved November 24, 2007, from www.glo110.blogfa.com/post-55.aspx

Ballantyne, W. M (1986); "The Constitutions of the Gulf States: A comparative Study". *Arab Law Quarterly,* Vol. 1 No. 2, pp. 158-176.

Barendt, E. (1998). *An Introduction to Constitutional Law.* Oxford: Oxford University Press.

BBC News (2006, February 9). *Qatar resolves citizenship issue.* Retrieved January 18, 2009, from http://news.bbc.co.uk/1/hi/world/middle_east/4698152.stm

Black, H. (1994). Black's Law Dictionary, Sixth Edition. Eagan, MN: West Publishers

Brand, D. (2005). Introduction to socio-economic rights in the South African Constitution. *Socio-economic Rights in South Africa,* 1-56.

Britannica Concise Encyclopedia (2006). *Nationality.* Retrieved May 1, 2009, from http://www.britannica.com/

Brown, N. (1997, August). Sharia and State in the Modern Muslim Middle East. Retrieved from *International Journal of Middle East Studies,* Vol. 29, No. 3, pp. 359-376: www.jstor.org/stable/164585

Center for Media and Democracy (2011, April). *Arab Spring.* Retrieved April 20, 2011, from SourceWatch: http://www.sourcewatch.org/index.php?title=Arab_Spring

Citizens Trade Campaign (2005, November 15). *Report of the Labor Advisory Committee for Trade Negotiations and Trade Policy (LAC).* Retrieved May 2, 2010, from Citizens Trade: www.citizenstrade.org/pdf/omanLACreport_11152005.pdf

Claiming Human Rights (2008, December 18). *Definitions of the right to a nationality*. Retrieved March 3, 2009, from http://www.claiminghumanrights.org/nationality_definition.html

Committee on the Rights of the Child (2001). *Reports by States: Oman. 28th session (Geneva, 24 September to 12 October 2001).* CRC/C/78/Add.1. Retrieved June 16, 2008, from International Service for Human Rights: http://olddoc.ishr.ch/hrm/tmb/ treaty/crc/reports/crc_23-41/CRC_28.htm#_ftn3

Committee on the Rights of the Child (2006). *Meeting of the 43rd Session (Geneva, 11 September–29 September 2006): Oman (second periodic report)*. Retrieved March 11, 2011, from http://olddoc.ishr.ch/hrm/tmb/treaty/crc/reports/crc_43/crc_43_oman.pdf

Council of Europe (1997, November 6). *European Convention on Nationality.* Retrieved April 13, 2008, from http://conventions.coe.int/Treaty/en/Treaties/Html/166.htm

Council on Foreign Relations (2005). *In Support of Arab Democracy: Why and How Report of an Independent Task Force No. 54.* Retrieved September 14, 2007, from http://i.cfr.org/content/publications/attachments/Arab_Democracy_TF.pdf

Crystal, J. (2005, July). *Political Reform and the Prospects for Democratic Transition in the Gulf.* Retrieved from http://www.fride.org/download/WP11_ReforPoli_ENG_jul05.pdf

Declaration of the American Independence (1776, July 4). Retrieved December 2, 2009, from Indiana University School of Law, Bloomington: http://www.law.indiana.edu/uslawdocs/declaration.html

Diwan of Royal Court (1996). *Royal Speech: Words and speeches of His Majesty Sultan Qaboos bin Said 1970-1995.* Muscat: Diwan of Royal Court.

Economist Intelligence Unit (2000). *Country Profile 2000: Oman.* London: EIU.

Economist Intelligence Unit (2001). *Country Report 2001: Oman.* London: EIU.

Economist Intelligence Unit (2009). *Index of Democracy 2008.* Retrieved June 13, 2009, from http://graphics.eiu.com/PDF/Democracy%20Index%202008.pdf

Economist Intelligence Unit (2010, Mar 09). *Oman politics: Unionised.*

Retrieved May 22, 2010, from Zawya: http://www.zawya.com/printstory.cfm?storyid=EIU20100401230354125&l=164500100309
Economist Intelligence Unit (2011). *Democracy Index 2010.* Retrieved March 22, 2011, from http://graphics.eiu.com/PDF/Democracy_Index_2010_web.pdf
European Centre for Parliamentary Research & Documentation (ECPRD) (2001). *Rules on Parliamentary Immunity in the European Parliament.* Brussels: Dick Toornstra.
Egypt State Information Service (2007). *Abdul Razeq Al-Sanhouri.* Retrieved May 02, 2007, from Egypt State Information Service: http://www.sis.gov.eg/Ar/Story.aspx?sid=28305
Encyclopædia Britannica (2011). *Arab.* Retrieved April 11, 2011, from EB: www.britannica.com/EBchecked/topic/31348/Arab
Fallon, R. H. (1997, Jan). "The Rule of Law" as a Concept in Constitutional Discourse. *Columbia Law Review*, pp. Vol. 97, No. 1, pp. 1-56. from http://www.jstor.org/stable/1123446.
Farahat, M. (2006, February). *State, civil society and the law: 'Notes on some aspects of the legislative discrimination against women in the Arab World' (in Arabic).* Retrieved October 3, 2010, from Studies Center; Working paper submitted for conference of civil society and the empowerment of Arab women – Bahrain: http://www.amanjordan.org/aman_studies/wmview.php?ArtID=1082
Final verdict: the Kuwaiti woman can travel without the consent of her husband. (2009, October). Retrieved from Ensaf: http://www.ensaf.org/articles/index.php?news=178
Freedom House (2008, April 29). *Freedom of the Press 2008 – Oman.* Retrieved January 22 , 2011, from Freedom House, Freedom of the Press 2008 – Oman, 29 April 2008, available at: http://www.unhcr.org/refworld/docid/4871f6242.html
Freedom House (2011). *Map of Freedom in the World.* Retrieved March 29, 2011, from http://www.freedomhouse.org/template.cfm?page=363&year=2011
Geck, W. K. (1966). Judicial Review of Statutes: A comparative Survey of present Institutions and Practices. *Cornell Law Quarterly,* 51, pp. 250-304.
Ghubash, H. (1997). *Oman – the Islamic Democratic Tradition: An Islamic*

Democracy (in Arabic). Beirut: Dar Alfarabi.

Goddard, H. (2002, January). Islam and Democracy. *The Political Quarterly,* Vol. 73, Issue 1, pp. 3-9.

Gulf Cooperation Council (GCC) (2004). *Counter-terrorism Agreement.* Retrieved from http://www.gcc-sg.org/indexd2c3.html?action=Sec-Show&ID=351

Hoffman, V. (2001). Ibadi Islam: An Introduction. Retrieved March 25, 2007, from *Islamic Studies, Islam, Arabic and Religion*, University of Georgia: http://www.uga.edu/islam/ibadis.html

Human Rights Committee (2002, November 22). *Concluding observations of the Human Rights Committee: Egypt-CCPR/CO/76/EGY. (Concluding Observations/Comments).* Retrieved May 20, 2010, from UN ICCPR: http://www.unhchr.ch/tbs/doc.nsf/385c2add1632f4a8c12565a9004dc311/89189f6057f03fdec1256c68002f1ec4?OpenDocument

Human Rights Education Associates (2007). *Freedom of Assembly and Association.* Retrieved April 13, 2010, from http://www.hrea.org/index.php?base_id=146

Human Rights First (2007, February 14). *The Neglected Right: Freedom of Association in International Human Rights Law.* Retrieved May 8, 2010, from http://www.humanrightsfirst.org/pubs/descriptions/neglrt.htm

Human Rights in Oman Blog (2010, April 25). *Digital repression in the Sultanate of Oman (in Arabic).* Retrieved January 2011, from http://humanrightsinoman.blogspot.com

Human Rights Watch (2000, October 2). *Kuwait: Promises Betrayed: Denial of Rights of Bidun, Women, and Freedom of Expression.* Retrieved January 30, 2009, from UNHCR Refworld: http://www.unhcr.org/refworld/docid/3ae6a87e0.html

Idris, J. (2004). *Shura and Democracy: A Conceptual Analysis.* Retrieved December 15, 2007, from Islamonline.net: http://www.islamonline.net/servlet/Satellite?pagename= Islam Online-English-Ask_Scholar/FatwaE/FatwaE&cid= 1119503544462

International Convention On the Elimination Of all Forms of Racial Discrimination (19 October 2006). *Concluding observations of the Committee on the Elimination of Racial Discrimination: Oman.* Geneva: United Nations.

International Federation for Human Rights (FIDH) report (2009, March). *Freedom of Association in the Arabian Gulf: The Case of Bahrain, Kuwait and Yemen.* Retrieved May 1, 2010, from http://www.fidh.org/IMG/pdf/etude.pdf

International Labour Organization (ILO) (2009). *Country Baselines under the 1998 ILO Declaration Annual Review (2000-2008): Oman.* Retrieved July 6, 2010, from http://www.ilo.org/wcmsp5/groups/ public/---ed_norm/---declaration/documents/publication/wcms_ decl_facb_omn.pdf

International Labour Organization (ILO) (2010). *Oman Observation(s).* Retrieved January 11, 2011, from http://www.ilo.org/ilolex/cgi-lex/commentplus.pl?Oman@ref

International Trade Union Confederation (ITUC) (2009). *Internationally-Recognised Core Labour Standards in the Sultanate of Oman: Report for the WTO General Council Review of Trade Policies of the Sultanate Of Oman.* Retrieved May 4, 2010, from http://www.ituc-csi.org/IMG/pdf/TPR_Oman.Final.pdf

Inter-Parliamentary Union (IPU). Second Regional Conference of Women Parliamentarians and Women in Decision Making Positions of the GCC States (2007). *Women Making a Difference in Parliament.* Retrieved May 12, 2008, from United Arab Emirates, 30-31 October 2007: http://www.ipu.org/splz-e/abudhabi07/information.pdf

Karam, A. (1999, October). *Strengthening the Role of Women Parliamentarians in the Arab Region: Challenges and Options.* Retrieved April 9, 2008, from UNDP: http://www.pogar.org/publications/gender/karam1/karama.pdf

Katz, M. (2004, September). Assessing the Political Stability of Oman. *Middle East Review of International Affairs,* 8 (3), 5-6.

Kuwait (1959). Kuwaiti Nationality Law No. 15/1959.

Langlois, A. J. (2003). Human Rights without Democracy? A Critique of the Separationist Thesis. The Johns Hopkins University Press, *Human Rights Quarterly,* Vol. 25, No. 4 (Nov. 2003), pp. 990-1019. From: http://www.jstor.org/stable/20069702

Layish, A. (2004). The Transformation of the Sharīʿa from Jurists' Law to Statutory Law in the Contemporary Muslim World. *Brill, Die Welt des Islams, New Series*, Vol. 44, Issue 1, pp. 85-113 from http://www.jstor.org/stable/1571336.

Lazarev, N. (2005). *Hohfeld's Analysis of Rights: An Essential Approach to a Conceptual and Practical Understanding of the Nature of Rights.* Retrieved from Murdoch University Electronic Journal of Law: http://www.austlii.edu.au/au/journals/MurUEJL/2005/9.html

Legal Information Institute, Cornell University, Law School (n.d.). *§ 1408. Nationals but not citizens of the United States at birth.* Retrieved May 1, 2009, from: http://www.law.cornell.edu/uscode/8/1408.html

Lewis, M. (2005). *Languages of Oman.* Retrieved May 04, 2007, from Ethnologue: Languages of the World: http://www.ethnologue.com

Mahmoud, H. (2009, July). *'The reality of civil work and its constraints in the Gulf States'; paper presented at GCC Volunteering Forum, Abu Dhabi, 2009.* Retrieved September 17, 2010, from Emaratalyoum website: http://www.emaratalyoum.com/local-section/2009-06-28-1.151713

Majlis Ash-Shura (2001). *Majlis Ash-Shura Formation 1997-2000 (in Arabic).* Muscat: Majlis Ash-Shura.

Majlis Ash-Shura (2004). *Majlis Ash-Shura Formation 2000-2003 (in Arabic).* Muscat: Majlis Ash-Shura.

Malik, M. (1981, August). The Concept of Human Rights in Islamic Jurisprudence. Retrieved from *Human Rights Quarterly*, Vol. 3, No. 3, The Johns Hopkins University Press: http://www.jstor.org/stable/761895

Manea, E. (2005). *Regional Politics in the Gulf: Saudi Arabia, Oman and Yemen.* London: Saqi Books.

Marashaha, M. (2005). Views Over the Basic Statute (in Arabic). *the Basic Statute Characteristics.* Muscat: School of Law, p. 14.

Marshy, M. (2005, April). *Freedom of Association with regard to Political Parties and Civil Society in the Middle East, North Africa, and the Gulf: A literature review.* Retrieved September 13, 2010, from International Development Research Centre (IDRC): http://www.idrc.ca/uploads/user-S/12018943281Pub_ Mona_ Marshy_doc.pdf

Miller, J. (1997, May/June). Creating Modern Oman: an Interview with Sultan Qabus. *Foreign Affairs,* 76 (3), pp. 13-18.

Minister of Social Development (2007). *Report submitted to Majlis Ash-Shura about the Ministry's Performance.* Muscat: Ministry of Social Development.

Ministry of Education (1997). Oman and the Abbasid State (in Arabic). In *Social Studies, "History", Middle School, 9th Edition.* Muscat.

Ministry of Information (2009). *Oman 2009.* Muscat: MOI.

Ministry of Information (2000). *Oman 2000.* Muscat.

Ministry of Manpower (2009). *Trade Unions Department.* Retrieved May 17, 2010, from http://www.manpower.gov.om/en/trade_union.asp

Ministry of National Economy (2008, April). *Manpower in Private Sector.* Retrieved December 12, 2008, from http://www.moneoman.gov.om/book/mb/Apr2008/T14.pdf

Ministry of National Economy (2011, June). *Facts & Figures 2010.* Retrieved from http://www.mone.gov.om/Publication Attachment/F&F %20BOOK2011.pdf

Montesquieu, C. (1748). *The Spirit of Laws: Book I. Of Laws in General.* Retrieved March 9, 2011, from the Constitution Society website: http://www.constitution.org/cm/sol_01.htm#003

Moqatel Encyclopedia (1960). *The Recommendations of the Sixth Conference of the Arab Experts on Social Affairs, (s1729/d p 34 / c 3) on 07/09/1960.* Retrieved May 12, 2010, from Moqatel Encyclopedia: http://www.moqatel.com/openshare/Wthaek/title/GamatDowal/AGamatDowal1730_87-1.htm_cvt.htm#1730

National Assembly of France (1789, August 26). *The Declaration of the Rights of Man and of the Citizen.* Retrieved April 2, 2011, from Human Rights and Constitutional Documents: http://www.hrcr.org/docs/frenchdec.html

Nizwa.net (2005). *The Traditional Aflaj Irrigation System.* Retrieved September 13, 2010, from Nizwa.NET: http://www.nizwa.net/agr/falaj/chapter1.html

Office of the Director General of Private Universities and Colleges (2009, September 24). Official Circular 60/2009. Muscat.

Olson, D. (1980). *The Legislative Process: a Comparative Approach.* New York: Harper and Row.

Oman: Looking forward to 2020 (1995). Facing the challenges: interview with Sultan Qaboos bin Said of Oman. Retrieved September 4, 2007, from *The Middle East*: http://www.thefreelibrary.com/Facing%20the%20challenges.-a018763792

Oman Newspaper (2010, November 18). *meeting with Ash-Shura Council Chairman (in Arabic)*. Retrieved February 8, 2011, from http://main.omandaily.om/node/35840

Oman Report (2011). *National report submitted in accordance with paragraph 15 (a)*. Retrieved February 6, 2011, from UN Human Rights Council – Tenth session: http://www.un.org/webcast/unhrc/archive.asp?go=110126

Omani Society for Authors and Writers (2011, March). Retrieved March 11, 2011, from Sablah Oman: http://Portal.s-oman.net/articles/201103/7219.htm

Popp, Georg (2008). *Tribal Society in Oman*. Retrieved from http://www.oman-tours.com/about-oman/people-overview/tribalsociety/

Rabi, U. (2002). Majlis al-Shura and Majlis al-Dawla: Weaving Old Practices and New Realities in the Process of State Formation in Oman. *Middle Eastern Studies*, Vol. 38 No. 4, pp. 41-50.

Rathmell, A., & Schulze, K. (2000). Political Reform in the Gulf: The Case of Qatar. *Middle Eastern Studies*, Vol. 36, No. 4, pp. 47-62.

Renteln, A. (1988). The Concept of Human Rights. *Anthropos*, Bd. 83, H. 4/6, pp. 343-364. Download from: www.jstor.org/stable/40463371

Reuters (2005, January 16). *UAE, Oman must make new move for FTA, says US*. Retrieved August 2, 2010, from Citizens Trade: http://www.citizenstrade.org/ctc/wp-content/uploads/2011/05/reuters_uaeomanlabor_01162005.pdf

Riphenburg, C. (1998). *Oman: Political Development in a Changing World*. Westport: Praeger.

Saudi National Society for Human Rights (2009). *Second Report on the Status of Human Rights in the Kingdom of Saudi Arabia 2008*. Retrieved May 17, 2010, from http://www.nshr.org.sa/FCKFiles/Second_Report_on_the_Status_of_Human_Rights.pdf

Sfeir, G. (1988). Source of Law and the Issue of Legitimacy and Rights. *Middle East Journal*, Vol. 42, No. 3, pp. 436-446, from http://www.jstor.org/stable/4327779.

Shehata, A. (October 2003). *A Guide to the Administrative Court in Oman.* Muscat: the Administrative Court.

Siegfried, N. (2000, October). Legislation and Legitimation in Oman: The Basic Law. *Islamic Law and Society,* 7 (3), 359-397.

Sulaiman, S. (1996). *Democracy and Shura.* Retrieved December 11, 2007, from Al-Hewar Center: http://www.alhewar.com/SadekDemAndShura.htm

Supreme Council of the Cooperation Council for the Arab States of the Gulf (GCC) (1984, 27-29 November). *The Closing Statement of the Fifth Session of the Supreme Council of the Cooperation Council for the Arab States of the Gulf (GCC).* Retrieved May 22, 2008, from http://www.gcc-sg.org/indexf3c2.html?action=Sec-Show& ID=107

UAE (17/1972). Federal Law Concerning Nationality and Passports, Issued on 18/11/1972. *Amended by Federal Law no. 10/1975 dated 15/11/1975.*

United Kingdom (UK) Border Agency, Home Office (n.d.). *What is British citizenship?* Retrieved May 1, 2009, from http://www.ukba.homeoffice.gov.uk/britishcitizenship/aboutcitizenship/

United Kingdom (UK) Parliament (2011). *Is a British Bill of Rights needed?* Retrieved from http://www.publications.parliament.uk/pa/jt200708/jtselect/jtrights/memo/britishbill/uc1802.htm

United Nations (1986, December 3). *Declaration on Social and Legal Principles relating to the Protection and Welfare of Children, with Special Reference to Foster Placement and Adoption Nationally and Internationally – A/RES/41/85.* Retrieved August 2008, 4, from http://www.un.org/documents/ga/res/41/a41r085.htm

United Nations (2011). Retrieved from Treaty Collection: http://www2.ohchr.org/english/bodies/ratification/index.htm

United Nations General Assembly (2004, October 1). *59th session of the UN General Assembly, UN Special Representative of the Secretary General on Human Rights Defenders Report (A/59/401).* Retrieved April 13, 2010, from UN: http://daccess-dds-ny.un.org/doc/UNDOC/GEN/N04/533/18/PDF/N0453318.pdf?OpenElement

United Nations, CEDAW (2009). *Declarations, Reservations and Objections to CEDAW: Oman.* Retrieved June 16, 2008, from http://www.un.org/womenwatch/daw/cedaw/reservations-country.htm

United Nations Development Programme (UNDP) (2005, April). *Human*

Rights in UNDP: Practice Note. Retrieved April 13, 2011, from www.undp.org/governance/docs/HRPN_English.pdf

United Nations Development Programme (UNDP) (n.d.). *Programme on Governance in the Arab Region: Oman.* Retrieved April 9, 2009, from http://gender.pogar.org/countries/theme.aspx?t=4&cid=13

United Nations Development Programme (UNDP). Arab Human Rights Index. *Reservations on Conventions: All Countries.* Retrieved June 2, 2009, from http://www.arabhumanrights.org/en/resources/reservations.aspx

United Nations Development Programme (UNDP). The Arab Human Rights Index. *Oman: Human Rights Profile.* Retrieved February 3, 2011, from http://www. arabhumanrights.org/en/countries/country.aspx?cid=13

United Nations High Commissioner for Human Rights (UNHCHR) (1983, July 29). *CCPR General Comment 11: (Article 20) Prohibition of Propaganda for War and Inciting National, Racial or Religious Hatred.* Retrieved from http://www.ohchr.org/Documents/Issues/Opinion/CCPRGeneralCommentNo11.pdf

United Nations High Commissioner for Human Rights (UNHCHR) (2006). *The Rights for Non-Citizen. HR/PUB/06/11,* downloadable from: www.ohchr.org/Documents/Publications/noncitizensen.pdf.

United Nations High Commissioner for Human Rights (UNHCHR) (2010, May 20). *2009 Report: Activities and Results.* Retrieved April 3, 2011, from http://unispal.un.org/UNISPAL.NSF/0/42FF510FF156E2FA8525772900646CC7

United Nations Human Rights Council – Tenth session (2011, January). *Unicef Inputs and Report on the Universal Periodic Review: Oman.* Retrieved February 6 , 2011, from http://lib.ohchr.org/HRBodies/UPR/Documents/Session10/OM/UNICEF_UnitedNationsChildren%27sFund_eng.pdf

United Nations Security Council (2004, August 23). Report of the Secretary-General: *The rule of law and transitional justice in conflict and post-conflict societies.* Retrieved January 21, 2011, from: http://www.unrol.org/files/2004%20report.pdf

U.S. Department of State, Bureau of Democracy, Human Rights, and Labor (2008, March 11). *2007 Human Rights Report: Oman.* Retrieved June

8, 2009, from U.S. Department of State: http://www.state.gov/g/drl/rls/hrrpt/2007/100603.htm

U.S. Department of State, Bureau of Democracy, Human Rights, and Labor (2010, March 11). *2009 Human Rights Report: Oman.* Retrieved October 12, 2010, from http://www.state.gov/g/drl/rls/hrrpt/2009/nea/136077.htm

U.S. Department of State, Office To Monitor and Combat Trafficking in Persons (2010). *Trafficking in Persons Report 2010: Oman.* pp. 258-260. Retrieved February 15, 2011, from: http://www.state.gov/documents/organization/143188.pdf

U.S. Department of State, Office To Monitor and Combat Trafficking in Persons (2010). *Tier Placements: Trafficking in Persons.* Retrieved January 13, 2011, from: http://www.state.gov/g/tip/rls/tiprpt/2010/142755.htm

Weis, P. (1962, October). The United Nations Convention on the Reduction of Statelessness, 1961. Retrieved from *The International and Comparative Law Quarterly*, Vol. 11, No. 4, Cambridge University Press on behalf of the British Institute of International and Comparative Law. pp. 1073-1096: Article Stable URL: http://www.jstor.org/stable/755987

Weissbrodt, D. (2008). *The Human Rights of Non-citizens.* New York: Oxford University Press

Weissbrodt, D. and Collins, C., (2006) The Human Rights of Stateless Persons, *Human Rights Quarterly*, Vol. 28, No. 1, February 2006, pp. 245-276.

Women Knowledge Network (2007, January 2). *Media Conference about Ash-Shura Council Elections 2007.* Retrieved 5 12, 2008, from Arab Woman and Political Participation website: http://www.awapp.org/wmview.php?ArtID=1588

World Audit (2010). *Democracy Table November 2010.* Retrieved April 9, 2011, from http://www.worldaudit.org/democracy.htm

Youngs, R. (1998). *English, French and German comparative Law.* London: Cavendish Publishing.

Appendix

Appendix 1: The Basic Statute of the State

ROYAL DECREE NO. (101/96) PROMULGATING THE BASIC STATUTE OF THE STATE

We Qaboos bin Said, the Sultan of Oman

Affirming the principles that guided the policies of the State in various fields during the past era;
Determined to pursue our efforts to establish a better future distinguished by further achievements for the benefit of the country and the citizens; Consolidating the international status that Oman enjoys and its role in establishing the foundations of peace, security, justice and co-operation among various countries and nations; and In pursuance of the public interest;

Decreed as follows:

Article (1): The Basic Statute of the State is hereby promulgated in accordance with the attached formulation.

Article (2): This Decree shall be published in the Official Gazette and shall come into force on the date of its issue.

Issued on: 24 Jumada Al Akhira 1417 A.H. Corresponding to:
6 November 1996 A.D.
This Decree was issued in the Official Gazette Annex No. (587)
Issued on 16 November 1996 A.D.[1]

Qaboos bin Said
Sultan of Oman

---

1 There is no official translation of the Basic Statute yet, this research used the translated copy from Oman's National Human Rights Commission website, downloadable from: <http://www.nhrc.om/images/The_Basic_Statue_of_the_State.pdf>

THE BASIC STATUTE OF THE STATE

CHAPTER ONE

The State and the System of Government

Article (1): The Sultanate of Oman is an Arab, Islamic, independent State with full sovereignty and Muscat is its capital.

Article (2): The State's religion is Islam and Islamic Sharia is the basis for legislation.

Article (3): The State's official language is Arabic.

Article (4): The Law determines the State's flag, emblem, insignia and national anthem.

Article (5): The system of governance is Sultani (Royal) and hereditary from the male descendants of Sayyid Turki bin Said bin Sultan, provided that whoever is chosen as the successor shall be a Muslim, judicious, of sound mind and the legitimate son of Omani Muslim parents.

Article (6): The Ruling Family Council shall, within three days of the throne falling vacant, determine the successor to the throne.

If the Ruling Family Council does not agree on the successor to the throne, the Defence Council shall confirm the appointment of the person designated by the former Sultan in his letter to the Ruling Family Council.

Article (7): The Sultan, before exercising his authority, shall, in a joint session of the Council of Oman and the Defence Council, take the following oath:

"I swear by Almighty Allah to respect the Basic Statute of the State and the Law and to fully safeguard the interests of the citizens and their freedom and to preserve the independence of the country and its territorial integrity."

Article (8): The Government shall continue to perform its functions as usual until the Sultan is selected and exercises his powers.

Article (9): Rule in the Sultanate shall be based on justice, Shura (consultation) and equality. Citizens have the right – in accordance with this Basic Statute and the conditions and provisions stipulated by Law – to participate in public affairs.

CHAPTER TWO
The Principles Guiding the State Policy

Article (10): The Political Principles:

- Preserving the State's independence and sovereignty, safeguarding its entity, security and stability and defending it against all aggression.
- Reinforcing ties of co-operation and reaffirming friendly relations with all countries and nations on the basis of mutual respect, common interest, non-interference in their internal affairs, adherence to the international and regional charters and treaties and generally recognized principles of international law conducive to the promotion of peace and security among countries and nations.
- Laying suitable foundations for consolidating the pillars of genuine Shura emanating from the country's heritage, values and its Islamic Sharia. Taking pride in its history and adopting the benefits of contemporary methods and instruments.
- Establishing a sound administrative system that guarantees justice, tranquillity and equality for the citizens and ensures respect for public order and the preservation of the higher interests of the country.

Article (11): The Economic Principles:

- The national economy is based on justice and principles of free economy. Its essence is the constructive and fruitful co-operation between public and private activity. Its objective is the achievement of economic and social development in order to increase production and raise the standard of living of the citizens according to the State's general plan and within the limits of the Law.
- Freedom of economic activity is guaranteed within the limits of the Law and the public interest in a manner that ensures the integrity of the national economy.
- The State encourages savings and supervises the regulation of credit.
- All natural resources and revenues therefrom shall be the property of the State which shall preserve and utilize them in the best manner taking into consideration the requirements of the State's national security and the interests of national economy. No concession or investment in any of the public resources of the country may be granted except by

virtue of a Law and for a limited period, provided national interests are safeguarded.

- Public property is inviolable. The State shall protect it and citizens and residents shall preserve it.
- Private ownership is safeguarded and no person shall be prevented from assigning his property except within the limits of the Law. No property shall be expropriated except for the public interest in cases stipulated by the Law and in the manner specified therein, provided that the person dispossessed shall be fairly compensated. Inheritance is a right governed by Islamic Sharia.
- Confiscation of property is forbidden. Specific confiscation as a punishment shall not be imposed except by judicial order, and in cases specified in the Law.
- Taxes and general charges are based on justice and the development of national economy.
- Imposition, amendment and cancellation of public taxes shall only be by virtue of a Law and no person shall be exempt from paying all taxes or part thereof except in cases specified by Law.
  It is not permissible to impose a new tax, fee or any right with retrospective effect whatever its type might be.

Article (12): The Social Principles:

- Justice, equality and equal opportunities for Omanis are the pillars of society guaranteed by the State.
- Co-operation and mutual compassion are intimate bonds among the citizens, and the reinforcement of national unity is a duty. The State shall prevent anything that might lead to division, sedition or disruption of national unity.
- The family is the basis of society and the Law regulates the means of protecting it, preserving its legal entity, reinforcing its ties and values, looking after its members and providing the suitable conditions to develop their potential and capabilities.
- The State guarantees assistance for citizens and their families in cases of emergency, sickness, disability and old age in accordance with the scheme of social security and shall work for the solidarity of the soci-

ety in bearing the burdens resulting from national disasters and catastrophes.

- The State cares for public health and the means of the prevention and treatment of diseases and epidemics. It endeavours to provide healthcare for every citizen and encourages the establishment of private hospitals, poly-clinics and medical institutions under its supervision and in accordance with regulations determined by Law. It also works towards the conservation of the environment, its protection and the prevention of pollution.
- The State enacts Laws for the protection of the employee and the employer and regulates the relationship between them. Every citizen has the right to pursue the profession he desires within the limits of the Law. It is not permissible to impose any compulsory work on anybody except by virtue of Law and only for performing a public service and in return for just remuneration.
- Public employment is a national service entrusted to those who carry it out. State employees, while carrying out their work, shall pursue public interest and service to society. Citizens are considered equal in taking up public employment in accordance with the provisions stipulated by Law.

Article (13): The Cultural Principles:

- Education is a fundamental basis for the progress of society sponsored by the State to be propagated and made accessible to all.
- Education aims to raise and develop the general cultural standard, promote scientific thought, kindle the spirit of research, respond to the requirements of economic and social plans and build a generation that is physically and morally strong that takes pride in its nation, country and heritage and preserves its achievements.
- The State provides public education, works to combat illiteracy and encourages the establishment of private schools and institutes under its supervision and in accordance with the provisions of the Law.
- The State fosters and preserves national heritage, encourages the sciences, arts, literature, scientific research and assists in their propagation.

Article (14): The Security Principles:

- Peace is the objective of the State, and the country's safety is a duty incumbent on every citizen.
  The Defence Council undertakes the consideration of matters related to preserving the Sultanate's safety and defending it.
- Only the State establishes the armed forces, public security organisations and any other forces. All these forces belong to the nation and their mission is to protect the State, ensure the safety of its territories, and guarantee the security and tranquillity of citizens. No organization or group is allowed to establish military or paramilitary forces. The Law regulates the military service, general or partial mobilization, and the rights, duties, rules of discipline of the armed forces, public security organizations and any other forces the State decides to establish.

CHAPTER THREE
The Public Rights and Duties

Article (15): Nationality is regulated by Law and it is prohibited to rescind or revoke it except within the limits of the Law.

Article (16): It is prohibited to deport or exile citizens or prevent them from returning to the Sultanate.

Article (17): All citizens are equal before the Law and share the same public rights and duties. There shall be no discrimination between them on the grounds of gender, origin, colour, language, religion, sect, domicile, or social status.

Article (18): Personal freedom is guaranteed according to the Law. It is unlawful to arrest, search, detain, imprison any person, or have his place of residence or freedom of movement or residence restricted except in accordance with the provisions of the Law.

Article (19): Detention or imprisonment in places other than those designated for such purpose under the laws of prisons – where health and social care is provided – is illegal.

Article (20): No person shall be subjected to physical or psychological torture, inducement or demeaning treatment and the Law stipulates the punishment for whoever commits such offences. Any statement or confession proven to have been obtained under torture, inducement, demeaning treatment or threats of any such acts, shall be rendered void.

Article (21): No crime or punishment is cognisable as such except by virtue of a Law, and there shall be no punishment except for acts subsequent to the Law coming into force wherein such acts are provided for. Punishment is personal.

Article (22): The accused is innocent until proven guilty in a legal trial in which the essential guarantees to exercise his right of defence according to the Law are ensured. It is prohibited to harm an accused either physically or mentally.

Article (23): The accused has the right to appoint a person capable of undertaking his defence during the trial. The Law defines the cases where the attendance of a defence lawyer on behalf of the accused is imperative, and ensures that for those persons who are financially unable, the means to seek judicial redress and defend their rights.

Article (24): Any person who is arrested or detained shall immediately be informed of the reasons for his arrest or detention. He has the right to communicate his circumstances to, or request assistance of, whomever he wishes in the manner regulated by Law. Such a person shall immediately be informed of the charges against him. He and his representative have the right to petition the court against the action restricting his personal freedom. The Law regulates the right of petition in a manner which ensures the disposal of such petition within a specified period, failing which he must be unconditionally released.

Article (25): Litigation is a protected right guaranteed to all people. The Law prescribes the procedures and conditions necessary to exercise such right. The State, as far as possible, shall guarantee the approximation of judicial bodies to litigants and the prompt adjudication of cases.

Article (26): It is illegal to conduct any medical or scientific experiment on any person without his freely – given consent.

Article (27): Places of residence are inviolable and accordingly, entry thereof is illegal without the permission of the legal occupant except in cases specified by Law and in the manner stipulated therein.

Article (28): The freedom to practice religious rites according to recognised customs is guaranteed, provided it does not disrupt public order or contradict with morals.

Article (29): The freedom of opinion and expression thereof through speech, writing or other forms of expression is guaranteed within the limits of the Law.

Article (30): The freedom of correspondence by post, telegraph, telephone or other means of communication is protected and its confidentiality guaranteed. Hence it is unlawful to monitor, search, disclose the confidentiality, delay or confiscate such correspondence except in cases specified by Law and in accordance with the procedures prescribed therein.

Article (31): Freedom of the press, printing and publishing is guaranteed in accordance with the terms and conditions specified by Law. Anything that leads to sedition, impairs State security or abuses human dignity or rights is prohibited.

Article (32): Citizens have the right to assembly within the limits of the Law.

Article (33): The freedom of forming societies on a national basis and for legitimate objectives and by peaceful means – provided that it does not conflict with the provisions and objectives of this Basic Statute – is guaranteed in accordance with the terms and conditions stipulated by the Law. It is prohibited to form societies the activities of which are hostile to the order of society, secret or of a military nature. It is illegal to force anyone to join any society.

Article (34): Citizens have the right to address public authorities on personal matters or matters pertaining to public affairs, in the manner and conditions designated by Law.

Article (35): Every foreigner legally present in the Sultanate enjoys protection for himself and his property in accordance with the Law. He shall uphold the society's values and respect its traditions and sentiments.

Article (36): Extradition of political refugees is prohibited. Laws and international agreements determine the rules for the extradition of criminals.

Article (37): Defending the homeland is a sacred duty, and coming forward to serve in the armed forces is an honour for the citizens regulated by Law.

Article (38): Preserving national unity and safeguarding the State's secrets is a duty incumbent upon every citizen.

Article (39): Payment of taxes and public dues is a duty according to the Law.

Article (40): Respecting the Basic Statute of the State, the Laws and orders issued by public authorities in implementation thereof, observance of public order and respect of public morals is a duty incumbent upon all residents of the Sultanate.

CHAPTER FOUR
The Head of State

Article (41): The Sultan is the Head of State and the Supreme Commander of the Armed Forces. His person is inviolable. Respecting him is a duty and his command must be obeyed. He is the symbol of national unity and the guardian of its preservation and protection.

Article (42): The Sultan discharges the following functions:

- Preserving the country's independence and its territorial integrity, protecting its internal and external security, safeguarding the rights and freedoms of citizens, ensuring the rule of law and guiding the State's general policy.
- Taking prompt measures to counter any danger threatening the Sultanate's safety, the integrity of its territories, the security and interests of its people or impeding the functioning of the State's institutions.
- Representing the State internally and towards other states in all international relations.
- Presiding over the Council of Ministers or appointing who is to preside.
- Presiding over the Specialized Councils or appointing who is to preside.
- Appointing Deputies of the Prime Minister of the Council of Ministers, Ministers and those of similar rank and relieving them of their posts.

- Appointing Under-Secretaries, Secretaries-General and those of similar rank and relieving them of their posts.
- Appointing senior judges and relieving them of their posts.
- Declaring a state of emergency, general mobilizations, war and concluding peace. The Law specifies the rules thereof.
- Promulgating laws and ratifying them.
- Signing international treaties and agreements according to the provisions of the Law or authorizing their signature and issuing decrees ratifying them.
- Appointing political representatives to other states and international organisations and relieving them of their posts in accordance with the limits and conditions stipulated by the Law, as well as accepting the credentials of representatives of other states and international organisations.
- Pardoning or commuting any sentence.
- Conferring orders of honour and military ranks.

Article (43): The Sultan shall be assisted in formulating and implementing the general policy of the State by a Council of Ministers and Specialized Councils.

The Council of Ministers

Article (44): The Council of Ministers is the body entrusted with the implementation of the State's general policies and in particular undertakes the following:

- Submitting recommendations to the Sultan pertaining to economic, political, social, executive, and administrative matters of concern to the Government including proposing draft laws and decrees.
- Protecting the interests of the citizens and ensuring the availability of necessary services to them, and enhancing their economic, social, health and cultural standards.
- Determining the objectives and general policies for economic, social, and administrative development and proposing the necessary means and measures for their implementation which ensures the best utilisation of financial, economic and human resources.
- Discussing development plans prepared by the competent author-

ities, submitting them to the Sultan for approval, and following up their implementation.

- Discussing proposals of Ministries relevant to their respective jurisdictions and taking appropriate recommendations and decisions in this regard.
- Supervising the functioning of the State's administrative body, following up the performance of its duties and co-ordinating among its units.
- General supervision of the implementation of the laws, decrees, regulations, decisions, treaties, agreements and courts' judgments in a manner that ensures adherence thereto.
- Discharging any other competences delegated by the Sultan or vested by the provisions of the Law.

Article (45): The Prime Minister shall preside over the Council's sessions and may entrust one of the Deputy Prime Ministers to conduct the sessions which he does not attend.

If the Prime Minister and his Deputies are absent, the Sultan will authorise whomever he deems appropriate to conduct the sessions.

Article (46): The Council's meetings shall be valid by the attendance of the majority of its members. Its deliberations shall be confidential and its decisions shall be made in accordance with the majority approval of attendees.

Article (47): The Council shall issue its internal regulations including its rules of procedure and shall have a Secretariat-General provided with a sufficient number of staff to assist it in performing its duties.

The Prime Minister, His Deputies, and The Ministers

Article (48): If the Sultan appoints a Prime Minister, his jurisdictions and competences shall be stipulated in the Decree appointing him.

Article (49): Any appointed Prime Minister, Deputy Prime Minister, or Minister shall be:

a. Of original Omani nationality in accordance with the Law.

b. Aged not less than 30 years of the Gregorian calendar.

Article (50): Before assuming their powers, the Prime Minister, his Deputies, and the Ministers shall take the following oath before the Sultan:

"I swear by Almighty Allah to be faithful to my Sultan and country, to respect the Basic Statute of the State and the State's applicable Laws, to fully protect its entity and territorial integrity, to guard its interests and those of its citizens and to perform my duties faithfully and honestly".

Article (51): The Deputy Prime Minister and the Ministers shall supervise their unit's affairs, implement therein the general policy of the Government, as well as establish the guidelines of the unit and follow up their implementation.

Article (52): Members of the Council of Ministers are collectively responsible politically before the Sultan for the implementation of the State's general policy. Each of them is individually responsible before the Sultan for the manner in which he performs his duties and exercises his authority in his respective Ministry or unit.

Article (53): Members of the Council of Ministers shall not combine their ministerial position and chairmanship of, or membership to, a board of directors of any public joint-stock company. The Government units which they are in charge of or supervise shall not deal with any company or establishment in which they have an interest whether direct or indirect. They shall always, by their conduct, pursue the interests of the country and work in furtherance of the public benefit. They shall not abuse their official positions in any form whether for their own benefit or the benefit of those with whom they have special relations.

Article (54): Emoluments of Deputy Prime Ministers and Ministers during their term of office and after their retirement shall be determined by orders of the Sultan.

Article (55): The provisions of Articles 49, 50, 51, 52, 53, and 54 shall apply to all those of a Minister's rank.

The Specialized Councils

Article (56): Specialized Councils shall be established, their competences determined and their members appointed by virtue of Royal Decrees.

The Financial Affairs

Article (57): The Law specifies the provisions relating to the following matters and the bodies responsible thereof:

- Collecting taxes, fees and other public monies and the procedures of their disbursement.
- Preserving and managing the properties of the State, the conditions for its disposal and the limits within which some of these properties can be assigned.
- The State's general budget and the final account.
- The autonomous and supplementary general budgets and their final accounts.
- The State Audit.
- Loans extended or obtained by the State.
- Currency, banks, standards, measures and weights.
- Matters pertaining to salaries, pensions, compensation, subsidies, and gratuities charged to the State's Treasury.

CHAPTER FIVE
The Council of Oman

Article (58): The Council of Oman shall consist of:

1. The Shura Council
2. The State Council

The Law shall specify the competences of each, its term, sessions, and rules of procedure. The Law shall also determine the number of its members, the conditions they should satisfy, the method by which they are selected or appointed, the reasons for their dismissal and other regulatory provisions.

CHAPTER SIX
The Judiciary

Article (59): The supremacy of the Law shall be the basis of governance in the State. The dignity, integrity and impartiality of judges guarantee the preservation of rights and freedoms.

Article (60): The judiciary is independent and its functions are exercised by the different types and levels of courts which issue judgments in accordance with the Law.

Article (61): Judges in their adjudication are subject only to the Law and cannot be removed except in cases determined by Law. No party may interfere in lawsuits or matters of justice. Such interference shall be considered a crime punishable by law. The Law shall determine prerequisites to be fulfilled by whomever exercises judicial functions, the conditions and procedures for appointing, transferring and promoting judges, the guarantees accorded to them, the cases where they cannot be removed from office and all other relevant provisions.

Article (62): The Law regulates the types and levels of courts and specifies their functions and jurisdiction. The military courts deal solely with military offences committed by members of the armed and security forces. Its jurisdiction cannot be extended to others except in the case of martial law and within the limits prescribed by Law.

Article (63): Court sessions are open unless the court decides to hold them in camera in the interest of public order or morals. In all cases the pronouncement of judgments must be held in open sessions.

Article (64): The Public Prosecution shall conduct criminal proceedings on behalf of the society, supervise criminal investigation, attend to the enforcement of criminal laws, the pursuit of the guilty and the execution of judgments. The Law regulates the Public Prosecution, its jurisdiction and specifies conditions and guarantees of those who discharge its functions.

- The public security bodies may, by a law, be exceptionally entrusted with conducting criminal proceedings in cases of misdemeanours and in accordance with conditions specified by the Law.

Article (65): The Law regulates the legal profession.

Article (66): The judiciary shall have a Supreme Council which shall supervise the proper functioning of the courts and auxiliary bodies. The Law shall specify its jurisdiction with regard to the job-related affairs of judges and the Public Prosecution.

Article (67): The Law regulates the settlement of administrative disputes through a panel or special court whose regulation and manner of exercising administrative judicature shall be specified by Law.

Article (68): The Law shall regulate the procedure for the settlement of conflicts of jurisdictions between judicial bodies and in cases of conflict of judgments.

Article (69): The Law defines the competences of the authority responsible for rendering legal opinions to Ministries and other government bodies, and the drafting and review of the draft laws, regulations and decisions. It also specifies the manner of representing the State and all public authorities and establishments before the judicial bodies.

Article (70): The Law appoints the judicial body entrusted with the settlement of disputes, which pertain to the extent of conformity of laws and regulations to the Basic Statute of the State and the provisions thereof. The Law also specifies the jurisdiction of such judicial body and its rules of procedure that is to be followed.

Article (71): Judgments shall be issued and executed in the name of His Majesty the Sultan. Abstaining from executing or obstructing the execution of these judgments by concerned public officials is a crime punishable by Law. The judgment creditor has the right in this case to file a criminal action directly before the competent court.

CHAPTER SEVEN

General Provisions

Article (72): The application of this Basic Statute shall not prejudice treaties and agreements the Sultanate has entered into with other countries, international institutions and organizations.

Article (73): No provisions of this Basic Statute shall be suspended except during periods of martial law and within the limits defined by Law.

Article (74): Laws shall be published in the Official Gazette within two weeks from the day of their issue. They shall come into force on the date of their publication, unless another date is specified therein.

Article (75): The provisions of the Law shall only apply to events subsequent to the date of their coming into force. They shall have no effect on events prior to that date unless otherwise stipulated therein. This exception shall not include laws relating to penal, taxation and financial dues.

Article (76): Treaties and agreements shall not have the force of Law until ratified. In no case shall treaties and agreements have confidential terms contradicting their declared ones.

Article (77): Whatever is stipulated by applicable laws, regulations, decrees, orders and decisions in force at the time when this Basic Statute comes into effect shall remain in force, provided they are not in conflict with any of its provisions.

Article (78): The competent bodies shall take steps for issuance of non-existing laws necessitated by this Basic Statute within two years from the date of its coming into force.

Article (79): Laws and procedures that have the force of Law shall conform to the provisions of the Basic Statute of the State.

Article (80): No authority in the State shall issue directives, regulations or decisions that contradict the provisions of the applicable Laws and decrees, or international treaties and agreements which are part of the Law of the Land.

Article (81): This Statute shall not be amended except in the manner in which it was promulgated.

Appendix 2: Royal Decree 99/2011 (amends Basic Statute of the State)[2]

We, Qaboos bin Said, Sultan of Oman, stemming from our belief in the importance of developing the Shura march in the country to serve the interests of the country and citizens and in confirmation of the importance of the participation of all individuals of society in the comprehensive development march in line with the requirements of the prospective development ... and having pursued the Basic Law of the State issued by the Royal Decree No 101/96.
And based on the public interest, decreed the following;

Article One: The attached amendments shall be introduced to the Basic Law of the State.
Article Two: Cancels all that contravenes with the Decree or its attached amendments or contradicts with their provisions.
Article Three: The Decree comes into force from the day following its date of publishing.

First: Replacing the Article No 6 of the Basic Statute of the State with the following:
Article (6). The Ruling Family Council shall within three days of the throne falling vacant determine the successor to the throne. If the Ruling Family Council does not agree on the choice of the successor to the throne, the Defence Council together with Chairmen of Majlis Ad-Dawla, Majlis Ash-Shura, Supreme Court and two of its oldest deputies, shall confirm the appointment of the person designated by His Majesty in his letter to the Ruling Family Council.

Second: A new paragraph shall be added to the text of the Article 42 of the Basic Statute of the State, as paragraph No 6, as follows: Establishing and

2 English translation of the full text of Royal Decree 99/2011 which amends the Basic Law of the State and confers more powers on the Majlis Ad-Dawla (upper council) and the Majlis Ash-Shura (elected representatives). Taken from the Oman Observer of 21st October 2011:
http://main.omanobserver.om/node/69298
http://www.newsbriefsoman.info/item/2011/10/royal-decree-992011-amends-basic-law-of-state-gives-greater-power-to-majlis

regulating the units of the state administrative apparatus and cancelling thereof.

Third: Replacing paragraph 4 of Article 44 from the Basic Statute of the State with the following text.

Discussing development plans prepared by competent authorities after it is reviewed by the Majlis Oman, submit the same to His Majesty for approval, and follow up their implementation.

Fourth: Replacing Article No 56 of the Basic Statute of the State with the following text:

Specialised Councils shall be established, their prerogatives specified and their members appointed by virtue of Royal Decrees, and shall be affiliated to the Council of Ministers unless the Royal Decrees providing for their establishment states otherwise.

Fifth: Replacing Chapter 5 of the Basic Statute of the State with a new chapter as follows:

Chapter 5: Majlis Oman.

Article 58: The Majlis Oman shall consist of:

1. The Majlis Ad-Dawla.
2. The Majlis Ash-Shura.

The Majlis Ad-Dawla

Article 58 (bis): The Majlis Ad-Dawla consists of a chairman and members not exceeding, including the chairman, the total number of Majlis Ash-Shura members, and shall be appointed by Royal Decree.

Article 58 (bis1): members of Majlis Ad-Dawla shall be selected from among the following categories:

- Former ministers, under-secretaries of the ministries, and their equivalents.
- Former ambassadors.
- Former senior judges.
- Retired senior officers.
- Those who are known for their competence and experience in the fields of science, arts, culture, and teachers of universities, colleges and higher institutes.
- Dignitaries and businessmen.

- Personalities who made great service to the nation.
- Whom His Majesty decides to choose and not from among the previous categories.

Article 58 (bis2): Without prejudice to Article 58 (bis1), the person who is chosen as a member of the Majlis Ad-Dawla shall be:

- Omani national.
- Not less than 40 Gregorian years of age on the date of appointment.
- Not ever been sentenced in a criminal case or in moral turpitude case or even in case of rehabilitation.
- Not affiliated to a security or military authority.
- Not placed under the guardianship as per a court judgement.
- Not having a mental illness.

Article 58 (bis3): The Majlis Ad-Dawla term is four years starting from the first meeting of the Majlis, and in any case not less than that of the Majlis Ash-Shura term.

Article 58 (bis4): The Majlis Ad-Dawla shall elect from among its members and for the duration of its term two deputies for the Majlis chairman; and if the seat of any of them falls vacant the Majlis shall elect another one to replace him until the end of its term. In all cases, the election shall be held by direct secret ballot and in absolute majority of the members.

Article 58 (bis5): The membership of the Majlis Ad-Dawla shall end due to the following reasons:

- The end of the Majlis' term.
- Exemption from membership.
- Death or total disability.

Article 58 (bis6): The Majlis Ad-Dawla member may ask for his exemption through a request to the Majlis chairman and the chairman in his turn will submit the same to His Majesty. In all cases, the Majlis Ad-Dawla member shall be exempted if he lost one of the conditions of the membership or lost confidence and esteem or violated the membership duties.

Article 58 (bis7): Only the two categories stipulated in item 5 and item 8 of Article 58 (bis 1) may combine the Majlis Ad-Dawla membership and public employments.

The Majlis Ash-Shura

Article 58 (bis8): The Majlis Ash-Shura shall consist of elected members representing all wilayats of the Sultanate.
The number of Majlis Ash-Shura members shall be determined so that each wilayat shall be represented by one member if that wilayat has a population not exceeding 30,000 on commencement date of candidature and two members if the number is more on that date.

Article 58 (bis9): The election of the Majlis Ash-Shura members shall be conducted through direct secret ballot and according to the election law.

Article 58 (bis10): The Majlis Ash-Shura candidate shall meet the following conditions:

- To be of originally Omani nationality.
- To be not less than 30 Gregorian years of age on commencement date of candidature.
- Shall hold an academic degree not less than general education certificate.
- Shall not been sentenced in a criminal case or in moral turpitude case or even in case of rehabilitation.
- Shall be on the election register.
- Not placed under guardianship as per a court judgement.
- Not having mental illness.

The member who finished his term may stand as candidate again for the Majlis Ash'shura membership.

Article 58 (bis11): The Majlis Ash-Shura term shall be four years starting from the first meeting of the Majlis, while the new Majlis election runs during the last 90 days of the ongoing term, and in case elections are not held at the end of the Majlis term or delayed for whatever reason, the existing Majlis shall continue working till a new Majlis is elected, and it is not allowed to extend the term of the Majlis unless there is a necessity and by virtue of Royal Decree. The extension shall not exceed one term.

Article 58 (bis 12): The Majlis Ash-Shura shall convene upon a call by His Majesty in an extraordinary session prior to the session set for election of the Majlis chairman and the two deputies for the same period of the chairman. The oldest member will chair the session. If the seat of any of the deputies falls vacant, the Majlis shall elect another one to replace him until the end of the term. The election shall be by direct secret ballot and with absolute majority of the Majlis members.

Article 58 (bis13): If the seat of any Majlis Ash-Shura member falls vacant before the end of the member term, the seat shall be filled by a candidate from the wilayat by reference to the Majlis election result for the same term. The first candidate on the list with the second largest number of remainder votes will fill the vacancy during 60 days of the vacancy reporting to the Majlis. The term of the new member shall be complementary to the membership term of his precedent. If the seat falls vacant six months before the end of the Majlis term, the seat shall not be filled.

Article 58 (bis 14): An independent and neutral higher committee chaired by one of the Vice-Presidents of the Supreme Court shall supervise the Majlis Ash-Shura election and take decisions on election complaints. The law shall specify how the committee shall be formed, its prerogatives and system of functioning.

Article 58 (bis 15): The membership of the Majlis Ash-Shura ends for the following reasons:

- The end of the Majlis term.
- Resignation.
- Death or total disability.
- Loss of membership.
- Dissolution of the Majlis.

Article 58 (bis16): The resignation from the Majlis Ash-Shura membership shall be submitted in writing to the Majlis chairman and he shall refer it to the Majlis, which shall decide to accept or reject the resignation. The Majlis bylaw regulates rules on this matter.

Article 58 (bis17): The membership of the Majlis Ash-Shura shall not be dropped unless the member lost one of the election conditions on which he has been elected or lost confidence and esteem or violated the membership duties. The loss of the membership requires the approval of two-third of Majlis members.

Article 58 (bis18): It shall not be permissible to combine the Majlis Ash-Shura membership and public employments. In case a public employee is elected to the membership of the Majlis, his/her service shall be considered terminated from the date of announcing the results of the election, and in case of contestation of his/her membership he/she retain his/her job without remuneration until a final decision is issued on the contest. In case the decision invalidates his/her membership and the decision of his/her win is revoked, he/she may return to his/her job and receive salary from the date of returning to work. In case the contest is rejected his/her service shall be considered terminated from the date of announcing the election results and shall receive an exceptional pension determined by the law on condition he/she has not less than 10 Gregorian years of service calculated in the pension on that date.

Article 58 (bis 19): His Majesty, in the cases which he appreciates, may dissolve the Majlis Ash-Shura and call for new election within four months from the date of dissolving.

Article 58 (bis 20): In open session, the members of Majlis Ad-Dawla and Majlis Ash-Shura, each before their respective council, shall take the following oath before assuming work in the council:
"I swear by Almighty Allah to be faithful to my Sultan and my country, to respect the Basic Statute of the State and the state's applicable laws, to preserve the state safety and the main pillars of the Omani society and its original values and to perform my duties in the council and its panels faithfully and honestly."
Before assuming his work in the council, the chairman of Majlis Ad-Dawla shall take the oath mentioned in the previous paragraph before His Majesty the Sultan.

Article 58 (bis 21): The chairmen of the Majlis Ad-Dawla and Majlis Ash-Shura, their deputies and the members of the two councils shall work for the interest of the country according to the laws in force and they shall not exploit in any form their membership for their own interest or the interest of those related to them or have a special relationship with them. The law shall determine works they shall not perform.

Article 58 (bis 22): The member of the Majlis Ad-Dawla and Majlis Ash-Shura shall not be blamed for his/her opinions or statements expressed before the Majlis or its committees on issues within the scope of the Majlis prerogatives.

Article 58 (bis 23): Except when caught in crime, any penal action against the member of the Majlises shall not be taken during the annual term unless there is prior permission from the Majlis concerned. The permission shall be issued by the Majlis' chairman when the council is in recess.

Article 58 (bis24): The memberships of the Majlis Ad-Dawla and Majlis Ash-Shura shall not be combined.

Article 58 (bis25): The Majlis Ad-Dawla and Majlis Ash-Shura shall each issue its bylaws. The bylaw determines proceedings of the council and its committees, maintaining order principles of debate, voting, and questioning for Majlis Ash-Shura and other prerogatives stipulated for the members and the penalties that may be imposed on a member in violation of proceedings or when being absent from sessions of the council or its committees without acceptable excuse.

Terms and prerogatives of the Majlis Oman

Article 58 (bis26): The ordinary term of the Majlis Oman shall not be less than eight months per year. The Majlis Oman convenes on His Majesty the Sultan's invitation in November every year. The ordinary session shall not be adjourned before the approval of the general budget of the state.

Article 58 (bis27): As exceptional from provisions of Article 58 (bis 26) His Majesty calls Majlis Oman for the first meeting after the general election of Majlis Ash-Shura within a month from the date of announcing the results of that election.

Article 58 (bis28): His Majesty may invite the Majlis Oman to convene outside its regular sessions in cases His Majesty considers appropriate.

Article 58 (bis29): The calling the Majlis Oman to convene or end ordinary or extraordinary sessions shall be according to proper legal procedures.

Article 58 (bis30): The Majlis Ad-Dawla and Majlis Ash-Shura shall convene at their respective venues in Muscat city and His Majesty may call for the Majlises to convene at any other place.

Article 58 (bis31): All sessions of the Majlis Ad-Dawla and the Majlis Ash-Shura shall be open sessions and closed sessions may be convened in cases of necessity and in agreement between the Council of Ministers and either of the two Majlises.

Article 58 (bis 32): A majority of members of the Majlis Ad-Dawla and Majlis Ash-Shura, including the chairman or one of his deputies, shall be present to constitute a sitting. If the majority of members are not present the sitting will be adjourned to the next sitting.

Article 58 (bis33): The decisions of the Majlis Ad-Dawla and Majlis Ash-Shura shall be passed by the absolute majority of the attending members except in cases that require qualified majority. If the votes are equal, the side that includes the chairman wins.

Article 58 (bis34): In case the Majlis Ash-Shura is dissolved, the Majlis Ad-Dawla session discontinues.

Article 58 (bis35): The draft laws prepared by the government shall be referred to the Majlis Oman for approval or amendment and then directly be submitted to His Majesty to issue them. In case of any amendments by the Majlis Oman on a draft law, His Majesty may return the same to the council for reconsidering the amendments and then shall be submitted again to His Majesty.

Article 58 (bis36): The Majlis Oman may propose draft laws and refer the same to the government for assessment and returning the same to the Majlis, procedures provide for in

Article 58 (bis35) shall be followed in approving, amending or issuing the said draft laws.

Article 58 (bis37): The draft laws shall be referred by the Council of Ministers to the Majlis Ash-Shura for approval or amendment within a maximum of three months from the date of referring. The same shall then be referred to the Majlis Ad-Dawla for approval or amendment within a maximum of 45 days from the date of referring. Shall the two Majlises disagree on the draft law the two council shall convene a joint session by invitation and under the chairmanship of Majlis Ad-Dawla Chairman to debate the differences and vote on the draft law in the same sitting. The decisions shall be issued by absolute majority of the present members, and in all cases the Majlis Ad-Dawla Chairman shall refer the draft to His Majesty along with the opinion of the two Majlises.

Article 58 (bis38): The draft laws of urgent nature shall be referred from the Council of Ministers to Majlis Ash-Shura for approval or amendment within a maximum of one month from the referral date and then shall be referred to the Majlis Ad-Dawla that should give a decision for approval or amendment within a maximum of 15 days from the referral date. The Chairman of the Majlis Ad-Dawla shall submit the same to His Majesty along with the two councils' opinions.

Article 58 (bis39): His Majesty may issue Royal Decrees that have the same power of law during the period when the Majlis Oman is in recess and when Majlis Ash-Shura is dissolved and Majlis Ad-Dawla sittings are discontinued.

Article 58 (bis40): Projects of development plans and the state annual budget shall be referred by the Council of Ministers to the Majlis Ash-Shura for debate and recommendation within a maximum period of one month from the referral date and then the same shall be referred to Majlis Ad-Dawla for debate and recommendation within a period of 15 days from the referral date. The chairman of the Council of Ministers shall return the same along with the recommendations of the two Majlises to the Council of Ministers. The Council of Ministers shall inform the two Majlises about the recommendations not adopted in this respect along with the reasons.

Article 58 (bis41): The economic and social draft agreements the government intends to make or join shall be referred to the Majlis Ash-Shura for consideration and the Majlis shall present conclusions reached by the Majlis on the same to the council of Ministers for appropriate decision.

Article 58 (bis42): State Financial and Administrative Audit institution shall send a copy of its annual report to the Majlis Ash-Shura and the Majlis Ad-Dawla.

Article 58 (bis43): On a request signed by at least 15 members of the Majlis Ash-Shura of any of the services ministers may be subject to interpellation on matters related to exceeding their prerogatives by acting in contrary to the law. The Majlis shall debate the same and submit the outcome to His Majesty the Sultan.

Article 58 (bis44): Services ministers shall report annually to the Majlis Ash-Shura on the stages of project implementation by their ministries. The Majlis may invite any of the service ministers for a report presentation and debate on matters within prerogatives of the ministry concerned.

Appendix 3: Human Rights Developments in Oman from August 2011 to early 2012

During the period from August 2011 to the beginning of 2012, significant changes have occurred in several laws and regulations governing the legislative, legal and administrative areas in Oman through royal decrees issued directly by the Sultan. Also, the same period witnessed elections for the Omani Shura Council for its seventh term (2012–2015) during October, and the outcome of this election was also of interest to researchers and observers.

The following papers illustrate briefly the most important developments and their impact on the human rights situation in Oman.

Shura Council Elections for the Seventh Term:

The election came after the reopening of the Council's membership from 26 March to 12 April. Such postponement by the authorities came after the Sultan's announcement of his intention to give legislative and auditing powers to the new term of the Council of Oman, and the appointment of a number of Shura Council members as ministers in the government in March 2011. It was an appropriate step to reopen the doors for Council membership to give opportunity to those who wished to run for candidacy after the announcement of these new developments, and there was a remarkable increase in the number of candidates – 1133 (almost a 70% increase from the number in 2007). This encouraged candidates to campaign and announce their plans and advertise themselves in the mass media in an unprecedented way in Oman, playing an important role in creating public awareness about the Shura Council.

What also emerged was an increase in women's interest in the elections and the significant support they received from the government, where several new faces participated and stood in some provinces, even in those conservative ones where the traditional tribal system predominated – 77 female candidates stood for election (almost 3.5 times an increase from the number of 21 candidates in 2007) – which gives an important view of women in the elections in general. Government support for women during this election was obvious in terms of providing a lot of conferences and media coverage of their role and encouraging citizens to give them the confidence in the realisation of this position, and encouraging college and university students to participate in the elections and to support women.

This election saw an official turnout of 76.6% according to official data (397,000 votes cast out of a total 518,000 enrolled), although reports in several regions told of a much lower turnout, reflecting differences in the degree of public confidence in the Majlis' ability to bring about genuine changes. In particular, the elections took place before the Sultan's concession of new powers to the Majlis al-Shura and the change of administrative divisions in Oman.

There are several outcomes of the electoral process of this election:

- The role of tribes emerged very significantly in the voting process. Tribal alliances may have decided several results beforehand. Tribes in a number of provinces mobilised their efforts and united their voices to the representative of the tribe, in order to win the provinces' seat for the tribe.
- For women, the results were disappointing compared to the expectations and aspirations of the government; only one was elected (out of 84 seats), a candidate from Seeb province of the capital Muscat.
- The election of three protesters who took part in demonstrations earlier this year.

Amendments to the Basic Statute of the State:

It is the first amendment to Oman's Basic Statute since its promulgation in 1996. The amendments by Royal Decree No. 99/2011 were declared immediately three days after the announcement of the Shura elections results; it seems that it was designed to fit with the election results. In addition to minor changes in Articles 6, 42, 44, and 56, the most changes introduced by the new Royal Decree cover fundamental ones with respect to Chapter Five of OBSS and its Article 58 (the Council of Oman), which became the longest Article of the OBSS from being the shortest one. These amendments came as a result of the earlier Royal Decree No. 39/2011, which gave legislative and auditing powers to the Council of Oman.

It is worth noting that most of these amendments and changes came as anticipated in the original research[3] as the Shura Council has not been granted full legislative power, but shares it with the Council of State, and

3 See 2.5 and Chapter 7 of the main research.

is tied by the approval of the Sultan who issues them by Royal Decree. Also, it is important to note that no changes have been introduced into the last article (Art. 81 OBSS), which is the essence of amending the Basic Statute.

The most noteworthy elements of the new amendment – to be analysed in more detail in a separate study – can be summarised as follows:

1. Giving the Council of Oman and the judiciary a role in confirming the appointment of the person designated by the Sultan in his letter to the Ruling Family Council, but without any substantial powers to veto; which was granted earlier to the Council of Defence alone – according to Article 6.
2. Listing new conditions for the membership of the Shura and the State Councils, the most important ones to mention being:
   a. Nationality requirement: native Omanis for the Shura Council without requiring such conditions for State Council membership (which opens the door to naturalised Omani).
   b. Educational Minimum Certificate: Requiring the General Education Diploma level of education as a minimum qualification to run for Shura Council Candidacy (after the recent elections results where several candidates were uneducated and where tribes were the decisive winning factor).
3. Electing the Chairman of the Shura Council from its members without the Sultan's intervention.
4. Exclusion of government control over the electoral process and introducing the election law with the establishment of a judicial committee to oversee elections and judge appeals.
5. Making all the Shura and the State Councils' sessions open to the public unless agreed between them with the Council of Ministers about the confidentiality of the sessions.
6. Granting the Council of Oman legislative and auditing powers, including:
   a) Acting as the middle link between the Council of Ministers and the Sultan to issue laws, by forwarding the draft law (those of ordinary or urgent nature ones) from the Cabinet to the Shura Council and the State Council and then bringing the draft law to the Sultan for promulgating and ratifying.

b) Receiving copies of the State Financial and Administrative Audit institution's annual reports.

c) The Shura Council's right to present its considerations on the economic and social draft agreements the government intends to make or join.

d) The Shura Council's right to interpellate any of the services' ministers by a request signed by at least 15 members.

These amendments are important developments in favour of the Council of Oman and in reducing the legislative power of the Council of Ministers. However, the legislative is still an absolute power of the Sultan based on the explicit text of Article 42 (paragraph 11) which has not undergone change by the new amendments, which provides the Sultan power to issue and ratify laws. In addition, Article 58 bis19 gave absolute powers to the Sultan to dissolve the Shura Council and call for new elections within four months. He has the right to issue decrees with the force of law between the Council of Oman terms and sessions, and during the dissolution of the Shura Council. (58 bis39)

On the other hand, it appears that there is a limitation to the legislative and auditing powers granted to the Council. For instance, in terms of the draft agreements that the government intends to make or join, though being considered as part of domestic law, the authority of the Shura Council is limited to the type of agreements, namely economic and social. Therefore, all the agreements with respect to foreign policy, military and security are outside the power of the Shura Council, and the government can act without referring to the Council, in addition to its jurisdiction limitation in this regard to express its views to the Council of Ministers without its mandatory right to approve or object. (58 bis41)

In terms of making the government accountable, the process of interpellation is limited to the ministers of services only (58 bis43) without the rest of the ministers or the whole Cabinet in general. Also, it is confined to matters related to ministers exceeding their prerogatives by acting contrary to the law, and there is no right to a vote of confidence or non-cooperation or to dismiss the minister from his post. Taking into account that the emphasis on the services' ministers without the rest of the ministers or the Cabinet itself reflects the role of the Sultan and his immunity, as he is the Prime Minister and he holds several non-service ministerial posts (Finance, Foreign and Defence).

In summary, the Sultan still holds the ultimate power to enact laws when the Shura Council conflicts with his desire by the dissolution of the Council. He also still retains a strong power of appointing the members of the State Council, who make up half of the Council of Oman, thus, reducing the number of strong conflicts within the Shura Council. However, in the case of adopting such a draft law, it might fail for one of the following reasons:

A The opposition by the State Council to the Shura Council, which requires having a joint session between the two houses with a joint vote with absolute majority.
B The Sultan may return the bill to the council for reconsideration, which sends a clear hint to both Houses of the Sultan's disapproval of the draft law.
C The Sultan may issue the law he desires without presenting it to the Council, using his power to issue laws when the Council of Oman is in recess.
D Dissolution of the Shura Council and, in turn, the State Council session discontinues.
E The Sultan's absolute power to amend the Basic Statute's articles, where he can limit or abolish the powers of the Council of Oman.

Conclusion

Oman is still feeling the atmosphere of the Arab spring, and the new developments may qualify it to occupy a better position on human rights protections in the Middle East. However, after almost 15 years of promulgation of the OBSS, the factors that influence Omani society and politics still exist today.[4] This is clear from the recent Shura Council elections results and the subsequent amendments of the OBSS and other laws.

It is important to note that the recent Royal Decrees declared during the last few months and which amended a number of aspects of the Omani legal system and law, have contradictory aspects on the subject of human rights. Although the Basic Statute amendments by Royal Decree No. 99/2011 were the biggest change to the Omani governmental system since 1996, awarding positive changes in the way of isolating the legislature

4 According to paragraph 2.1.4 of the research which focuses on the tribe, religion and geographical areas and their impact on Omani society.

from the executive branch, and in terms of giving auditing and legislative powers to the Council of Oman, such as the Interrogation right, and electing the Chairman of the Shura Council without the intervention of the Sultan. This was followed by the issuance of new substantial changes concerning the restructuring of regional administration (Royal Decree No. 114/2011) by forming a new administrative structure reflecting the distribution of administrative authorities in the whole country. Royal Decree No. 116/2011 promulgates Municipal Council's Law which is another and promising batch of popular participation in Oman, where it gives the public the right to be part of those councils by elections similar to the Shura Council, albeit with less power. It is another step towards democracy by increasing the field of public participation in different aspects.

Royal Decree No. 86/2011 is another important step for human rights protection, which states the withdrawal of all reservations Oman has made on the Convention on the Rights of the Child, but without withdrawing the reservation on Article 14 on the right of choice of religion.

On the other hand, other recent laws are sending different messages and are not in line with the above-mentioned developments or with the principle of human rights protection, such as:

- Royal Decree No. 95/2011 on amending the Press and Publications Law, which came to modify some of the deficiencies resulting from the original law to criminalise the publicising of official documents on the Internet, although internet usage is governed by a different law. This amendment came as a result of the case of one of the activists who published an official governmental circulation that restricted the work of the most famous radio broadcast programme.[5]
- Royal Decree No. 59/2011 on amending some provisions of the Law of Criminal Procedure, which came as a result of the demonstrations and sit-ins. The decree has given some prosecution powers to the military and police personnel.
- Royal Decree No. 96/2011 on modifying the Omani Penal Law and the Law of Criminal Procedure, which came to criminalise unauthorised assemblies and emphasises the sanctions and penalties for different types of demonstrations, sit-ins, road blocking, and resistance to au-

5 See section 3.2.2, p. 94 (Freedom of Expression and the Media).

thority and arrest. This clearly came as a result of the last demonstrations in Oman.

In conclusion, a paradigm shift has been observed with regard to the size of the powers and responsibility given to the Shura Council during this period and which will qualify it in the future to assume the legislative authority and to transfer Oman to the constitutional monarchy. Nevertheless, according to other recent decrees, there is still clear governmental hesitation to protect civil liberties, mostly those of intellectual freedom and expression. This makes the development of human rights and freedoms in Oman in the near future rest in the hands of the Council of Oman (mostly the Shura Council). If the council succeeds in its task to change the laws which hinder the rights and freedoms in Oman, this will result in promising expectations of human rights. Otherwise, its failure will make the Sultan – as used to be the case – the last resort for human rights development, and that – without a doubt – will make the transition to the constitutional monarchy stage take much longer.